Mysteries of the Past

Great Mysteries

Aldus Books London

Mysteries of the Past

by Stuart Holroyd
and David Lambert

Series Coordinator:	John Mason
Editor:	Nina Shandloff
Designer:	Ann Dunn
Research:	Frances Vargo
Editorial Consultant:	Beppie Harrison

SBN 490 004350

First published in United Kingdom
in 1979 by Aldus Books Limited
17 Conway Street, London W1P 6BS

Printed in Hong Kong

Introduction

Why is it that the riddles of the past seem more compelling than any modern puzzle? Is it because they have remained unsolved for so long? Some, such as the massive Egyptian pyramids with their hieroglyphic inscriptions and the "standing stones" of Stonehenge, have been the focus of travelers' interest since they were first opened up to scholars. Others—including the myths of King Midas' golden touch, the tower of Babel, the Jewish martyrs of Masada, and King Arthur's Camelot—are the subject of dedicated research outside the gaze of the public eye. In both cases the theories, frequently conflicting and sometimes controversial, depend on the work of archaeologists. Their fascinating evidence is examined in detail in each chapter, and there are also general discussions of underwater and contemporary land investigations. Archaeology has now become a booming industry, attracting enormous public interest in exhibitions and support for international crusades to preserve temples and monuments now many centuries old. This book tells the exciting, sometimes amazing story of the mysteries of the past.

Contents

Chapter 1
The Puzzle of the Pyramids

It was Napoleon who initiated European interest in the mysteries of ancient Egypt. His 1798 campaign brought nearly 200 scholars and artists to the richest spectacles of the ancient world. Moreover, the booty of objects, drawings, and above all writings brought back fired European scholars everywhere with a new curiosity. The unanswered questions were innumerable: how had the primitive ancient Egyptians erected vast pyramids and temples, colossal statues, the enigmatic sphinx? What was the purpose of all these monuments, uncannily preserved in the hot dry air of the Egyptian desert? Inscriptions were everywhere and these must hold the key. But what did they say?

Ten thousand colorful horsemen turned out to defend the city of Cairo against Napoleon's expeditionary force on July 12, 1798. This army of Mamelukes, the foreign mercenaries who ruled Egypt for the Turkish emperor, was a formidable sight. Exhorting his troops before the engagement that became known as the Battle of the Pyramids, Napoleon coined a memorable and rousing phrase. "Soldiers," he cried, "remember that from the top of these monuments 40 centuries are looking down upon you." In fact at that time the pyramids of Giza were about 4500 years old. But considering that Egyptology only began with Napoleon's conquest, 40 centuries wasn't a bad estimate.

The object of Napoleon's expedition to Egypt was to threaten British India. Militarily, however, it was a failure, but it had more success in its secondary purpose, which was to open up the ancient and mysterious land of Egypt to European scholarship. A contingent of nearly 200 scientists, scholars, and artists accompanied the army, and one of Napoleon's first acts when he entered Cairo was to requisition five large mansions to accommodate what he called the "Institute of Egypt." Over the next year the French troops pushed into Upper Egypt, but always they were accompanied by scientists and artists who collected, measured, investigated, and sketched the antiquities of the Nile valley.

Among these "learned civilians" from France was a former courtier and diplomat named Vivant Denon. A dilettante in the

Opposite: the Great Pyramid, the tomb of Cheops. Ever since the time of Herodotus and other Greek visitors in the 5th century B.C., the group of three pyramids at Giza has attracted much attention—particularly this one, largest of the three. It was erected at the beginning of the 4th dynasty (2720–2560 B.C.) and took 20 years to build, rising to a completed height of 481 feet and measuring 755 feet along each side at the base.

Above: *Battle of the Pyramids, July 1798* by the French painter Baron Louis-François Lejeune. The battle began when 25,000 French troops, demoralized, hungry, and exhausted after a 10-hour march, were ordered by Napoleon to face a force of Egyptians which he overestimated to number 78,000. A percentage of Cairo's defenders were Mamelukes, foreign mercenaries in the pay of Egypt's Turkish rulers. These exotic mounted horsemen, who wore multicolored turbans and floating, gold-embroidered caftans, fought very bravely but were no match for the French firepower.

Right: Napoleon's staff, which included many "learned civilians," surveying Egyptian antiquities.

Sketches of Old Egyptian Sites

Below: Baron Dominique Vivant Denon. He was struck by the extraordinary beauty of Egyptian works of art "with no extraneous ornaments or superfluity of lines." His two-volume illustrated description of Bonaparte's campaign in Egypt was an instant best seller in Europe; Denon was later made a baron by the emperor and became superintendent of the Louvre museum in Paris.

arts, it was his work in Egypt that gained him lasting fame. He was enraptured by all that he saw. "One has to rub his eyes to be sure that he is not in a dream," he wrote on the day he first saw the ancient city of Thebes. Of the temple at Dendera he wrote: "What uninterrupted power, what wealth, what abundance, what superfluity of resources must have belonged to a government that could raise an edifice like this." But the awe of the tourist soon gave way to the passion of the artist, and Denon sketched all the relics he encountered in the minutest detail. Future Egyptologists were to be greatly indebted to him, for many of the things he drew were later pillaged or destroyed.

So painstaking was Denon's work that he copied exactly the mysterious inscriptions on the Egyptian monuments, though neither he nor any of the scholars of the Institute of Egypt had any idea what they meant. The ancient civilization of the Egyptian pharaohs was as strange and remote to the inhabitants of Egypt as it was to their conquerors, but the Frenchmen, sons of 18th-century European Enlightenment, were dedicated to the

Discovery of the Rosetta Stone

task of bringing all areas of human knowledge under their sway. They recognized that the script known as *hieroglyphics*, from Greek words *hieros* meaning sacred and *glyphein*, to carve, must be the key to the mysteries of this land of massive monuments.

It was in the summer of 1799 that one of Napoleon's officers of engineers made the most important find of the whole expedition. Pierre Bouchard was in charge of construction work at a French fortification near Rosetta, about 40 miles from Alexandria, when one of his soldiers drew his attention to a basalt stone that he had dug up. It was about the size of a tabletop and it was divided into three sections of engraved writing. The bottom section was in Greek, and therefore was readable. The top section was in the enigmatic hieroglyphic script in which figures of animals, birds, and human beings were mingled with abstract symbols. The middle section was in a kind of writing known as *demotic*, a simplified and popular form of hieroglyphic used for everyday purposes by the ancient Egyptians. It was a fair assumption that

Below: Denon's drawing of mummies he found while with Napoleon's forces in Egypt.

Right: Napoleon's forces in Egypt, 1798. The "learned civilians" or "savants" who accompanied them were not favorites with the lower ranks of the French army, who were convinced that the "graybeards" had been brought along solely to locate hidden treasure.

the three sections contained the same text. If this were so it might be possible to use the Greek to decode the hieroglyphics. The Rosetta stone was sent to Cairo and Napoleon gave orders for casts of it to be made. This made it possible for copies of the texts to be sent to France where excited scholars vied with each other to be the first to crack the code of the pharaohs. It was as well for French scholarship that the casts and copies were made. When the French had to capitulate to the British fleet at Alexandria in 1801 and negotiate for the safe conduct of their "learned civilians" back to France, surrender of the Rosetta stone was part of the price. It is now in the British Museum in London.

One of the scholars on Napoleon's Egyptian expedition was the mathematician and physicist Jean-Baptiste Fourier. Soon after his return from Egypt, Fourier was inspecting a school in Grenoble when he came across an 11-year-old boy prodigy named Jean-François Champollion who had recently taken up the study of Hebrew after already mastering Latin and Greek.

Below: "The Pursuit of Knowledge" by Gillray, from the book *On the Education of the Crocodile*. A crocodile seizes a member of the Institute in a satire on the activities of Napoleon's savants in Egypt, whose functions were to "civilize the natives" and to copy or draw the many undeciphered inscriptions and monuments they saw. Once the "learned civilians" had landed in Egypt they were not issued rations or sleeping quarters, and when he pulled out of Egypt Napoleon left them to the British.

Left: the Rosetta stone, scientifically the most sensational discovery made by the French in Egypt. A broken 3-foot slab of black basalt engraved in three languages, its importance lay in the comparison that could be made between the undeciphered hieroglyphics and the Greek proclamation of the same words. The stone was surrendered to the British who shipped it to Portsmouth, England in 1802 and deposited it with the Society of Antiquarians in London. It was later transferred to the British Museum.

Above: Jean-François Champollion (1790–1832), acknowledged as having laid the foundations of Egyptology by cracking the code of the language of hieroglyphics. A child prodigy in the study of ancient languages, he studied Coptic for many years and published a dictionary and grammar for the language. Champollion worked for 14 years from a plaster cast of the Rosetta stone without ever seeing the stone itself. Below: Thomas Young (1773–1829), who in 1812 acquired a copy of the Rosetta stone. A man of considerable learning (he was an eminent physicist) and wide interests, he probably helped Champollion to make his breakthrough in the translation of hieroglyphics.

The boy spoke of his fascination with ancient languages, so Fourier invited him to his home and showed him his Egyptian collection. "Can anyone read them?" Champollion asked when he saw the cryptic hieroglyphs. When Fourier told him that nobody could the boy said solemnly, "I am going to do it."

With extraordinary single-mindedness, Champollion prepared himself to fulfill this ambition. He studied Denon's profusely illustrated account of his travels, and he added to his linguistic repertoire Arabic, Syrian, Chaldean, and then Coptic. This last was a language directly descended from ancient Egyptian. The initial optimism of scholars as to the possibility of deciphering the hieroglyphs with the help of the Greek text of the Rosetta stone had proved mistaken. Some small progress was made with the interpretation of parts of the demotic text—the middle and best preserved section of the Rosetta stone—by the French orientalist Sylvestre de Sacy and by a Swedish diplomat, Johann David Åkerblad. The top section of hieroglyphic script continued to baffle scholars.

The main reason why it baffled them was that they regarded the hieroglyphs as a form of picture-writing in which the recognizable figures stood for what they represented and the more abstract symbols had some religious significance. This view of the matter went back to a Greek writer of the 4th century A.D. named Horapollo, and because of its antiquity and plausibility nobody had thought to doubt it. After all, the very term "hieroglyph" means "holy writing." Champollion's first important discovery was that there was a difference between the sacred sculptural emblems of the Egyptians and their hieroglyphic texts, although they both made use of animal and bird figures. Champollion formulated and worked on the assumption that the hieroglyphs were phonetic symbols, and it was his persistent following up of this idea that ultimately led to the breakthrough that made him the father of Egyptology.

In fact Champollion was not entirely original in his approach. Some writers have claimed that an Englishman named Thomas Young was the first man who saw the light. Young was a man of multiple talents who made significant contributions to theoretical physics as well as to the study of languages. He worked with the Rosetta stone and also with the text of an obelisk from Philae in Egypt which stood (and still stands) in the grounds of the country estate of a Mr. Bankes at Kingston Lacey in Dorset, England. Young worked out that certain groups of symbols in the ancient texts, which were formed in oval "cartouches," would be the names of rulers, and he proposed that names of foreign origin would have been rendered phonetically. Following this line of reasoning, Young correctly identified the names Ptolemy and Berenike. He also established other principles that were later proved correct. For instance, he suggested that hieroglyphic scripts could be read either from left to right or from right to left, and that the correct beginning of a line was indicated by the way the bird or animal figures faced. What he didn't see was that it was not only foreign names that were represented phonetically in the texts, but that the hieroglyphs were all phonetic symbols.

It was the text of the obelisk in Dorset that enabled Champollion to make his discovery of the key to the hieroglyphs. He

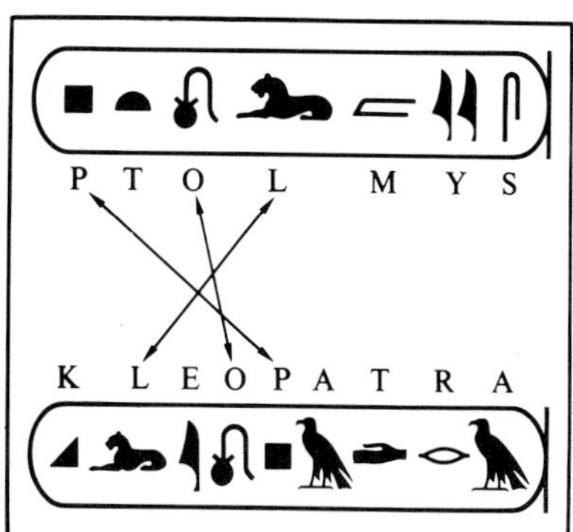

Naming Ptolemy and Cleopatra

Far left: the obelisk from Philae in the grounds of a country estate at Kingston Lacey in Dorset, England.

Above left: companion of the cartouches of the royal names Ptolemy and Cleopatra. These names, with their three common letters P, O, and L, provided Champollion with his first breakthrough in deciphering the hieroglyphics.

Left: relief of Cleopatra showing her cartouche, the oval shape enclosing her name. A loop of double-thick rope with knotted ends was simplified to form a line, probably signifying the all-embracing rule of the pharoah.

identified on it, in another cartouche, the name Cleopatra. Then when he compared the signs that rendered Ptolemy with those that rendered Cleopatra he found that three of them were common to both names. Moreover these symbols occurred in roughly the positions corresponding with the positions of the letters P, O, and L in the names. Having found this lead, he was able to surmise or narrow down the possibilities of what other hieroglyphs stood for what letters in the names. In this way Champollion took his first steps toward translating the language of the ancient Egyptians. Turning his attention to another and older text, he was able to make out the signs that spelled the name Rameses which was given to 11 of the pharaohs. Therefore he established that phonetic symbols had not only been used for the names of foreign rulers but also for those of Egyptian rulers. Further long and patient research led him to the conclusion that hieroglyphics were not "holy writing" but the written form of a real language that dealt with everyday things.

Champollion realized the ambition of his boyhood 20 years after he had announced it to Fourier. It was in 1822 that he read his historic paper on the hieroglyphs to a French learned society. Then in the years 1828–29 he led a scientific expedition to Egypt,

Europeans as Treasure Seekers

where his ability to read the writing on the ancient stones astonished 19th-century Egyptians and enabled him repeatedly to confirm his ideas and to identify and date the great monuments and relics by reading their inscriptions. Champollion laid the foundations of Egyptology, although when he died at the age of 42 many European scholars mocked his ideas and dismissed him as mad. It was not until 1866, when another engraved text in the three languages of the Rosetta stone was found by a German, Richard Lepsius, that Champollion was proved right beyond dispute. Lepsius placed on one of the Giza pyramids a tablet bearing the name of the sponsor of his 1843–45 expedition, King Frederick William IV of Prussia, and written in hieroglyphic script—an act which paid tribute to the scholar Champollion quite as much as to the Prussian king.

While men like Champollion and Young were puzzling over the cipher that would open the mysteries of ancient Egypt, others were making a more direct approach to those mysteries, and at the same time making fortunes for themselves out of valuable Egyptian antiquities. One of the most important of these treasure seekers was an extraordinary Italian adventurer named Giovanni Belzoni who had started his career as a strong man in a London circus billed as "The Patagonian Sampson." But Belzoni's first experience among the monuments of the ancient Egyptians was typical of many later explorers. When in 1818 he found his way into the burial chamber of Chephren, builder of the second pyramid of Giza, he found it empty. Robbers had taken its contents during the Middle Ages, so his only satisfactions were to scrawl his name boldly on the wall of the sacred place—the inscription is still there today—and to go down in history as the first man to discover an ancient Egyptian burial chamber in modern times. But Belzoni was a man who looked for more substantial rewards for his efforts. After all, he had gone to Egypt in the first place to seek his fortune, not to establish a

Above: Richard Lepsius (1810–1884), a German Egyptologist who led a Prussian expedition to Egypt and Nubia which was the first to arrange material scientifically. As a result the number of known pyramids was increased to 67, and knowledge of the Old Empire was extended to as far back as the 4th millenium B.C.

Right: the pyramid built by Chephren at Giza, first explored in 1818 by Giovanni Belzoni.

Left: Abu Simbel, the temple cut from rock by Rameses II. It was Giovanni Belzoni who cleared the sand which covered it, and he also shipped to England a stone head of the pharoah like that of this colossal figure. When the Aswan Dam was planned in more recent times the endangered temple was cut into 30-ton blocks and rebuilt beyond the reach of the waters of the Nile.

Below: Belzoni exploring tombs in search of antiquities for Henry Salt. Many of the tombs he entered had been only partially rifled by tomb robbers of the past due to the ingenuity of the original architects and their designs.

scholarly reputation. He had the good fortune to meet and befriend the British consul general, Henry Salt, who was running a profitable sideline in buying Egyptian antiquities for patrons in England. Belzoni became Salt's chief collector, and in the course of traveling around Egypt looking for bargains he happened to make some important discoveries. He was not only the first modern European to explore the interior of a pyramid, but was also the first to enter the temple at Abu Simbel. He was also the discoverer of the tomb of Seti I in what became known as the Valley of the Kings near Thebes in Upper Egypt, where he acquired for Salt a *sarcophagus* or stone coffin which is today in the Soane Museum in London.

Many of the exhibits in the Egyptian gallery of the British Museum are there thanks to Belzoni's energy. He was not daunted by size. One of his first commissions from Salt was to get a giant stone head of the pharaoh Rameses II that was lying in the sand at Thebes. Another was to bring an obelisk down the Nile by barge from Philae. On this second errand Belzoni came into conflict with the agents of the French consul general, Bernardino Drovetti, who was also in the looting and shipping business.

Above: Belzoni's method of transporting the stone head of the Rameses II colossus from Thebes in preparation for shipping it to England. His interest in such problems of transport was foreshadowed when he first arrived in Egypt—to demonstrate a hydraulic machine of his own invention.

Below: Mehemet Ali (ca. 1769–1849), Albanian founder of the royal house of modern Egypt. He first went to Egypt as an officer of the Ottoman forces mobilized to fight Napoleon in 1798. He occupied Cairo in 1805 after the evacuation of the French army, and in 1806 the Turkish sultan was forced to confirm him as pasha.

Shots were fired, but Belzoni retained his trophy. In this way, the Italian adventurer contributed indirectly to the solution of the riddle of the hieroglyphs, for this particular obelisk was the one destined for Mr. Bankes' estate in Dorset and which helped Champollion to make this breakthrough. On another occasion an obelisk Belzoni was transporting fell into the Nile, but while a less enterprising man would have left it there Belzoni managed to get it out again.

The massive size of many of his Egyptian acquisitions was a problem that never seemed to trouble Belzoni. Nor was the original purpose of the buildings and antiquities, whether religious or funerary. He never appears to have shown much curiosity about or admiration for the people who many thousands of years ago had built the magnificent temples, tombs, and statues of the Nile valley. He appears to have been completely without superstition or any other fear. The following extract from one of his accounts of a particularly tough tomb-looting expedition gives us a good idea of the man's nerve: "I sought a resting place and found one; but when my weight bore on the body of an Egyptian, it crushed it like a band-box. I naturally had recourse to my hands to sustain my weight, but they found no better support; so that I sank altogether among the broken mummies, with the crash of bones, rags, and wooden cases, which raised such a dust as kept me motionless for a quarter of an hour." If there ever was such a thing as "the mummy's curse," which was said to threaten later robbers and explorers of the Valley of the Kings, the brash giant Belzoni must have been immune to it.

Between 1804 and 1844 the ruler of Egypt on behalf of the Turks was another adventurer, a former coffee dealer from Albania named Mehemet Ali. His chief concern was to get his country modernized and he had little interest in its antiquities. It was left to others to protest about the wholesale robbery of the land of the pharaohs, which at the rate it had reached in the 1820s and 1830s would soon have scattered the relics so far and wide that scholars trying to solve the mysteries of ancient Egypt would have been frustrated. Remarkably preserved by the sand

and the hot, dry climate was evidence of a great civilization raised by men more than 4000 years ago that had flourished for thousands of years, a civilization capable of engineering feats that would even discourage a modern contractor, and possessed of artistic and religious traditions that seemed strange to Europeans but were clearly consistent and long-established. The relics of this early peak of human civilization had obviously been pillaged down the centuries, but in the first decades of the 19th century the rich and insatiable European and American collectors had encouraged the plundering. The traffic in treasures reached such proportions that before long there would be little left except the most massive and enigmatic relics of all, the great pyramids themselves. At this time two things were badly needed. First, some control of the traffic in Egyptian antiquities; secondly, some attempts to undertake systematic archaeological field work and to apply the new knowledge of hieroglyphic script to the task of understanding ancient Egyptian culture and history.

Howard-Vyse and Mykerinos' Tomb

Above left: the pyramid of Mykerinos and his queen, the third and smallest of the Giza pyramids, first identified by Colonel Howard-Vyse.

Above: Colonel Richard Howard-Vyse (1784–1853) in 1830. He was to spend over £10,000 exploring the pyramids, to which he was attracted by "the remote antiquity and uncertainty of their origin, and . . . the peculiarity of their mysterious construction." His greatest prize, the sarcophagus of Mykerinos, was lost when the ship carrying it back to England sank in a storm off the coast of Spain.

In the 1830s a British army officer, Colonel Richard Howard-Vyse, teamed up with a civil engineer, John Perring, to investigate the pyramids. This was one of the first expeditions motivated by the quest for knowledge rather than profit, but if Vyse's motives were more admirable than Belzoni's his methods were scarcely less crude. He correctly identified the smallest of the Giza pyramids as that of the ancient king Mykerinos, but in an attempt to get into the burial chamber he damaged the pyramid with explosives.

It was the three-year expedition of Champollion's disciple Richard Lepsius in 1843–45 that was the first real archaeological exploration of the land of Egypt. Lepsius discovered the remains of 30 formerly unknown pyramids, which meant the total of known pyramids was 67. He traveled all over the land copying down or taking casts of hieroglyphic inscriptions on buildings and statues. By translating them and comparing and cross-relating their sources Lepsius gradually built up a view of the panorama of Egyptian history. He explored no less than 130 *mastabas*, the strange rectangular buildings with sloping sides that the ancient Egyptians had erected over the tombs of important people. On

Mariette and the Cult of the Bull

Right: wall painting from the tomb of Khnumhotep near Beni Hasan on the Nile, recreated from the original tracings and notes of Richard Lepsius' Prussian expedition. It shows the arrival of a caravan of Semitic nomads in Egypt and dates from the time of Sesostris II around 1895 B.C.

Below: Auguste Mariette (1821–81) at the age of 30. A dedicated Egyptologist, he campaigned to conserve antiquities for Egypt—an aim which was met with varying response from the Egyptian rulers and the disapproval of other foreign collectors.

the vast empty plain where once had stood Akhetaton, capital city of the heretic king and religious genius Akhnaton, he found relics with inscriptions that provided insights into the character and thought of that strange inspired ruler. Lepsius took a wealth of information back to Germany with him in 1845, as well as a wealth of antiquities which furnished the Egyptian Museum in Berlin. In addition, he established the foundations of the study of ancient Egyptian history with his books, *Egyptian Chronology* (1849) and *The Book of Kings* (1850).

In 1850 a young Frenchman, Auguste Ferdinand Mariette, arrived in Egypt on a mission to catalog manuscripts in Coptic monasteries and to buy for the Louvre Museum in Paris ancient Egyptian documents known as *papyri*, from the material on which they were written, made from thin strips of a grasslike plant called papyrus pressed together and dried. The monks were suspicious of him, however, because some years before an Englishman had gone around on a similar pretext and had proceeded to get the monks drunk in order to steal their manuscripts. Having met resistance to his project everywhere, Mariette went to Cairo, where one evening he climbed to the top of the citadel and had an experience that changed his life. As he described it later: "Suffused in golden dust and in the fiery red glow from the setting sun, the pyramids, massed together, presented an imposing spectacle, which overwhelmed me and absorbed me with a force almost painful in its violence."

Giving up the hunt for manuscripts, Mariette boldly put the funds the authorities of the Louvre had furnished him with to another purpose. One day he was walking among the ruins of Sekkara, a town about 15 miles from Cairo, when he noticed, near the great step pyramid of Zoser, a sphinx partly buried in the sand. On it he read a hieroglyphic inscription referring to Apis, the sacred bull of a cult that had been centered at the nearby city of Memphis. Mariette then remembered a passage from the Greek geographer, Strabo, who was born in about 58 B.C. Strabo described the burial ground of the sacred bulls of Memphis, where in his own day there had been an Alley of Sphinxes, most of them even then nearly buried in sand. Mariette had one of

Left: ancient Egyptian writing implements. From left to right they are: wooden palette; porcelain palette; inscribed wooden palette; inscribed wooden palette with reeds for writing; wooden palette of the reign of Amenophis III; ivory palette; bronze inkpot and chain; and a roll of blank papyrus. Scribes used pointed reeds as pens and palettes for holding ink. Black ink was made of soot mixed with water or vinegar and was used for writing on papyrus—pressed dried strips of a grasslike plant.

those intuitions that have often led to great archaeological finds. He felt sure that he was standing on the sacred site, and he backed his hunch by using his funds to hire Arab workers. He excavated an avenue 600 feet in length flanked by 140 sphinxes and with the remains of a temple at each end. In the temples and in several tombs he found a wealth of artifacts connected with the cult, as well as some fine statues such as the figure of a seated scribe which is today one of the treasures of the Louvre.

Not surprisingly, the French authorities approved Mariette's employment of their funds and provided him with more money to continue his excavations. In one of the temples he found a steep shaft leading down to the burial chambers where the succes-

Below: the step pyramid of Zoser at Sekkara, near the site of Mariette's avenue of sphinxes.

The Tomb of Ti

Right: 1.5-foot-high statue of a seated scribe found at the Serapeum site by Mariette and now at the Louvre museum in Paris. As keepers of all records, scribes held an important place in Egyptian life and wielded a power of which they were well aware. One boasted, "It's the scribe who imposes taxes . . . who commands the whole country." Another considered a book "more effective . . . than a decorated tombstone."

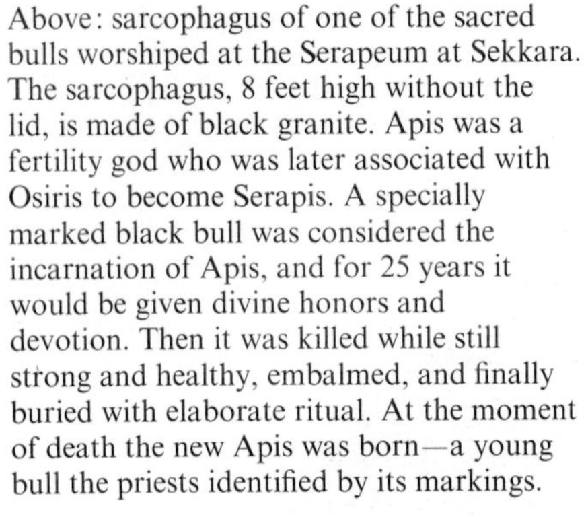

Above: sarcophagus of one of the sacred bulls worshiped at the Serapeum at Sekkara. The sarcophagus, 8 feet high without the lid, is made of black granite. Apis was a fertility god who was later associated with Osiris to become Serapis. A specially marked black bull was considered the incarnation of Apis, and for 25 years it would be given divine honors and devotion. Then it was killed while still strong and healthy, embalmed, and finally buried with elaborate ritual. At the moment of death the new Apis was born—a young bull the priests identified by its markings.

sion of sacred bulls of Apis had been ceremonially buried over centuries. Eventually he excavated galleries stretching underground for about 1000 feet, opening onto which were burial chambers containing the immense stone sarcophagi in which the sacred bulls had lain. Each sarcophagus had been covered with a heavy stone slab, but most of these had been pushed aside by tomb robbers centuries ago. Only two of the sarcophagi were unopened, and in them Mariette found intact the original burial regalia of the sacred bulls.

The Serapaeum, as this site is called after the god Serapis, was in its day the most sensational excavated find in the history of Egyptian archaeology. With its discovery Mariette began a career of 30 fruitful years in Egyptology. He campaigned widely and successfully for conservation of the antiquities of Egypt, and when the Egyptian authorities formed an Institute of Egyptian Antiquities in 1857 Mariette was appointed its director and the chief supervisor of all excavations. He investigated many important sites, and made one other major find: the tomb of a great courtier and landowner named Ti. The tomb was situated near the Serapaeum, but it was considerably older and was judged to date from about the same period as the great pyramids of Cheops, Chephren, and Mykerinos at Giza. Its chief interest was its wealth of well preserved decoration. The narrative friezes and reliefs on the walls of the burial chamber and the corridor leading to it gave a vivid and detailed picture of daily life in ancient Egypt. Here were depicted the activities of farmers, shipbuilders, foresters, stone masons, leather workers, and gold-smelters. Here too were illustrations of Ti's own domestic and official life which showed him to have been a very powerful lord in a feudal-type society. The tomb of Ti gave a fascinating insight into the life of the period when the pyramids had been built, but at the same time it increased the mystery of those colossal structures, for it posed a central question: how could a people with only a rudimentary technology have succeeded in building them?

Mariette did not believe that much could be learned from the pyramids themselves, and it was not until a year before his death that he turned his attention to them. In 1880 he opened a minor pyramid at Sekkara, and he had a stroke of luck comparable to that of his first discovery. The small pyramid turned out to be a royal tomb.

It was Mariette's successor as director of the Institute, another Frenchman, Gaston Maspero, and his assistant Brugsch who made the next great discovery in Egyptian archaeology. The royal burial chambers in the great pyramids and in the Valley of the Kings all turned out to be empty when they were explored. It was naturally assumed that their contents, including the mummified royal remains, had all been pillaged centuries ago. Powdered mummy had been in great demand as a remedy for all kinds of diseases in the European Middle Ages. So when Maspero found intact the mummies of 36 kings, queens, princes, and high priests, including the illustrious Rameses II, Seti I, Tuthmose II, and Amenophis I, he won renown in the history of Egyptology.

The circumstances of Maspero's find were curious and dramatic. Noticing that some fine funerary objects and papyri were turning up regularly on the private market in Egyptian antiquities, Maspero decided that someone had found a rich tomb and was plundering it. His investigations led him to an Arab family, one of whose members was induced to talk and to lead the authorities to the secret hiding place of the loot. It was just outside the Valley of the Kings, and was a most cunningly concealed hiding place. Access was gained only by descending between the walls of a precipice to the hidden entrance to a well. Leading from the interior of the well there were underground passages which led eventually to a funerary chamber. Inside this chamber was an astonishing sight. Not only was the ground littered with valuable objects and works of art, but also from floor to ceiling were piled sarcophagi and boxes of mummies. All of these were carefully marked with their names and among them were some of the most famous rulers of Egyptian antiquity. When the contents of the royal mass tomb were transferred by barge down the Nile to Cairo, funeral salutes were fired by the Egyptian villagers, while women followed along the bank wailing and tearing their hair as if in mourning for their own rulers.

Tomb plundering had been a problem at the very time when the royal tombs in the Valley of the Kings had been constructed. This fact is proved by surviving contemporary documents announcing dire punishments for tomb robbers. The royal tombs

Above: a scene of herdsmen and their cattle crossing a river, from a frieze found in the tomb of the landowner Ti.

Below: the mummy of Set I, one of the 36 found by Gaston Maspero and his assistants in a funerary chamber just outside the Valley of the Kings. It is now in the Cairo museum.

The Pyramidology of Piazzi Smith

Right: Emil Brugsch, assistant to Maspero, who was first shown the burial chamber of the royal mummies at Deir-el-Bahri.

Above: Charles Piazzi Smyth, who made important contributions to the science of spectroscopy as well as astronomy. He believed that the "sacred cubit" unit of measurement used by the builders of the Great Pyramid of Cheops was the same length (25.025 inches) as that used by Moses to construct the tabernacle and by Noah in the building of the Ark. In the process of trying to prove some of his theories he performed the first systematic analysis of the Great Pyramid using modern measuring equipment.

were probably situated together in the Valley so that the living successors of the royal dynasty would be able to protect them. After all it would be in their own interest to do so because they too in turn would need protection. There are indications that the system worked relatively well for a time, but with inevitable dynastic changes, wars, and the occasional accession of weak rulers, there was obviously no guarantee of the eternal repose for their mortal remains that the great kings had hoped for. It must have been at a time when a collapse of authority was foreseeable that a ruler, or possibly an assembly of priests, had removed the royal mummies that Maspero found to the obscure communal tomb outside the valley, for there they might have a chance of resting in peace even though not in the splendour they had originally provided for themselves. It is ironical that in this land where stood the most monumental tombs the world had ever seen the rulers that enjoyed the longest uninterrupted repose after death had been bundled unceremoniously together in an obscure hole in the ground.

It seemed that nearly every new discovery in Egyptology raised some new question about the pyramids. Were they really just monumental tombs, the egomaniacal creations of ancient kings bent on feathering the nests of their eternal souls? Not every European scholar thought so. One man who thought that at least one of the pyramids at Giza was much more than this was the Astronomer Royal for Scotland, Charles Piazzi Smyth, who in 1874 published a curious and apparently scholarly book titled *Our Inheritance in the Great Pyramid*, which became an international best seller.

Wherever there are intriguing mysteries and reliable information is meager, eccentric theories flourish. Nowhere has this been more true than in the case of the puzzle of the pyramids. Piazzi Smyth set out for Egypt in 1864. His object was to measure the exact dimensions of the Great Pyramid at Giza, tomb of the

Above: the pyramids at Giza from the south. The Great Pyramid (of Cheops) is the one farthest away from the camera. All three pyramids were plundered long ago, and they no longer reach their original heights. The Great Pyramid, for example, is now 30 feet shorter than when it was built. Surrounding the three monumental structures are fields of flat-topped mastabas used for the burial of relatives or officials of the kings.

pharaoh Cheops. Ten years later, when he published his book, he had decided that the Great Pyramid had great significance for Christians and that its structure could even reveal future events. Briefly, Piazzi Smyth found, in its dimensions and alignments and those of its internal chambers and passages the encoded history of the human race from Old Testament Biblical times down to the future Second Coming of Christ. The Scot has had many followers down to modern times, and in recent years the so-called science of "pyramidology" has enjoyed a boom. The ideas of the eccentric 19th-century astronomer have been combined with the theory of the modern German writer Erich von Däniken that the pyramids were built by space men. This makes a heady mix of speculation indeed. But perhaps Piazzi Smyth's major importance was that his theories brought to Egypt the man who was to become the greatest Egyptologist of all, the British archaeologist William Flinders Petrie. Petrie arrived in Egypt in 1880 at the age of 27. His father, a supporter of Piazzi Smyth's idea that the Great Pyramid was divine revelation in stone, encouraged him to make the trip. He believed that the young man, who had already made a reputation for himself with his precise and detailed survey of Stonehenge, would be able to confirm the measurements on which the Astronomer Royal's theories were based. But Petrie was, at the least, skeptical of Piazzi Smyth's and his own father's views, and so it was that he went to Egypt determined to settle once and for all the puzzle of the pyramids.

Chapter 2
The Pyramids Explored

What were the pyramids built for—and how? What methods were used to preserve so successfully the bodies of the dead? What exactly was the belief that made the living mourners place mummified food, exquisite scale models, and priceless objects of all kinds in the tombs of their dead? This chapter takes as its central theme the Egyptian cult of the dead and the evidence built up about it by scholars and archaeologists who, armed with the key supplied by Champollion and other philologists, set about solving the puzzle. Its culmination is the discovery, in 1922, of what Egyptologists had dreamed of for years—a royal tomb untouched by robbers, the world-famous tomb of Tutankhamen.

One still, moonlit night in 1880 a white figure emerged from one of the tombs near the base of the Great Pyramid of Cheops, scrambled over the great stones and climbed to the entrance to the chambers of the dead. Then it disappeared. An observer might well have thought that he had seen a ghost. What in fact he would have seen was a stark naked Englishman. William Flinders Petrie, just arrived at Giza, had encamped in one of the mastabas and was impatient to begin the survey of the Great Pyramid. He went naked because of the heat, and even so when he emerged after midnight he was sweating profusely and had an aching head. He was satisfied with the night's work, though, when he went back to his mastaba. By the light of a smoking lamp he copied out and put in order the notes he had made inside the pyramid.

Night after night Petrie worked in the stifling corridors and chambers of the pyramids. His work led to the publication of his book, *Pyramids and Temples at Gizeh*, in 1883. His findings are generally considered to have demolished Piazzi Smyth's theory that mysteries and messages were encoded in the measurements of the Great Pyramid. But he had demonstrated that it was a building of sublime symmetry and proportions and a consummate feat of engineering genius. Petrie became the man most intimately acquainted with the pyramids of Egypt, and throughout his life he denounced the fantasies of pyramidologists. A tale he enjoyed telling was how he once caught a pyramidologist

Opposite: Queen Ankhesenamun anointing her husband's collarette in a scene decorating the back of Tutankhamen's plated throne. Sheets of gold and silver, colored glass paste, glazed ceramic, and inlaid calcite are the materials used. The sovereigns are each marked with their names.

Above: Sir William Flinders Petrie (1853–1942) in 1923. Before making his first scientific survey of Giza in 1880 Petrie had surveyed several ancient British sites including Stonehenge. During his 60-year career as an Egyptologist he founded the British School of Archaeology in Egypt, and he is considered the father of modern scientific archaeology.

filing down a projecting stone in order to make its measurement conform to his theory.

One overwhelming fact that is difficult to reconcile with the claims of mystical pyramidology is that the Great Pyramid of Cheops is only one of more than 60 pyramids scattered throughout Egypt. This implies that it is a cultural artifact of a historical people and not a building raised on the precise instructions of God Almighty. Petrie, in his 60-year career in Egyptology, investigated all the pyramids, and put forward his own hypotheses as to when, how, and why they had been built.

The oldest structure, he believed, was the pyramid at Medum, which doesn't look much like a pyramid at all today, but more like an immense square tower. This tower structure, Petrie believed, was the central core of the building. Beneath and in the middle of it was the tomb chamber, the entrance to which was by way of a long sloping passage which leveled off below the chamber and then rose vertically into it through the floor. The building had been begun, he suggested, as a mastaba, which had been enlarged by heightening it and adding a coating. This pro-

Right: the square structure at Medum which Petrie believed might be the oldest structure found to date in Egypt, a prototype for the later monuments at Giza.

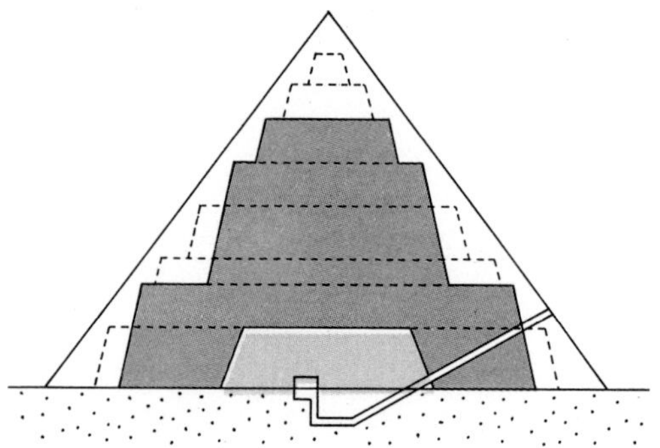

Below: diagram showing the development of Medum from a mastaba to the familiar step-pyramid shape.

Petrie's Theory of Medum Tower

cess of heightening and extending had been repeated seven times, resulting in a high, stepped mass of masonry. The same process was exemplified more clearly in the better preserved step pyramid at Sekkara. The pyramid shape, Petrie thought, might have come about rather by chance as the original structure was added to. This idea was supported by the fact that the internal masonry lining the descending passage showed clear discontinuities at points corresponding to where the entrances would have been at the different stages of construction. This observation indicated that for a time the stepped structure had been regarded as the building's ultimate form. Eventually a true pyramid would have been achieved by adding a uniform slope of masonry from base to top. Whether this stage had actually been reached at Medum was dubious, though, for it was possible that the disaster of its collapse had occurred before the building was complete. The internal stresses set up in such an immense mass of masonry were such that the very precise calculations of angles, tolerances, and the load-bearing capacity of foundations needed to be made to ensure against collapse. Medum probably taught the pyramid builders valuable architectural lessons which they applied in the later construction of the pyramids at Giza.

In most pyramids the sepulchral chamber is below ground level, sometimes cut out of the rock base on which the structure rests, but in the Great Pyramid of Cheops there are two chambers actually in the pyramid as well as one beneath it. In fact the subterranean chamber is unfinished, and the upper ones, known as the king's and the queen's, were originally extremely well hidden. A long descending passage, as at Medum, led from the outer face of the pyramid on the north side down to the subterranean chamber. At a point along this passage there was access through

Below: diagram of a section of the inside of the Great Pyramid of Cheops. Petrie surveyed and measured the entire building in an attempt to prove or disprove Piazzi Smyth's pyramidologist theories. He was impressed to find the layout of the Great Pyramid "a triumph of skill. Its errors, both in length and in angles, could be covered by placing one's thumb on them."

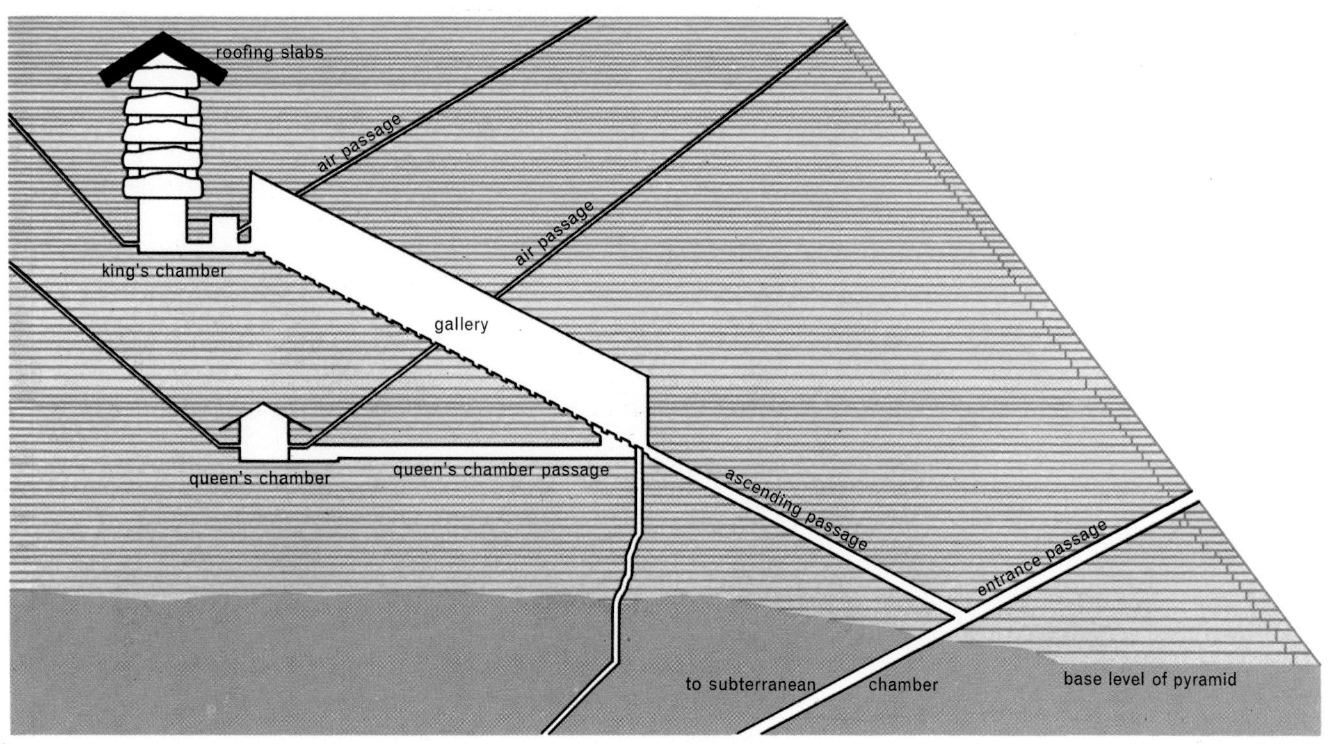

The Ingenuity of the Tomb Robbers

Right: Arabs exploring the Grand Gallery of the Great Pyramid. Its overall length is 157 feet; the walls are 28 feet high, rising vertically in seven courses of polished limestone. The gallery narrows from 62 inches wide to 41 inches at the top.

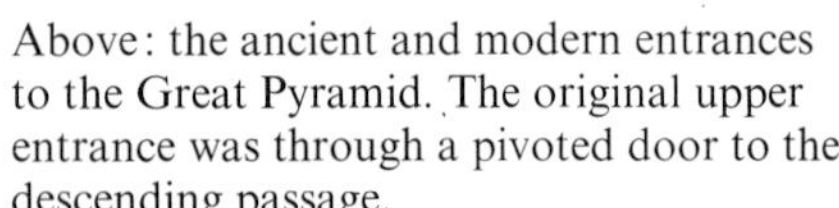

Above: the ancient and modern entrances to the Great Pyramid. The original upper entrance was through a pivoted door to the descending passage.

the roof to an ascending passage. This access was plugged with a granite block so that probably the descending passage and subterranean chamber were constructed to mislead possible intruders. Another passage branching off the ascending passage and leading to the queen's chamber was also blocked. The indications were that the pyramid was an artificial mountain in the middle of which Cheops had hoped that he and his regent would be securely concealed from intruders for ever. And when we recall that originally the entire outer casing of the immense structure was of smooth fine stone, immaculately jointed and highly finished, and that the small sealed entrance to the descending passage was hidden somewhere behind this facing, we can understand the virtual impossibility of the would-be tomb robber's task. It was probably only when dynastic changes made the pyramids things of no concern to the rulers of Egypt, and their fine casing stones were plundered for other building projects, that the tomb robbers had any hope of gaining access to the treasures walled up with the dead pharaohs.

Petrie's explorations brought him to feel admiration for the

Left: detail of the Abbot papyrus in the British Museum, London. It records part of an early tomb robber's confession. The symbol for pyramid—a rectangle laid on its long side, with a triangle atop it—can be seen near the right end of the third line from the bottom.

patience, stamina, and ingenuity of the pyramid thieves. In 1889 he tackled an apparently intact and previously unidentified pyramid further up the Nile. Failing to find any sign of the usual entrance on the north side, he carefully examined the east side. Again there was no sign of an entrance. He decided to dig a tunnel straight through to the middle. This task took weeks, but eventually he reached the wall of the burial chamber. This was breached, but to begin with the hole was not wide enough for Petrie to get in, and he had to send a small Egyptian boy in with a light. The light revealed two sarcophagi, both of which were empty and had obviously been plundered. Also, water had seeped into the chamber. When eventually Petrie entered he found that he had to wade, and to explore the floor he had to use a hoe. His work was rewarded with the finding of some small objects that enabled him to identify the pyramid as that of Amenemhet III, a pharaoh who had reigned from 1849 to 1801 B.C. This was an archaeological coup, but Petrie had become fascinated with the question of how the robbers got into the well-hidden chamber, and he continued his investigations to try and find the answer.

Eventually he found a cunningly concealed entrance to the pyramid on the south side. Retracing the route the thieves had taken was a difficult and sometimes dangerous business. At times the archaeologist had to crawl on his stomach through low passageways covered with mud. He found that the architects of the pyramid had been unbelievably ingenious in devising means of frustrating would-be intruders. A flight of stairs came to a dead end in an empty chamber, from which there seemed to be no way forward. But the ceiling proved to be an immense trapdoor. This gave access to another passage, which had obviously been filled with great blocks of stone, which the robbers had had to move before continuing along the passage, to find themselves in a second blind room. Having found their way forward from here, they came to a third, and so on. Amenemhet III had certainly been determined never to be disturbed in his burial chamber deep inside his pyramid. Petrie could not help admiring the robbers whose determination and ingenuity had matched those of the pharaoh and his architects.

People who put forward occult theories of the nature and purpose of the pyramids tended to base their arguments on the fact that it was impossible that such enormous and elaborate

Below: bust of Amenemhet III, a pharoah of the 12th dynasty, showing him in priestly robes. Petrie discovered objects which enabled him to identify the tomb in which the bust was found.

Above: painting from the papyrus of Hunefer of the 19th dynasty, showing the ceremony of "The Opening of the Mouth." Performed when a funeral procession arrived at the tomb, it was a ritual remembrance of the visit of the Egyptian god Horus to his father Osiris to bring the news that his murder had been avenged, his killer Set defeated, and Horus had attained his rightful place. The touching of the dead person's lips with a ceremonial adze insured the resurrection of his soul.

structures should be merely tombs. And certainly the investment of wealth and labor that went into their construction does seem absurd compared with the object of keeping the mortal remains and some of the property of a king safe from thieves. But we tend to look at the phenomenon from our point of view, and consider that only the most self-centered and ruthlessly despotic ruler would be capable of such an extravagant act of folly. Evidence such as Petrie found in the pyramid of Amenemhet III, indicating the pharaoh's paranoid terror of having his mortal remains disturbed, does suggest, however, that the pyramids really were just tombs, and when we also take into account the nature of ancient Egyptian religion and belief in the afterlife the idea becomes less preposterous.

No archaeological discovery has cast more light on the ancient Egyptian cult of the dead than that of the tomb of Tutankhamen. Excavated in the years 1922–26 by a former assistant of Petrie's, Howard Carter, this site yielded the richest-ever find in the history of Egyptology and made the obscure adolescent pharaoh the best-known figure from Egyptian history. For a century Egyptologists had dreamed of finding the pharaoh's tomb unmolested by robbers, and the possibility that such a thing existed was beginning to look very remote indeed when Carter made his incredibly fortunate strike. The astonishing wealth of this tomb of a ruler who could never have been more than a puppet of the powerful priesthood made people wonder what fabulous treasures must have furnished the sepulchral chambers of more illustrious pharaohs. It also helped them to understand the lure

Untouched Tomb of Tutankhamen

that had driven the tomb robbers to overcome all the difficulties that had been put in their paths.

In 1914 a British amateur in archaeology, the Earl of Carnarvon, obtained a concession to dig in the most intensely excavated site in the whole of Egypt: the Valley of the Kings. Gaston Maspero, who signed the authorization, assured Lord Carnarvon and his archaeological aide, Howard Carter, that there could not possibly be anything more to find in the Valley. Carter recalled, however, that the same thing had been said when the American archaeologist Theodore Davis had obtained his concession in 1902. Over the 12 succeeding seasons Davis had unearthed three important new tombs and found the coffin and mummy of the heretic King Akhnaton. It was certain of Davis' secondary finds that gave Carter the idea that the tomb of Tutankhamen might be in the Valley. A cup buried under a rock, a broken gilded box found in a small rock tomb, and some large earthenware jars containing funerary material—all these finds bore the name Tutankhamen and suggested the existence of his tomb somewhere in the vicinity.

Carter and Carnarvon started digging in 1917 and continued for five seasons with little success. A small deposit of alabaster jars bearing the names of the pharaohs Rameses II and Meremptah were found, but nothing else of note came to light in the entire triangle of their concession. There was some debate whether they should devote a sixth season to the site or move on to a more promising one elsewhere. Finally they decided to put in a final season as there were still some areas where they had not dug.

Immediately below the entrance to the tomb of Rameses VI there were some ancient workmen's huts erected on a foundation of flint boulders, originally to accommodate laborers in the tomb of Rameses. Eventually the only spot left unexcavated was directly underneath the huts, and late in his last season, after Lord Carnarvon had gone back to England, Carter ordered them to be demolished. When the first one was taken down there was

Above: photograph from the Griffith Institute of the Ashmolean Museum, Oxford, England, showing the royal cemetery in the Valley of the Kings. Taken on the Carter-Carnarvon expedition, this photo shows the relative position of the tombs of Tutankhamen and Rameses VI.

Left: wall painting from the tomb of Haremheb, discovered by Theodore David in 1908. Haremheb was an army general who took the throne at the end of the 18th dynasty. He is depicted twice in this section, with his cartouche above him. The god Horus and his mother Isis are with him.

Golden Shrine of the Boy-King

revealed beneath it a step cut into the rock. Two days of feverish excavation revealed a stairway leading down beneath an overhanging rock. At the end of it the upper part of a sealed doorway was disclosed. A peephole drilled in the door revealed beyond it a passage filled with rubble. Carter could scarcely control his excitement. The seals on the door indicated that this was the tomb of an important person, and the presence of the huts above it showed that it had not been entered since the days of Rameses VI. Feeling that such a potentially important find should be shared with his sponsor, Carter telegraphed Carnarvon to come from England, and filled in the excavation again to await his arrival. He would have been less in suspense if he had first cleared another few inches down the doorway, for there, quite distinctly, was the seal of Tutankhamen.

Nearly three weeks later Carnarvon arrived from England and the excavation was resumed. It took workmen several days to clear the rubble in the passage beyond the door, and when they had done so a second sealed door was revealed. When a hole big enough to shine a light through was made in this door the most fantastic sight ever to meet the eyes of an archaeologist was revealed to Carter. In the chamber beyond were a golden throne, golden couches, alabaster vases, statues, animal heads, and gold snakes, as well as a piled-up profusion of boxes and caskets. Only there was no sign of a sarcophagus, and when the excavators broke into the room they found that it was only an antechamber and in two of the walls there were other sealed and plastered doorways.

Below: photograph from the Griffith Institute, Ashmolean Museum, showing the top of the unexcavated stairway leading to Tutankhamen's tomb in the Valley of the Kings. This was the way the entrance was first seen.

Above right: photograph from the Griffith Institute, Ashmolean Museum, showing the antechamber of the tomb of Tutankhamen as it was found by Howard Carter.

At this stage further progress was delayed by the fact that the crowded antechamber could not be cleared until its contents had been cataloged and photographed, and in some cases given special preservative treatment because of their fragile state. This work required experts from all over the world, and once again the excavation was filled in until a team capable of doing the job properly could be assembled. Three months passed before one of the sealed doors from the antechamber was breached. Shining his light through the first hole made in the door, and moving it around in all directions, Carter announced to the assembled scientists and officials that he seemed to be looking at a wall of solid gold. When eventually the entire doorway was cleared, Carter and Carnarvon were the first to enter the room beyond, and when they did so they found that the apparent wall of gold was a huge shrine that nearly filled the room. Moving with extreme care to avoid damaging priceless funerary gifts, they went to the eastern end of the shrine. Here there were two great bolted doors, which when opened revealed a second shrine, also with great doors that were sealed as well as bolted. Deciding to leave the seal intact and the pharaoh undisturbed for the time being, they then went to the other end of the sepulchral chamber, where they found a low door giving entrance to yet another room, a small one but furnished with greater treasures than had been found elsewhere in the tomb: exquisite figures in gold of guardian gods and goddesses, and miniature shrines with funerary statues of Tutankhamen adorned with emblems of the underworld.

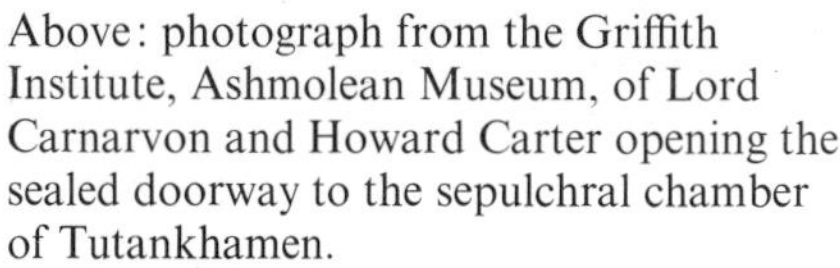

Above: photograph from the Griffith Institute, Ashmolean Museum, of Lord Carnarvon and Howard Carter opening the sealed doorway to the sepulchral chamber of Tutankhamen.

Left: the goddess Isis, from the shrine of Tutankhamen, carved in wood and overlaid with gold. There was a tradition that she protected the dead Osiris with long feathery wings that she was able, as the Great Enchantress, to grow. Another story says that with her wings she attempted to give back to him the breath of life. Here Tutankhamen is portrayed as Osiris.

Below: figure of Tutankhamen on a leopard, one of the many ritual statuettes found in his tomb. The king is borne on the back of an animal considered benevolent which protects him from evil in the afterlife.

Right: photograph from the Griffith Institute, Ashmolean Museum, showing the first sight of the sarcophagus which filled the entire area of the fourth and innermost shrine of Tutankhamen's tomb.
Far right: photograph from the Griffith Institute, Ashmolean Museum, showing a wreath, garlands of olive and willow leaves, and the linen shroud covering the second coffin in the shrine of Tutankhamen.

Above: photograph from the Griffith Institute, Ashmolean Museum, showing the roof of the fourth and innermost shrine, on slings, being prepared for removal to the antechamber.

At this stage, after a series of distinguished visitors had seen the tomb, the excavation was closed down again. Two years passed while the Egyptian government made up its mind whether the concession should be extended, and an international commission sat to adjudicate how the finds should be divided. During this time Lord Carnarvon died in a Cairo hotel of an infection caused by a mosquito bite, and the myth of "the curse of the pharaohs" was born. It was the winter of 1925–26 before investigation of the tomb could be resumed. Returning to the sealed second shrine, Carter entered it only to find within it a third. His own words describe the next stage:

"With suppressed excitement I carefully cut the cord, removed that precious seal, drew back the bolts, and opened the doors, when a fourth shrine was revealed, similar in design and even more brilliant in workmanship than the last . . . An indescribable moment for an archaeologist! What was beneath and what did that fourth shrine contain? With intense excitement I drew back the bolts of the last and unsealed doors; they slowly swung open, and there, filling the entire area within, effectually barring any further progress, stood an immense yellow quartzite sarcophagus . . . Especially striking were the outstretched hand and wing of a goddess sculptured on the lid of the sarcophagus, as if to ward off an intruder. It symbolized an idea beautiful in conception, and, indeed, seemed an eloquent illustration of the perfect faith and tender solicitude for the well-being of their loved one, that animated the people who dwelt in that land over 30 centuries ago."

The lid of the sarcophagus weighed over half a ton and hoisting tackle had to be brought into the chamber in order to lift it. First

Opening the Sarcophagus

Left: the upper part of the second mummiform sarcophagus containing the solid gold sarcophagus. Made of compact wood covered with sheets of gold, it is inlaid with multicolored glass paste and semiprecious stones. It depicts the mummified figure of Osiris, arms crossed on his chest, holding his insignia. He is wearing the nemset or headdress, the wide collar, and the long beard of the gods. On his arms are the two animals of the monarchy, the vulture and winged cobra. The face has an expression of suffering emphasized by the yellowish color in the cornea of the eyes.

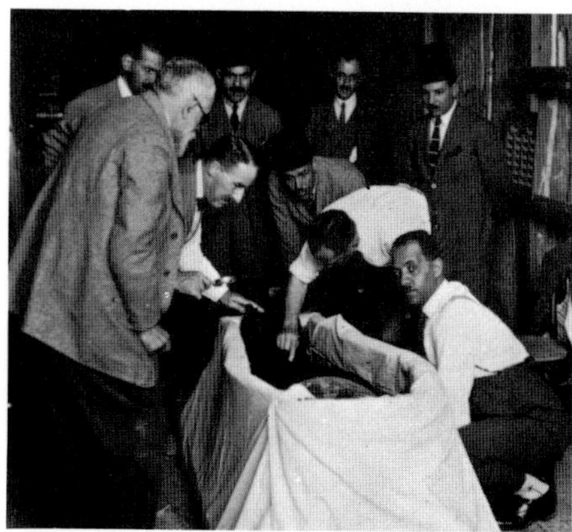

Above: photograph from the Griffith Institute, Ashmolean Museum, showing the first incision in the wrappings of the royal mummy by Dr. Douglas Derry, professor of anatomy at the Egyptian University. The mummy of Tutankhamen filled the interior of its gold coffin, which measured 6 feet 1 inch in total length.

the four shrines had to be carefully dismantled and removed, and as this was being done Carter noticed that each of their 80 component parts was numbered, but some of them had been assembled wrongly, and his feelings of admiration for the original craftsmen and of scorn for the workmen were as if they were his contemporaries. When at last the heavy lid of the sarcophagus was raised all that could be seen was something bundled in linen cloths. These were removed to reveal a golden effigy of Tutankhamen on the lid of a coffin. This proved to be the lid of the first of three coffins, each one nested within the other, and each decorated with an effigy of the king, wearing and surrounded by symbols of the religion of Osiris. The innermost coffin was made of solid gold and the mummy was covered by a mask of beaten gold portraying the youthful king probably as he had looked in

Tutankhamen as the God Osiris

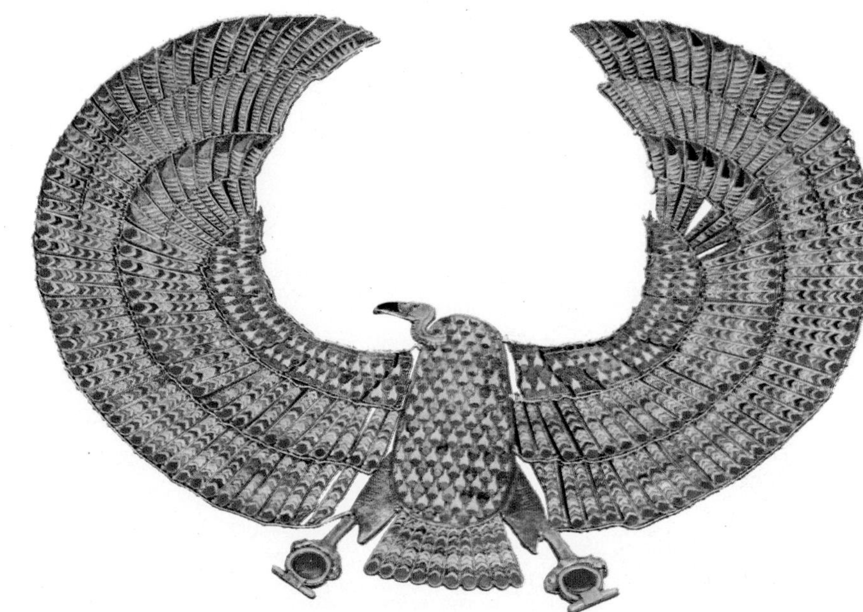

Right: the flexible collar of Nekhebet from the king's mummy, composed of 256 separate gold plaques—engraved on the back and minutely inlaid on the front with opaque glass imitating turquoise, red jasper, and lapis lazuli—and carnelian. The vulture symbolizes the southern goddess Nekhebet.

life. The one disappointment of the whole fabulous find was that the actual mummy was in a worse state of preservation than those of the other pharaohs that had been found in the communal tomb, for the embalming substance that had been poured liberally over it had caused it to be carbonized. Unwrapping the linen bindings covering the body was a delicate task. Each turn brought to light some golden amulet, symbol, or magic sign. In all, 143 pieces of jewelry were found among the winding sheets wrapped around the mummy, all of them placed in accordance with ritual procedures prescribed in the *Egyptian Book of the Dead.*

No archaeological find had given Egyptologists more information about the ancient Osirian religion and the Egyptians' beliefs about death and the afterlife than Howard Carter's discovery of the tomb of Tutankhamen. The fabulous wealth of the funerary gifts, and the meticulous care and craftsmanship that went into all the preparations, particularly of the mummy itself and its nest of coffins, all indicate an assured belief in the survival of the king in the company of the gods after the ending of his earthly reign. Clearly it was of primary importance that a great king should have a send-off into the next life, where he would keep company

Below: the mummiform image in miniature of King Tutankhamen lying in the position of the god Osiris. The bed suggests the elongated body of an animal of the cat family, and it is reminiscent of the gilded bed on which the coffins were placed in the stone sarcophagus. On either side of the dead king two birds, one of which has a human face, are stretching a protective wing over the torso of the figure.

Above: a supplicant kneeling before Osiris, Judge of the Dead, in a Book of the Dead. These books were collections of spells meant to help the dead person on his journey through the underworld with its many dangers and demons. This is an illustration from the Book of the Dead of Ani the scribe.

with the immortal gods, befitting the rank he had had on earth and guaranteeing him a corresponding rank in the afterworld. A fulsome welcoming by the great gods was also anticipated, and engraved on gold plaques in Tutankhamen's coffin were speeches of the sky and the Divine Mother: "I reckon your beauties, O Osiris, King Kheperunebre; your soul lives: your veins are firm. You smell the air and go out as a god, going out as Atu. Osiris, Tutankhamen. You go out and you enter with Ra . . .

In this speech Tutankhamen is identified with Osiris, the god of the dead and of resurrection in Egyptian religion. An ancient myth related how the fourth of the divine pharaohs, Osiris, who had brought the arts of civilization to the land of Egypt, had been murdered by his evil brother, Set, and his dismembered body scattered about the land. His wife and sister, Isis, had collected the fragments and bound them together again (which is probably why the bodies of mummies were bound), and by magical means had restored him to eternal life. Thereafter he had ruled in the afterworld as the judge and lord of the dead. Historians of religion have suggested that Osiris was a vegetation god, and the theory would appear to be supported by the most curious finding in the tomb of Tutankhamen. In an oblong box there was a wooden frame made in the shape of the god Osiris, which had been hollowed out, filled with silt from the Nile and planted with corn. This had been moistened and the life-size figure had become green and living, symbolizing the resurrection of Osiris and Tutankhamen.

The wealth of everyday objects and practical things like chariots and oars among Egyptian funerary equipment were provided to make possible the safe journey of the deceased through the underworld prior to his joining Osiris in the Fields of Yalu (the Elysian Fields of Greek religion) or the sun god Ra in his solar boat. Resurrection of the physical body laid in the tomb was not anticipated, but the Egyptians believed that man had a counterpart body, or double, which they called the Ka. This had all the characteristic attributes of the person and was believed to

Pyramids in the Cult of the Dead

Below: wooden model of a ship of the dead, from around 1400 B.C. These were often left in tombs for travel in the afterlife. The mummy, adorned with the likeness of Osiris, rests between the mourning figures of the goddesses Isis and Nephthys.

be able to eat and drink and enjoy the fragrance of incense. In early Egyptian tombs plentiful supplies were provided for it and a special area was set apart for its use.

Dwelling in the Ka was the Ba, or soul, which could be corporeal or incorporeal at will, could leave the tomb, and in fact spent most of its time existing in glory in heaven, but it would occasionally revisit the entombed body, which it sometimes reanimated. A third component part of man was the Khu, or spiritual intelligence, which was believed to be a luminous etheric body that also lived with the gods. When the physical body died these other immortal and incorruptible parts were believed to be born from it, and it was to provide for their needs and glorification that tombs were so elaborately and richly furnished.

Egyptian religion changed and evolved but the most constant and fundamental aspect of it was the cult of the dead. The tomb of the great lord Ti, which the Frenchman Mariette excavated, as well as many other tombs of nobility, shows that immortality was not considered a privilege only of kings, but was believed to be available to everyone in a manner befitting his station in life if only he made appropriate preparations for a good burial. A text that has come down to us from the age of the pyramids provides an insight into the ceremonies that took place at an Egyptian burial ceremony:

"Remember then the day of burial, the passing into beatitude; when the night shall be devoted to thee with oils and with bandages . . . There is a procession to be made of thee on the day thou art reunited with the earth: thy mummy-case of gold, with head of lapis-lazuli, a heaven [shrine] above thee—the while that thou art placed upon the hearse, and oxen drag thee. Then shall musicians await thy coming, and the dance of the *Muce* be performed at the door of thy tomb. The words of offering shall be pronounced on thy behalf, and victims slaughtered at the door of thy stele."

There can be little doubt that the pyramids were monumental tombs in which the early pharaohs sought to protect themselves and their provisions for life in the next world by heaping a mountain about their hiding place and having the only entrance concealed and disguised. In the most interesting book on the pyramids, first published in London in 1974 by the German-born physicist Kurt Mendelssohn, a very well-documented and persuasive case is made for the proposition that the main object of pyramid construction was the creation of a work program which effected an historic social transition: the change from a rural economy to a new form of community life, the nation-state. "Pyramid-building was a milestone in the history of man because it was his first true application of large-scale technology," Mendelssohn writes, and he argues that this development was undertaken with a view to effecting a transformation of the social order and creating administrative institutions and a class of people possessing administrative skills. This solution of *The Riddle of the Pyramids* (the title of Mendelssohn's book) has in its favor, he argues, the fact that "it does not contradict the well-established fact that the pyramids were funerary monuments."

The reason that really massive pyramid building was confined to a relatively short period of time was because its purpose as a

Left: wall painting in the inner chamber of the tomb of Nekhtamun of the 19th dynasty, at Deir-el-Medina. Here Anubis, the jackal-god of mummification, prepares to take Nekhtamun to the seat of judgment.

Above: limestone relief from the tomb of the landowner Ti. Serving girls, personifying Ti's estates, carry baskets filled with produce. At first the denial of death was limited to the pharoah and his family, but by the end of the Old Kingdom the belief had widened to include nobles. Servants whose functions might be useful to their departed masters were depicted or mentioned in their tombs.

work program to effect a social transition was accomplished in that time. So Kurt Mendelssohn argues, and it is difficult to dispute his conclusions, because there is no kind of evidence that can be found and used against him. The pyramid building program must surely have brought about a change in the social order, but whether this change was foreseen and planned, and whether the religious significance of the pyramids was secondary to it, is debatable. The evidence of the archaeological finds in and around the Valley of the Kings would support the point of view that the building of pyramids stopped because living pharaohs discovered that there was no way of securing them against the determination and ingenuity of tomb robbers. They therefore chose to build for themselves less conspicuous tombs underground in the desert with no surface marking to betray their existence. For most of them this too proved an ineffectual means of ensuring eternal repose for their mortal remains and the preservation of their treasures, but by a near miracle one of them did survive to provide our age with an unprecedented glimpse of the splendor and the mystery of civilization in Egypt more than 3000 years ago.

Chapter 3
Secrets of the Standing Stones

Few ancient monuments are more puzzling than the great circles, avenues, and groups of "standing stones" scattered around western Europe. Stonehenge in England and Carnac in France—these are the most impressive, but they are found around the Mediterranean coast, along the Atlantic coast, across the British Isles, into Scandinavia. What were they built for? Recently, scholars have made some extraordinary claims for these stone clusters. One American has even described Stonehenge as a kind of neolithic computer designed to predict with amazing accuracy the movement of sun and moon. Others have found similarities between the European stones and the vast Maya structures at Chichen Itza. What is the truth?

One summer evening in 1934, after a hard day's sailing up the west coast of Scotland, an Oxford University professor took his boat into Loch Roag on the Isle of Lewis to find an anchorage for the night. A full moon was rising over the hills, and silhouetted against it was a most impressive sight: the tall standing stones of Callanish, the ancient monument that has been called the Scottish equivalent of Stonehenge.

Professor Alexander Thom went ashore, and, standing in the middle of the mysterious stone circle, he noticed that according to the pole star the structure was aligned due north-south. This observation fascinated him, for he knew that in the days when the stone circle was constructed there was no pole star because its constellation hadn't reached its present position. He wondered whether the alignment was a chance occurrence or had been deliberately planned. If it was deliberate it would probably be found at other megalithic sites. Thom decided to check whether it was, and thus began 30 years of painstaking study, involving survey work at no fewer than 450 sites in remote spots in the British Isles, which led to the publication in 1967 of his book *Megalithic Sites in Britain*, and in 1971 of *Megalithic Lunar Observations*. It also led to a revolution in thinking about European prehistory. It had previously been assumed that barbarians had inhabited Western Europe in prehistoric times, when civilization had first arisen in the Middle East. Thom's findings demanded a radical change of this view. "I'm an en-

Opposite: the standing stones of Callanish. Situated on a low promontory of land at the head of Loch Roag, sheltered from the harsh waves that break along the Atlantic coastline of Lewis, the dense noncircular ring of stones measures about 40 feet across.

The Megaliths of Western Europe

Below: Professor Alexander Thom at work measuring a trilithon at Stonehenge. He is not only convinced that all the standing stone structures are astronomical observatories of great precision, but also that they were constructed according to a standard unit of measurement—the megalithic yard.

Above right: the Rudston monolith near Bridlington, Yorkshire, England. This gigantic stone, a menhir, is the tallest standing stone in Britain. It measures 25.5 feet high (above ground), 6 feet wide, and 2.25 feet thick and weighs about 40 tons. The stone rears up from among the graves close by a Norman church and there is said to be as much of it underground as above, which is probably why it was left standing when the church was built. It dates back to 1600–1000 B.C. Legend says the Devil threw the menhir at Rudston church in order to destroy it but missed.

gineer," he wrote, and indeed his professorship was in engineering. "I'm certain these people were too—and proud of it."

By "these people" Thom meant the megalith builders. The word *megalith* comes from two Greek words meaning simply "large stone," and its adjective is used for a variety of structures from single standing stones known as *menhirs*, to structures in which three standing stones support an immense capstone, known as *dolmens* or *cromlechs*, and to piles of rough stones burying a tomb or serving as a memorial or landmark, known as *cairns*, and of course stone circles. Professor Glyn Daniel of Cambridge has estimated that there must be between 40,000 and 50,000 megalithic tombs or temples in Western Europe. The question of who built them has given rise to at least as much speculation and controversy as any other question in archaeology.

The phenomenon is not exclusive to Western Europe, but it is peculiarly concentrated there, particularly in the form of menhirs and stone circles. The practice of building tombs of stone—and dolmens are thought to have been tombs—is a

Above left: Lanyon Quoit, a dolmen or roofed stone structure. It was reerected in the early 19th century after it had fallen in a storm. The uprights may have been damaged, because before the storm it had been possible for a man to ride through the dolmen on horseback. Traces of the earth mound which once covered the stones can be seen close by.

Above: Clava cairns, near Culloden battlefield, 5.5 miles east of Inverness, Scotland. A cairn is a megalithic tomb covered by small stones. These, dating from the early Bronze Age, are some of the most extensive in Scotland.

Left: drawing of a Bronze Age burial in a tumulus. Funeral practices varied from burying to burning the bodies, but most tombs would eventually be sealed.

natural development from cave burial. As such it might be expected to occur spontaneously in different parts of the world. But the erection of single standing stones, or avenues or circles of them, is a practice that at first consideration appears rather pointless. As the French archaeologist Professor P. R. Giot wrote of the standing stones: "Whether isolated or in groups, they remain enshrouded in mystery. This is no doubt why their study has, unjustifiably, been comparatively neglected. . . . With the very limited evidence at his disposal, the interpretation of single menhirs is one of the archaeologist's nightmares."

The mystery is deepened when we think of the labor involved. All other archaeological evidence bears witness to the fact that the inhabitants of Western Europe at the time when the megaliths were erected were neolithic farmers living in small communities who possessed only the most primitive tools and technology. Professor Richard Atkinson, the Englishman who excavated around Stonehenge, estimated that the transport of the 81 sarsen stones from Avebury, some 15 miles away, would have taken 1500 men working continuously for 5.5 years. And the construction of nearby Silbury Hill (which is not a megalith but is of the same period) he reckoned would have taken 18 million man-hours. In the 1830s a capstone from a megalithic tomb near Saumur in France was moved to serve as a bridge. It took 18 pairs of oxen and enormous rollers, each consisting of four oak tree trunks lashed together, to shift it. The great stone known as the Grand Menhir Brisé in Brittany, which now lies broken on the ground, weighed about 380 tons and stood 60 feet high. In the famous nearby avenues of menhirs at Carnac there are no fewer than 3000 great stones. The labor involved in erecting them, and the thousands of other stones and stone structures in

Right: a 19th-century artist's view of Bronze Age men moving massive menhirs. According to modern research he was correct in assuming the stones were moved on rollers, but he underestimated the number of men (at least 1000) and ropes that would have been required.

Right: ancient Britons building Stonehenge. Pickaxes like that shown here, made of red deer antler, have been found in the circular ditch surrounding the temple area at Stonehenge. These tools would have been used for digging holes and ditches and for banking up the earthwork.

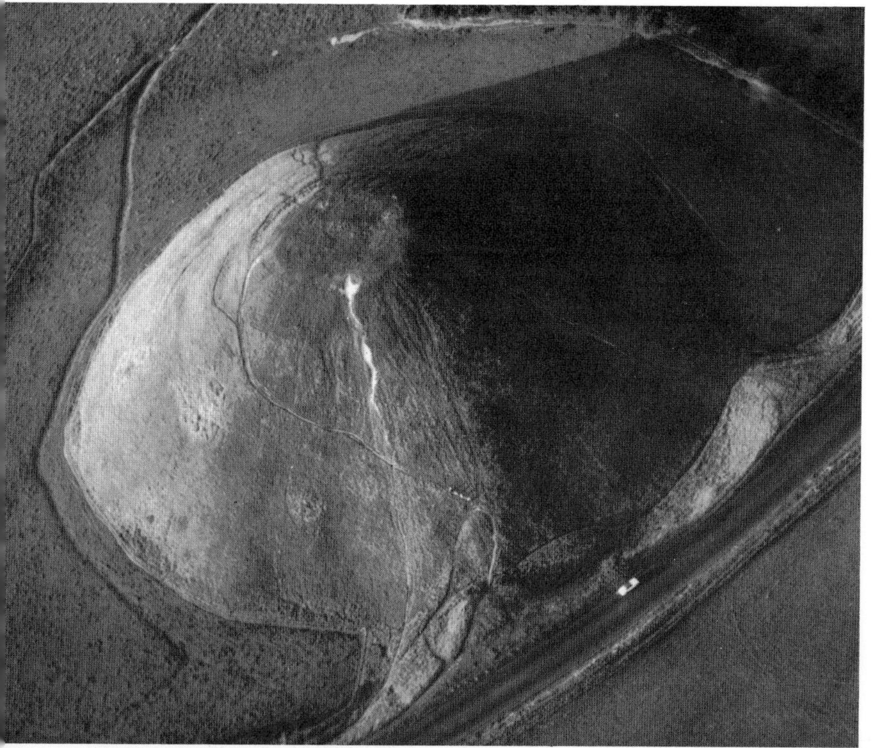

How Were They Constructed?

Left: Silbury Hill near Marlborough, Wiltshire, in southwestern England. Measuring 130 feet high, covering an area of 5.25 acres, and with a diameter of just over 100 feet across its flat top, Silbury Hill is the largest prehistoric man-made mound in Europe. The most popular archaeological theory is that it was a gigantic burial mound—according to legend a King Sil was buried there on horseback. Radiocarbon dating in 1968–9 attributes the construction of Silbury Hill to around 2750 B.C., earlier than was previously thought.

Left: the Le Menec stone alignments, avenues of stones near Carnac on the southern coast of Brittany. A 19th-century observer recounted how "the extraordinary view of that regiment of stones, the startling army of shapeless rocks so symmetrically aligned, filled me with astonishment." The most striking feature of all the Carnac alignments is the way the megaliths decrease in size quite regularly from the enormous boulders that begin each series of avenues to the last small stones, only 2 to 3 feet high.

Brittany and the British Isles, was prodigious. The idea that they were erected by giants or magicians long prevailed, and a form of it has even been seriously proposed by a present-day British writer on the subject, John Michell. But if we do not allow ourselves flights of fancy about supernatural engineering we must assume that the megaliths were erected by manpower. The question of why such prodigious manpower was put to such a purpose then becomes one of the most intriguing puzzles that enigmatic relics of the ancient world pose for modern man.

John Aubrey, the celebrated 17th-century English antiquarian and diarist, was out hunting with some friends just after Christmas, 1648 when they came to the village of Avebury. There Aubrey experienced a revelation. He realized that he was standing in the middle of an immense prehistoric temple. Where others saw, and for centuries had seen, only a lot of old stones and a few mounds, Aubrey saw evidence of a grand design. The design

Romans or Druids?

Right: aerial view of Avebury in Wiltshire, England. Silbury Hill is nearby. The great temple of freestanding megaliths was probably erected around 2500 B.C. The avenue of stones once ran from Avebury into the dip of the valley and up the other side to the flat top of Overton Hill.

Below: Inigo Jones, the 17th-century architect who, on the instructions of King James I, drew reconstructions of the megaliths of Stonehenge.

stands out quite clearly on a modern aerial photograph, even though today there are far fewer stones at Avebury than there were in Aubrey's day, thanks to the efforts of such men as the 18th-century farmer known as "Stone-Killer Robinson." He devised a means of breaking them up by toppling them into fiery pits and administering a dash of cold water and a hammer blow.

The Avebury circle is so large that the medieval village has grown up within it. It was its size that had hidden it from view and made its component stones seem a mere random assembly. Stonehenge, however, could not be ignored. Standing on the open Salisbury Plain, its great stones clustered in an obviously man-made design, it invited speculation about the men who had built it. The 12th-century English historian Geoffrey of Monmouth had written that it was built about A.D. 470 as a memorial to 460 ancient British chieftains massacred by Hengist the Saxon. His view prevailed, for lack of a more authoritative one, until the 17th century, when British royalty began to take an interest

Right: reconstruction of Stonehenge by Inigo Jones, characterized by a classical symmetry he believed was due to its Roman builders. He declared that the Romans "only amongst all the nations of the universe" could have created such a wonder.

in Stonehenge. King James I of England visited it, and had his architect Inigo Jones make drawings showing its original construction. Jones expressed the opinion that it had been built by the Romans in the first or second century A.D. in honor of the god Coelus, and that it could not possibly have been built by the "savage and barbarous" early Britons. They, he said, would have been quite incapable of achieving such "stately structures, or such remarkable works as Stonehenge." John Aubrey was less scornful of the early Britons, or of their priests, the Druids. When asked by King Charles II to survey the site and write an account of it, he stated that its history went back beyond Saxon and Roman times. Referring to both Avebury and Stonehenge, he wrote that since the Druids were "the most eminent order of priests among the Britons, it is most likely that these monuments were the temples of the priests of the most eminent order, the Druids, and it is strongly to be presumed that they are as ancient as those days."

Aubrey's view was taken up and elaborated in the next century by Dr. William Stukeley, whose book, *Stonehenge, a Temple restored to the British Druids*, was extremely influential. It inspired so much other fanciful literature about Druids and their practices that the popular view has prevailed down to our day

Above: a Druid priest as drawn by Dr. William Stukeley in the early 18th century. He declared in his work of 1740 that Stonehenge was "the metropolitical Church of the chief Druid of Britain . . . This was the *locus consecratus* where they met at some great festivals of the year, as well as to perform the extraordinary sacrifices and religious rites, as to determine causes and civil matters."

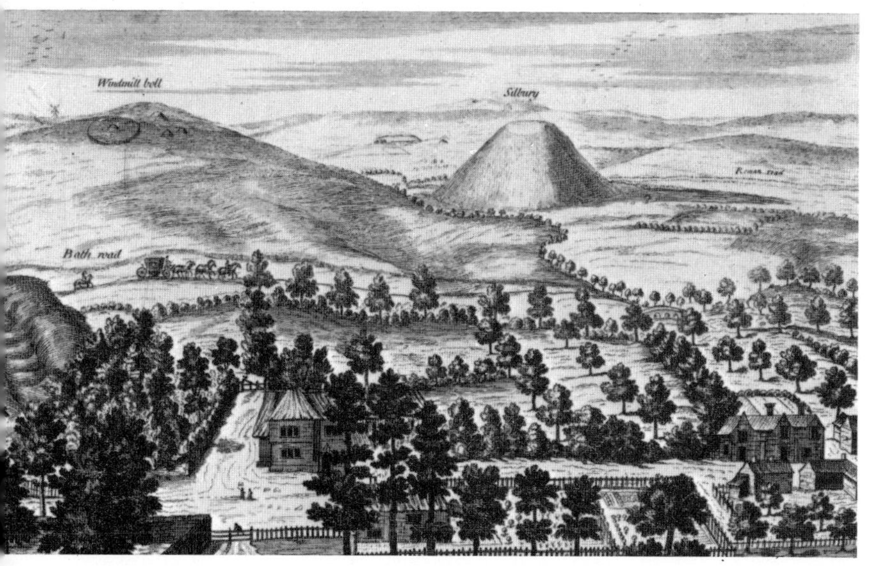

Left: Avebury and Silbury Hill as drawn by Stukeley for inclusion in his book, *Stonehenge, a Temple restored to the British Druids*. Stukeley was forced to watch helplessly as for 30 years the local farmers and builders periodically toppled and smashed the great stones to clear land for plowing or as an easy source of building material.

that Stonehenge was erected by Druids for purposes of ritual sacrifice and sun worship. The discovery that it might have been used to predict eclipses has been, as it were, added to this view by proposing that the possession of such an expertise would have enabled the Druidic priesthood to manipulate ignorant people by demonstrating apparant magical powers over the heavenly bodies. We know about the historical existence of Druids from references in the writings of Julius Caesar. Possibly Stonehenge and other monuments throughout Britain were used by them, but they certainly did not erect the megaliths, and Stonehenge was built much earlier than 460 B.C., as Stukeley had conjectured.

Archaeology as a scientific study could not make much pro-

Carbon Dating

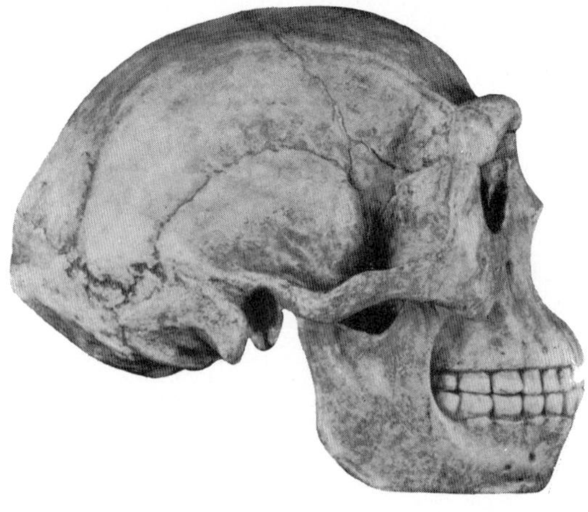

Above: reconstructed skull of Peking Man, made up of pieces from both male and female skulls. Peking Man lived about 220,000 years ago, and he discovered how to control and use fire.

gress until the late 19th century. Then the mind of Western man gradually became emancipated from the Biblical version of prehistory as it had been interpreted by Archbishop Ussher of Armagh, Ireland, whose calculation that Man had been created on October 23, 404 B.C. had been adopted as dogma by the Church. When the findings of geology, and of fossil remains testifying to human life on earth thousands of years ago, combined with evolution theory to overthrow this dogma, the way was open for a scientific study of prehistory. The most obvious area for the pursuit of this study was the Near and Middle East, for there relics were conspicuous, varied, and well preserved. Moreover there were traditions and written records to guide archaeological field work and to help interpret its findings. Western Europe, by comparison, was unspectacular and unpromising. Its enigmatic clusters of rough stones, its great mounds and chambered tombs, could not be related to contem-

Right: one of the three Mnajdra temples on the coast of Malta, dating from 2800 B.C. Malta has several magnificent open-air megalithic temples which do not seem to have been built as tombs. The stones have been worked with a sharp tool to give a special texture to the surfaces. The dome-like structures at Mnajdra were probably originally roofed over.

porary historical or literary records, and their existence was not obviously inconsistent with the idea that the people who built them were superstitious barbarians. The Swedish archaeologist Oscar Montelius expressed the prevailing view when he wrote in 1908: "At a time when the people of Europe were, so to speak, without any civilization whatsoever, the Orient and particularly the Euphrates region and the Nile were already in enjoyment of a flourishing culture."

This view led to the idea known as the theory of *diffusionism*. This suggested that civilization had first arisen in Mesopotamia and Egypt about 3000 B.C. and that aspects of it had gradually spread westward. Archaeological findings appeared to support this view. For example, it was possible to trace the spread of the practice of burial in chambered tombs from the Aegean via Malta, Spain, Portugal and France, to Britain and Scandinavia. And as the British archaeologist Sir Mortimer Wheeler wrote in 1925: "The general analogy between the *mastabas* (of Egypt) and many types of chambered tomb is too close to be altogether accidental." Evidence of the achievements distinctive of high

civilizations, such as sculpture, fine metalwork, and sophisticated decorative art and design, was not to be found among the relics of Western European prehistory.

The conclusion that "megalithic culture" was derived from but greatly inferior to the high civilizations of Mesopotamia, Egypt, and the Aegean was a natural one to make. It is only quite recently that it has been proved to be untenable and the diffusionist theory in its simple form has now been discredited.

The discovery in 1949, by the American chemist Willard Libby, of a means of dating prehistoric relics by measuring the amount of radioactive carbon-14 they contain, signaled a revolution in archaeology. At first the radiocarbon dating technique seemed to confirm established ideas, and the few anomalies it threw up could be ignored. Some archaeologists were skeptical of its reliability. They pointed out for instance that although we know that the building of the Great Pyramid was begun about 2600 B.C., the radiocarbon technique of dating yielded the result 2200 B.C. It was not until 1967 that the reliability of the technique was established beyond dispute. Then not only was the error in dating the Great Pyramid explained but at the same time prevailing ideas about the relative antiquity of Near, Middle Eastern, and Atlantic European artifacts were confounded.

In California there grows a tree known as the bristlecone pine. Some of these trees are 5000 years old, and as they grow one ring on their trunks each year their age can be precisely known. In 1967 Professor Hans Suess conceived the idea of taking tree-ring samples and comparing their known calendrical ages with the ages yielded by radiocarbon dating. If the latter technique were accurate, the ages should of course correspond. It turned out that they didn't correspond, but that the discrepancy between the two dates was a factor that varied predictably, becoming larger the further back in time. This meant that the old radiocarbon dates were wrong, and that, in order to correct them, dates of around 1000 B.C. had to be pushed back by 200 years and at about 3000 B.C. by nearly 1000 years. This meant that, when the original radiocarbon data for the Great Pyramid was corrected, the new date coincided with the known historical date.

Above left: carbon-dating equipment consisting of a cabinet which houses a Geiger counter. This measures the relative radioactivity of materials.

Above: Dr. Willard F. Libby of the University of Chicago's Institute for Nuclear Studies, who in 1949 discovered that radioactive Carbon-14 in nature could be used for dating the distant past.

Below: bristlecone pines (*Pinus aristata*) in the White Mountains of California. These trees are the oldest in the world, and by counting their annual rings their precise age can be determined. These figures can then be compared with those produced by carbon dating.

Calculating the Megalithic Yard

Below: the egg-shaped stone circle at Castle Rigg, Cumberland, 1.5 miles east of Keswick. It is composed of 38 stones, has a rough diameter of 110 feet, and has a flattened edge. According to Professor Thom the circles were deliberately flattened in order to use whole numbers of megalithic yards as both diameter and circumference.

But when megalithic sites were radiocarbon dated they proved to be considerably older than the eastern civilizations that they were supposed to be derived from. Megalithic chambered tombs turned out to date from 4500–4000 B.C., long before the building of the Egyptian *mastabas* and of the round tombs found around the Aegean. And the first construction at Stonehenge itself was found to be at least contemporary with, and probably earlier than, the Great Pyramid of Cheops. The signs were that an indigenous culture had evolved independently in Western Europe in prehistoric times.

The year 1967 was an exciting year for students of European prehistory. In addition to the evidence of the unsuspected antiquity of megalithic artifacts afforded by the new dating estimates there came evidence of their unimagined mathematical and geometrical properties. For that year Professor Thom published his *Megalithic Sites in Britain.*

For years following his first insight at Callanish, Thom, assisted at first by his sons and later by his grandsons, had carried surveying equipment to remote megalithic sites and taken careful measurements. As he completed an increasing number of surveys, it became clear that the sites had been chosen and the stones located by men who had a knowledge of astronomy as well as of geometry and mathematics. They had also possessed sophisticated techniques and equipment. "Some sites," he wrote, "for example Avebury, were set out with an accuracy approaching 1 in 1000. Only an experienced surveyor with good equipment is likely to attain this sort of accuracy. The differences in tension applied to an ordinary measuring tape by different individuals can produce variations in length of this amount or even more."

Thom's main discovery was the "megalithic yard," the unit of measurement used by the prehistoric builders. This unit, the equivalent of 2.72 feet, together with another unit that was precisely 2.5 times the megalithic yard and which he called the "megalithic rod," Thom found to be a constant feature of the dimensions of all the stone circles he surveyed. The radii and circumferences of the structures, as well as the distances between individual stones, were found to be always multiples of the megalithic yard. Thom's surveys revealed that a majority of the structures were not exact circles. Some were egg-shaped, some elliptical, some flattened on one side, and some elongated. But whatever its shape the circumference and radius of each stone "circle" was measurable in whole numbers of megalithic yards. And always the accuracy was uncanny. It was inconceivable that this accuracy was due to chance. Thom made his discovery when surveying sites in Scotland, which being more remote are generally more intact than those further south. But as his studies progressed he found that all megalithic sites from Brittany, France to the Orkneys, the islands off northern Scotland, were all laid out according to a consistent principle of measurement. He concluded that there must have been a prehistoric culture on the European coast of the Atlantic Ocean of considerable sophistication and with some kind of central administration. For if the measuring instruments used in the construction of the megaliths were not officially standardized and issued, but were obtained by each local community copying from its neighbor's, there would certainly be a greater degree of localized error and variation than was in fact found.

When Thom first announced his findings, most archaeologists were skeptical and some were positively hostile. His findings were of course irreconcilable with the picture of Neolithic man and his culture in northwest Europe that had emerged from decades of orthodox archaeological research. But *Megalithic Sites in Britain* was such a scholarly and exhaustive study, so unsensational in its presentation and impeccable in its mathematics, that its findings could not be dismissed as nonsense. An independent mathematician, Professor David Kendall of the Statistical Laboratory at the University of Cambridge, subjected Thom's figures to a series of tests using a computer. Kendall reached the conclusion that there was no more than a one percent chance that the dimensions of the stone circles could have been achieved without the common unit of the megalithic yard. Thom was vindicated and historians had to start revising their ideas.

The revision demanded by the new evidence was not a minor one. One fact that had to be taken into account in it was that the

Left: the Rollright Stones, a circle near Oxon in Oxfordshire, England. There are about 70 stones in the circle called the King's Men, and a few yards away stands a single stone called the King Stone.

Below left: stone circle called the Merry Maidens at Boleigh, Cornwall, in southwestern England. Comprising 19 stones in a ring about 75 feet across are the petrified "dancing maidens." Two outlying stones to the north are known as the "Pipers" while to the west is the "Fiddler."

Below: the collapsed stones of Arbor Low, near Middleton, Derbyshire, England. The site consists of an earth circle with a large cairn built over the bank to the south, situated on the moors at over 1000 feet above sea level. There are about 50 blocks of weathered limestone, which from the air resemble a huge clockface.

Above: Woodhenge on Salisbury Plain, a pattern of post holes first discovered from the air in 1925 and subsequently excavated by M. E. Cunnington and his wife. They left small concrete posts to mark the positions of the holes. The Cunningtons pointed out that the long axis of the post setting indicates midsummer sunrise.

megalith builders had understood the principle of Euclidean geometry 2000 years *before* Euclid, who lived in about 300 B.C. Within the stone "circles" Thom discovered geometrical figures formed by key features which were measured in whole numbers of megalithic yards. Of all possible triangles there are a limited number with sides measurable in whole numbers. We call them Pythagorean triangles, but the megalith builders had apparently had them all worked out long before Pythagoras. At Avebury, for instance, Thom found that "the basis of the design is a 3,4,5 triangle set out in units of exactly 25 MY (megalithic yards) so that all the resulting shapes come out in multiples of 5 or 10." At Woodhenge, another site on Salisbury Plain, there are five concentric circles with perimeters measuring exactly 40, 60, 80, 140, and 160 MY, and with internal dimensions based on the Pythagorean triangle 12, 35, 37. At Stonehenge there is an outer ring known as the Aubrey Holes (after John Aubrey, who first drew attention to them), and the holes numbered 56, 7, and 28 define the points of a perfect Pythagorean right-angled triangle with sides of 40, 96, and 104 MY, as does every other corresponding set. Thom found comparable symmetries between features in all the megalithic sites he surveyed, and concluded that the megalith builders had been experienced and clever geometers and mathematicians. It appeared that they had varied the shapes of their stone "circles" by way of experimenting with different geometrical figures, and setting and solving for themselves a number of geometrical problems.

It was surely inconceivable, though, that the tremendous physical effort involved in erecting the megaliths should have been invested in mere intellectual exercises, or even in laying down demonstrations of, or "teaching machines" for, mathematical and geometrical principles for the benefit of future generations. Clearly, there must be more to them than that. And of course there was. There was the knowledge of astronomy that their siting and construction testified to.

It was the Englishman William Stukeley in the 18th century who first observed that Stonehenge is aligned to the midsummer sunrise. In 1901 Sir Norman Lockyer, director of the Solar Physics Laboratory at South Kensington, London, published a book showing that Stonehenge and many other similar monuments were aligned on many of the stars as well as on the sun. Then in the 1920s Admiral Boyd Summerville surveyed 90 sites and announced that "In every instance . . . orientation of one kind or another has been found." So when Thom began his work he had guidelines and precedents for considering the megaliths as devices for calendrical calculation and astronomical observation. It was well known that by taking sight-lines from particular marked positions in stone circles to natural or man-made features of the landscape precise observations could be made, for instance of the sun at the solstices and equinoxes. These annual phenomena perhaps require a little explanation. The *solstice* occurs twice a year in northwest Europe, once in summer when the sun reaches its maximum distance from the equator on about June 21, and once when it reaches the tropic of Capricorn to begin its journey back again around December 21. The *equinox* also occurs twice a year, when the sun crosses the equator, making the night equal in length to the day. These equinoxes occur about March 21 and September 23 of each year. But the full extent of the megalith builders' astronomical knowledge was not known, and it astonished Thom himself when he found unequivocal evidence of it.

The cycle of the sun's positions throughout the year is simple and constant, but the moon is quite a different matter. In fact its cyclic pattern cannot even be understood without taking into account a period of 18.6 years. Over this period it first rises and sets in extreme northerly and southerly positions. Then it moves inward from these extreme positions for a period of 9.3 years and outwards toward them again for a second 9.3-year period. Astronomers call the extreme positions reached by the moon every

Plotting the Path of the Sun

Below left: Stonehenge was probably built in the chalk and limestone hills of Wiltshire because the surrounding lowlands were then covered with a thick oak forest. Stones for the monument came from as far away as the Presely Mountains in Wales.

Below: modern Druids celebrating the summer solstice at Stonehenge. They perform rituals which have supposedly survived since the original Druids—priests, teachers, healers, and sacrificial murderers—lived in Britain.

Prediction of Eclipses

Below: a lunar eclipse. Professor Gerald Hawkins of Boston University believes that the "Aubrey Holes" at Stonehenge can be used to predict eclipses and follow other activities of the moon's cycles. In his book *Stonehenge Decoded* he describes a 1961 midsummer sunrise when he became convinced that he should investigate all the principal sight lines incorporated in the monument for astronomical possibilities.

9.3 years its major and minor "standstills." For a few days on either side of these standstills it is possible to observe a small perturbation of the moon's orbit, generally known as the moon's "wobble," which is caused by the gravitational attraction of the sun. It was thought that this phenomenon had first been observed at the end of the 16th century of our era, but Thom discovered clear evidence that the megalith builders had known about it. Evidence that they possessed this knowledge lay not only in their great observational exactitude and subtlety, but also their ability to predict eclipses. For it is when the moon's perturbation is at its greatest that eclipses occur.

The size and location of the fallen Grand Menhir Brisé near Carnac in Brittany, France had always been a mystery. Thom's survey of the region revealed that its purpose had been to pinpoint to within a fraction of a degree the moon's major and minor standstills and the exact amount of its perturbation. The megalith served as a foresight marker for the points of rising and setting of the moon at the extremes of its 18.6-year cycle. The eight different points that an observer would occupy in order to use the megalith in this way, one of which was as far as ten miles away from it, were predicted by Thom. At four of these sites prehistoric markers in the form of mounds or stones were found.

The power to predict is the main criterion that science demands a hypothesis should satisfy. Thom's predictions in this case and several others greatly enhanced the credibility of his astonishing disclosures. For instance, at Kintraw in Argylle, Scotland there is a single tall standing stone in a field. Thom predicted that this stone would align with a point on the horizon between two mountain peaks where the sun would have set at the midwinter solstice, and he indicated a point on a steep slope at a distance from the stone which would have been the observation point from which this alignment was obtained. Excavations were carried out at the point he indicated. The archaeologists were astonished to find an artificial platform of rubble with two massive boulders situated at one end where the observation point would have been. With such evidence, the astronomical theory of the function of the megaliths became virtually irrefutable.

Thom was not alone. There were other distinguished professors canvassing the astronomical theory in the 1960s. Gerald Hawkins, professor of astronomy at Boston University, Massachusetts, studied Stonehenge with the help of a computer. Hawkins came up with evidence that alignments of distinctive features of the Stonehenge complex pointed to all major astronomical events. He also observed that the number 56 is almost exactly three times the 18.6 years of the moon's cycle, and showed how the 56 so-called "Aubrey Holes" at Stonehenge could be used to predict eclipses. England's most famous astronomer, Professor Sir Fred Hoyle, supported Hawkins' theories. He restated the basic and most fundamental problem posed by the megaliths as a whole when he wrote that the construction of Stonehenge demanded "a level of intellectual attainment orders of magnitude higher than the standard to be expected from a community of primitive farmers."

So we still come back to the original mystery, the original question: who were the megalith builders? The archaeological

evidence shows that without doubt the standing stones of northwest Europe were erected at a time when the lands were inhabited by uncivilized Stone Age farmers. The properties which we can now see that the megalithic structures possess must have been beyond the comprehension of such people, and therefore we have to assume that there existed in their midst an intellectual elite, or priesthood, which coordinated its efforts over centuries. Their object was to achieve the knowledge and establish the traditions that it did, and to do so it commanded the services of a substantial labor force. Such an elite, supported by tribute and taxes paid by the farming communities that made up the population, is known to have existed in other parts of the world, such

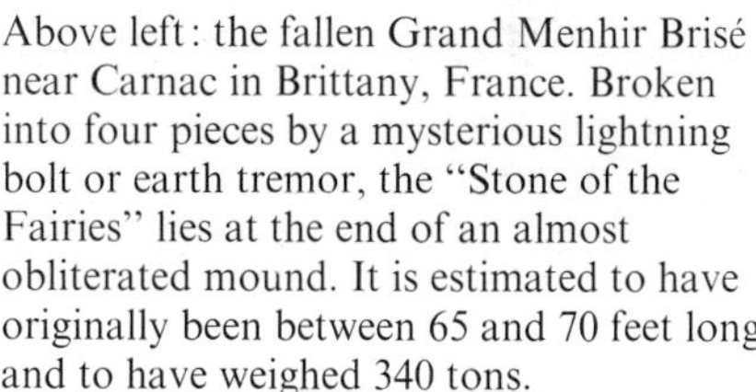

Above left: the fallen Grand Menhir Brisé near Carnac in Brittany, France. Broken into four pieces by a mysterious lightning bolt or earth tremor, the "Stone of the Fairies" lies at the end of an almost obliterated mound. It is estimated to have originally been between 65 and 70 feet long and to have weighed 340 tons.

Above: Professor Thom at the Grand Menhir Brisé. According to him, the months or years that were probably spent erecting the menhir were only the culmination of decades of astronomical calculation aimed at locating the right site for such a marker. The builders may have wanted an accurate lunar predictor that could provide complete information about the moon's full 18.6-year cycle.

Left: the site of the single standing stone, 11 feet high, at Kintraw, Argyll, Scotland. Looking southwest the prominent peaks of the island of Jura can be seen 28 miles away. Excavations carried out by Dr. Euan MacKie in 1970–1 showed evidence of a man-made platform, quite possibly for an observation point.

Above: handmade model of a masked Maya priest, probably dressed for a sun cult ceremony. Excavation of British Neolithic sites such as Durrington Walls seems to show that they are wooden British equivalents of the Maya stone ceremonial sites of Central America. This is evidence of the existence of similar priestly hierarchies.

as among the Maya people of Central America. In a recent book on the megalith builders Dr. Euan MacKie of the University of Glasgow, Scotland has argued that we may in fact have archaeological evidence of the existence of an intellectual elite in Western Europe in Neolithic times which has hitherto been otherwise and wrongly interpreted.

In the winter of 1850 a tremendous storm lashed the Orkney Isles. On the western coast of the largest island it washed away some sand dunes to reveal the stone foundations of an ancient building. Later excavation of this site showed that it was a complex of buildings, some of which appeared to have been built for individual occupation and others for communal use. There were

Right: Skara Brae in the Orkney Islands off the northern coast of Scotland. Its name is Scottish for "hilly dunes," and the entire settlement was hidden under those dunes for millenia before a storm exposed it. The village is remarkable because it is the most fully preserved Neolithic site yet found in Europe and also because it is built entirely of stone. The settlement consisted of 10 stone houses connected or separated by stone walls and linked by stone valleys. They were furnished with stone beds and benches.

signs that a disaster had occurred there at the time when it was inhabited, and which had resulted in its abandonment. Some pottery found on the site was flat-based and decorated with deep grooves and abstract reliefs, unlike anything found anywhere else, and archaeologists long assumed that Skara Brae, as the site was called, was an isolated Neolithic farmers' village. A similar settlement, with the same type of pottery, was found on another Orkney island, Rousay, in the 1930s, and in the same decade Grooved Ware pottery, as it became known, was found at Clacton in Essex, which exploded the myth that it was a unique

Stone Village of Skara Brae

Orkneyan artifact. More Grooved Ware was found when Woodhenge on Salisbury Plain was excavated in the 1960s and other sites in southern England have since yielded more examples, particularly the site known as Durrington Walls, also on Salisbury Plain. Radiocarbon dating showed that the settlements at Durrington Walls and at Skara Brae had flourished at the same time, and the similarity of their artifacts suggested that Skara Brae had been something more than an isolated farming settlement. An ingenious study of the food refuse—in the form of animal bones—of the settlement at Durrington Walls, and a comparison of it with the refuse from another Neolithic site, the nearby Windmill Hill causewayed camp, has shown that the

Above: the Ring of Brogar at Stennes on the Orkney mainland. This imposing megalithic circle repeats some of the essential features of Avebury, over 900 miles to the south. Probably about 60 stones originally stood here, of which 27 remain.

Durrington Walls inhabitants enjoyed a different diet from that of the ordinary members of a Neolithic community, an interesting discovery which strongly suggests that they were members of an elite class.

At Stenness, near Skara Brae, there is a stone circle, and at Quanterness, also nearby, a chambered cairn has been found. Dr. MacKie has suggested that the three sites are related, and that his theory explains another mystery posed by megalithic remains. This is the question of who was buried in the great chambered tombs. It used to be assumed that these were the burial places of whole Neolithic communities. But as radiocarbon dating has shown that burials in particular places were spread over very long periods of time, the probability is that the few hundred occupants of these tombs found throughout the British Isles were a very select group. Therefore it seems likely that they were, in fact, members of a kind of intellectual theocracy, a class of priest-architect-designer-astronomers who were the megalith builders themselves.

Chapter 4
Three Mysterious Kings

Archaeology often consists of finding the reality behind the myth. The stories of the Trojan War and of King Minos and the Minotaur are good examples. This chapter looks at three legendary kings: Midas of Phrygia, whose touch turned everything to gold; Gyges, who made Sardis, capital of Lydia, one of the richest cities of the ancient world; and Croesus of Lydia, whose name is still today a byword for massive wealth. They all ruled in Asia Minor at a time when its southwest region was enjoying a period of extraordinary prosperity. What else do we know about them? In this chapter fact is sifted from fable. The results are fascinating.

To have the "Midas touch" is generally accounted a blessing. It wasn't such a blessing to Midas himself. According to the ancient legend, Midas was the son of the goddess Cybele by Gordius, the Phrygian king who devised the Gordian knot. He himself in due time became King of Phrygia, and proved a wise and good ruler. He won the favor of the god Dionysus by rescuing the drunken Silenus, the gross old man who had been Dionysus' tutor, from peasants who had tied him up on the banks of the Sangarius. As a reward Dionysus granted Midas a wish. The king wished that everything he touched should be turned to gold. He soon regretted making this wish, though, for he was unable to eat because his food turned to gold. He prayed to Dionysus, who told him to dive into the Pactolus river, which he did, and thereafter the river flowed with gold dust.

This legend is historically interesting because it commemorates a civilization about which very little is known. Phrygia was situated in central Anatolia in what is today Turkey. Modern archaeology has shown that a high civilization flourished there for several centuries from about the middle of the 8th century B.C. Archaeologists used to think of this area as one of transit between Europe and Asia. It is only since 1950, when a team of American archaeologists led by Professor Stuart Young of the University of Pennsylvania began excavating the site of the Phrygian capital of Gordium, that historians have realized that there were prosperous ancient civilizations in Anatolia.

Opposite: illustration by Walter Crane showing Midas turning his beloved daughter into gold. The gift bestowed on him by the god Dionysus not only made it impossible for him to eat, he also could not touch his family in affection. The details of the various Midas stories are recounted by the Roman poet Ovid in his *Metamorphoses* II.

Above: Midas as Mita of Mushki, receiving an embassy from his ally Urartu. The two countries had a common enemy in Assyria and around 720 B.C. they joined forces.

Below: bed of the celebrated river Pactolus of Lydia which rises on Mount Tmolus and flows past Sardis into the Hermus. Its gold had been exhausted by the time of the Roman emperor Augustus.

Below right: a brick house of Gordium in the time of King Midas. The slots in the brickwork were for wooden beams for reinforcement. The house consisted of two large rooms each with a circular hearth. The smaller room opened to an extensive stone courtyard paved with pebble mosaic. At the back of the house and along its west side were small storerooms, probably added at a later date.

Assyrian annals of the 8th century B.C. speak of a ruler called "Mita of Mushki" as one of their most powerful enemies in the north. This king has been identified with the one the Greeks called Midas and credited with the foundation of Phrygian civilization. Many experts today believe that Phrygian culture contributed to the development of early Greek civilization, for when Phrygian and Greek architecture of the 7th and 8th centuries B.C. are compared, the Phrygian is seen to be manifestly superior. Phrygian pottery and metal work of the period too is often very fine. As a considerable number of Phrygian metal objects have been found in and around Greece but no corresponding Greek products of the same period have been unearthed in Phrygia, the case for Phrygian influence on Greek culture would appear to be strong.

The legend of the Midas touch and of the Pactolus flowing with gold dust is believed to be based on the fact that in ancient times the rivers of Anatolia did in fact carry down great quantities of gold and that the prosperity of the region was founded on this happy phenomenon. The Phrygian capital was situated on the river Sangarius, which is today called the Sakarya. Gordium was obviously an important center, for one of the things that has been unearthed there is a section of a great highway, known as the Royal Road of the Achaemenid Persian emperors. This came from Susa, in what is today southern Iran, crossed the Sangarius at Gordium, and continued to Sardis, the capital of neighboring Lydia.

When Greek and Persian structures of later periods had been cleared away, the Gordium archaeologists found ample evidence that the Phrygians had been great architects. There were remains of military, civil, and religious buildings. In one there was found a great hall paved with an intricate mosaic of colored pebbles, the earliest example of this technique that has ever been discovered. But the richest discoveries were made in the burial mounds just outside the city. The Phrygians had buried important people in tomb-chambers made of timber which were roofed and then covered with tons of earth. The biggest of such burial mounds or *tumuli* found at Gordium was originally called the "Tomb of Midas," and was a mound some 170 feet high and 800

Midas and the River of Gold

feet in diameter. American archaeologists located the burial chamber by drilling down into it from the top of the mound. When they had done this they dug a horizontal tunnel toward it. They found that the chamber of timber had been surrounded by a stone wall and covered with an inner mound of stone rubble in order to bear the tremendous weight of the earth piled above. The wall had to be breached and a good deal of the rubble removed before the archaeologists gained access to the inner chamber. Because these operations weakened the support it was with some apprehension that they finally ventured to enter. They were hardly reassured when they found that part of the roof had already fallen in. They had to construct temporary supports before they could investigate the contents of the chamber.

Just under the spot where the wall had been breached, the Americans found the skeleton of a Phrygian king lying on an immense bed, which had collapsed, but which was covered with 20 rich coverlets. The floor was strewn with bronze vessels that had apparently been on a structure of shelves which had also collapsed. There were ornamented copper cauldrons standing on iron tripods against the walls, which had apparently originally been filled with food and drink. But there were no objects made of gold among the funerary relics. Considering the reputation of the fabled Midas the American archaeologists found this rather puzzling and disappointing.

There is a second legend associated with this mysterious ruler. It was said that he was once called upon to judge the comparative skills of the god Apollo on the lyre and the satyr Marsyas on the flute. He declared Marsyas the winner, and Apollo vindictively rewarded him with a pair of ass's ears. Midas hid his affliction under his Phrygian cap, and the only person who knew about it

Below left: the rock-hewn monument known as the "Tomb of Midas" at Yazilikaya, Turkey. The vertical rock face is sculptured to represent the end façade of a gabled building and decorated with geometrical ornament in relief to represent terracotta tiles.

Above: bronze vessels of the 8th century B.C. found in the tumulus at Gordium. Three bronze cauldrons and hundreds of smaller bronzes were cluttered over the floor of the tomb where they had fallen off iron nails on the walls or wooden tables which had collapsed under their weight.

The Legends of Midas and Gyges

Right: *The Judgment of Midas* by the 17th-century Italian painter Domenichino, illustrating the musical competition between the god Apollo and the satyr Marsyas. When Midas chose Marsyas as the winner Apollo gave him the ears of an ass.

was his barber, whom he swore to secrecy. The barber, however, found it very difficult to keep the extraordinary secret to himself, and to gain some relief he dug a hole in the ground and confided it to the earth. But reeds grew from the spot and whenever they were rustled by the wind they could be heard to say, "King Midas has ass's ears." Midas, according to the legend, killed himself in desperation by drinking the blood of a bull.

Very often the traditional heroes of one culture are portrayed as devils or buffoons in another, and this preposterous tale is probably a Greek attempt to discredit a foreign ruler whose achievement in establishing Phrygian civilization was one of the outstanding individual accomplishments of the ancient world. At Gordium the American archaeologists found a terracotta bust of Midas, portraying him with two immense ears, but it was of late date and Greek origin and obviously not a confirmation of the legend but rather a product of it.

The kingdom next to Phrygia to the west, Lydia, began its golden age a little later. It is believed that Midas died in about 695 B.C., and that Gyges, the first ruler of the great Mermnad dynasty in Lydia, assumed power in about 687 B.C. Since about 1200 B.C. Lydia had been ruled by a dynasty known as the Heraclids, for they were supposed to be descended from the god-hero Heracles. He had been sold as a slave to Omphale the Queen of Lydia and had then become her lover. The last of the Heraclids, King Candaules, was apparently murdered and usurped by Gyges, and the Greek writers Plato and Herodotus relate different fantastic accounts of how the dynastic change came about.

In Plato's tale, Gyges was a shepherd who fell into a chasm after a thunderstorm and an earthquake, and there found a bronze horse with a dead man inside. There was a gold ring on the dead man's finger. Gyges took it and found that the ring could be manipulated so as to make its wearer invisible. He immediately conceived and carried out a bold plan. He used the magical property of the ring to enable him to gain admission to the queen's bedchamber, became her lover, and then murdered the king and took his place.

Herodotus' account is somewhat less fabulous and makes Candaules' folly as much the cause of his downfall as Gyges' ambition. Gyges, in this story, was originally a courtier and favorite of King Candaules. The king was so proud of the beauty of his wife, Toudo, that he wanted to boast of it to another, and obliged Gyges to play the voyeur so that he could see her naked.

Below: early 19th-century painting by the Englishman Sir William Etty of *Candaules, King of Lydia, showing his Wife to Gyges.* According to Herodotus, the king one day said to his favorite, Gyges: "It appears you don't believe me when I tell you how lovely my wife is. Well, a man always believes his eyes better than his ears; so do as I tell you —contrive to see her naked."

Sardis and the Delphic Oracle

Gyges was reluctant to comply, and when he did he was discovered by the queen, who was angry but at the same time flattered and attracted to him, and who gave him a choice between instant death or murdering her husband and taking his place both in her bed and on the throne. He naturally took the latter option, and thus began the great Mermnad dynasty.

These are fantastic tales, but the common factor of Gyges' violent usurpation of Candaules and annexation of his wife are probably historically true. Herodotus' account of events immediately following the coup also rings true. Though Gyges held the reins of power, the Heraclid faction had considerable support and was a threat to the security of his regime. In order to avoid civil war the two sides agreed to put their claims to the arbitration of the Delphic oracle. The oracle declared in favor of Gyges, who showed his gratitude by endowing the Delphic shrine with generous gifts of silver and gold: an act of realpolitik which showed shrewdness in consolidating his power.

Gyges' wealth became legendary. A contemporary Greek poet, Archilochus of Paros, wrote: "Naught care I for the wealth of Gyges, lord of Sardis." He may not have cared, but great rulers like the Assyrian Assurbanipal and the Egyptian pharaoh Psammetichus certainly cared for the military and political power that Gyges came to wield through the deployment of his wealth. In his reign of some 35 years he made the Lydian capital of Sardis a city of international importance both politically and socially. Diplomacy and generalship must have been among his accomplishments, but the gold of the Pactolus, the legendary river on which the city of Sardis was situated, was the foundation upon which his prosperity and power were built. It was in his reign that the mining of gold began from the mountains whence

Right: the temple of Apollo at Delphi where Gyges consulted the oracle, said to have been discovered when some goats strayed into the mouth of the cave and went into convulsions. The oracle answered in favor of Gyges, but the priestess added that the Heraclids would have their revenge on him after five generations.

Above: Sardis, capital of Lydia. Gyges made it a city of great influence and wealth, and it was one of the earliest seats of the Christian religion. The city was destroyed in the wars of the Middle Ages.

the torrent of the Pactolus carried the precious metal down to enrich the sands of Sardis.

If it was personal ambition that drove Gyges to seize the throne of Lydia, that ambition became identified with the national cause during his reign. Though he was reputed eventually to have become a shrewd economist and wise ruler, Gyges began his reign as an aggressive expansionist. Sardis lay about 65 miles inland from the Aegean coast. Between Lydia and the coast there were a number of small Greek city states, such as Miletus, Magnesia, Smyrna, and Colophon. Probably realizing that if Lydia were to prosper commercially it would need access to the sea, Gyges led military campaigns against these coastal Greek city states. At the same time he sent envoys to conciliate the more powerful city states of mainland Greece and further generous offerings to keep the Delphic oracle well disposed toward him. Although success attended most of his military enterprises, he was not always triumphant. The Roman historian Plutarch retells a story of a shameful Lydian defeat. They had laid siege to the city of Smyrna and sent to its ruler, Philarchus, a demand that the women of Smyrna should be sent out to them. The Smyrneans had just decided to agree to this humiliating condition when a slave girl suggested to Philarchus that instead of sending out their wives and daughters the Smyrneans should dress up slave girls in fine clothes and send them out. This was done, and when the Lydians were exhausted from their dalliance with the slave girls the Smyrneans attacked and overcame them.

The Lydians' love of luxury was famed among the Greeks at a later period, and this story, which Plutarch quoted from a Smyrnean historian, may well be simply propaganda reproduced. The fact that Gyges' troops were no mere pleasure-lovers is suggested by their keeping at bay the wild tribesmen of the north, the Cimmerians, who terrorized the cities of Asia Minor in the 600s B.C., seeming to appear suddenly from nowhere, indulge in an orgy of plunder, murder, destruction, and rape, and then dis-

Burial Mounds of King Gyges

appear as suddenly and mysteriously as they arrived. But when the Cimmerians fell upon Sardis in 657 B.C. they met strong and determined opposition and were defeated. The success emboldened Gyges and consolidated his power, and for the remaining 12 years of Gyges' reign Sardis was a proud and prosperous city. But in 645 B.C. a more massive and ferocious force of Cimmerians attacked, Sardis was sacked, and Gyges himself killed. The ruthlessness of the sacking was indicated by the recent discovery by archaeologists of the skeleton of a little girl killed by the collapse of a burning house.

The Mermnad dynasty consisted of a succession of five kings: Gyges, Ardys, Sadyathes, Alyattes, and Croesus. The Cimmerian conquest proved only a temporary setback for the Lydians. Gyges' son, Ardys, reestablished Lydian morale and continued to fight fiercely against the Greek city states of the coast. He also had a fine tomb built to house his father's remains, with a colossal burial mound or tumulus raised above it to commemorate his greatness.

In the 1960s an American archaeological expedition began to investigate the royal cemetery to the north of Sardis. There, among about 100 burial mounds, three are conspicuous by their immense size, and the middle one of these is believed to be the tomb of Gyges. It is about 130 feet high and 650 feet in diameter. When a tunnel was bored into this mound it was discovered that other tunnels had penetrated it, and there were signs that these had been made by tomb robbers in Roman times. The most interesting discovery, though, was of a substantial wall of limestone blocks comprising a circular structure of about 300 feet in diameter erected deep within the tumulus. On a number of these blocks an incised monogram was found. The monogram is cryptic and a number of alternative ways of reading it have been suggested, the most plausible of which is that it spells "Gugu," which was the name by which Gyges was known in Assyrian records of the period.

Tunneling was continued beyond the inner wall and reached the center of the mound, and a number of other exploratory

Right: the Gygean lake and site of the "Thousand Tombs." Excavated by a team of American and Turkish archaeologists in the 1960s, the burial mounds to the north of Sardis may include the tomb of Gyges himself. No actual burial chamber was found, but this may be because tomb robbers had preceded them or because the chamber was situated in a place not likely to attract the attention of visitors.

tunnels were dug around the center, but no actual burial chamber was found. In other Lydian tombs burial chambers have been found situated off-center, sometimes at a considerable distance, no doubt in order to trick robbers and other intruders, so perhaps King Gyges' skeleton remains undisturbed to this day beneath the great tumulus at Sardis.

The grandeur of Lydia under the Mermnads lasted less than 200 years, and it ended when its civilization and influence had reached their very height in the fifth generation under King Croesus. This king, whose name has been synonymous with fabulous wealth for 2500 years, succeeded to the throne of Lydia in 560 B.C. at the age of 35. He began his reign by completing the work that Gyges had started and the other Mermnad rulers had continued: the subjection of the Greek cities of the coast and extension of Lydian sovereignty to the Aegean in the west, the Mediterranean in the south, and the Hellespont in the north. Eastward he subdued all the nations up to the river Halys, and at the height of his power was master of an area about half the size of modern Turkey.

Above: the giant tumulus at Lake Gyges today. According to Herodotus, the mound was raised by the joint labor and contributions of tradesmen, craftsmen, and prostitutes of Lydia. The amount of work done by the prostitutes was calculated to have been the largest.

The Pactolus river and the golden mountain of Tmolus continued to disgorge their wealth, Lydia prospered too by trade and Croesus invited philosophers and great men from all over the Greek world to visit Sardis and view its splendors. Legend has it that one of these visitors was Solon, the lawgiver of Athens, a man famed for his wisdom, and that an interesting discussion took place between him and Croesus. After showing Solon around his treasuries, Croesus asked him who he thought was the happiest man he had ever met. Solon answered without hesitation that Tellus of Athens was, because he had lived in a lovely

Right: *Croesus and Solon* by the 17th-century Dutch painter Hendrick van Steenwyck the Younger. Croesus showed his wealth to the Athenian lawgiver Solon and asked who was the happiest man he had ever seen. Croesus expected that he himself would be named, but instead Solon pointed out the transience of material wealth.

Below: the fabled wealth of Croesus. Both Plutarch and Herodotus tell the story of the meeting between the wise Solon and the rich king Croesus.

city, had lived to see his sons and grandsons grow to manhood, and had died gloriously and with honor, defending his city. "Who, then, was the second happiest?" asked Croesus, clearly angling for flattery. But Solon calmly answered that he thought perhaps Cleobis and Biton were, because they had enjoyed wealth, health, and public acclaim in their lives and had died in their sleep in the temple of the goddess Hera after sacrificing and feasting. No longer containing his annoyance, the king then demanded of Solon why he took no account of Croesus' own happiness. The Athenian explained that such was the jealousy of the gods, and so subject to change was human life, that it was impossible to call any man happy until his life was done and he had died a happy death. Croesus, according to Herodotus' telling of this story, angrily dismissed Solon from his court and declared that he considered him foolish to take no account of present happiness and success.

In Herodotus' histories it is always difficult to distinguish fact

Who is the Happiest Man?

Left: Cyrus the Great, founder of the Persian empire and conqueror of Lydia in 546 B.C. He took Croesus prisoner. In the Old Testament of the Bible he is the "Cyrus the King" who ordered the rebuilding of the Temple in Jerusalem. He was considered by the Greeks to be a model ruler.

from fable, for many of his tales are obviously told in such a way as to point a moral. Because Herodotus is our main source of knowledge of the life of the last Lydian king, the historical Croesus remains something of a mystery. He presented such a dramatic example of the downfall of the mighty that a philosophically-minded, moralizing historian like Herodotus could hardly resist embroidering his narrative. He tells us that after his interview with Solon, the king was disturbed and he had a dream in which he saw his son Atys killed by an iron weapon. Fearing that this was a prophetic dream, Croesus forbade Atys to lead the army, had all iron weapons removed from his apartments, and to compensate Atys and divert his attention he contracted a marriage for him. Some time later Croesus received a request to send Atys and some companions to hunt down a wild boar that was terrorizing a region. He was reluctant to do so, and when Atys protested he explained to him about the dream. The young man still insisted on going, and pointed out that as a boar does not have tusks of iron he would be quite safe. Croesus relented, but as a precaution sent a Phrygian prince, Adrastus, as his bodyguard. When eventually the boar was brought to bay, Adrastus hurled his javelin at it but missed his aim and killed Atys by mistake, thus fulfilling the king's prophetic dream.

This story is so obviously an illustration of Solon's teaching about the unpredictable nature of human fortune that we cannot be certain that Atys ever really existed. Herodotus goes on to say that Croesus spent two years mourning his son's death, and was eventually awakened from his resultant apathy by news of the conquests of Cyrus the Persian. Here Herodotus undoubtedly reports authentic history, for the growing power of Cyrus at this time was a matter of concern not only in Lydia but also in Greece, Egypt, and Babylon.

In order to determine whether he should make war on Cyrus, and whom he should ally himself with if so, Croesus decided to

Above: Croesus brought before Cyrus after Lydia was overrun by the Persians. The funeral pyre behind him is ready to be set afire.

consult an oracle. But first he conducted a test to find out which of the oracles was likely to be the most reliable. He sent envoys to famous oracles throughout Greece and even to one as far away as Libya, and instructed them simultaneously to ask the oracles, at a certain time 100 days after their departure from Sardis, to specify what King Croesus was doing at that particular moment. When the prearranged time came, Croesus was cutting up a tortoise and a lamb and boiling them in a bronze cauldron. Two of the oracles tested gave the right answer—a remarkable feat of clairvoyance—and one of them was the oracle at Delphi.

Perhaps recalling his ancestor Gyges' happy dealings with the Delphic oracle, Croesus sent sumptuous gifts to Delphi before putting his question. He received the reply that if Croesus made war on the Persians he would destroy a great kingdom, and that he should seek to ally himself to the strongest of the Greek states. Delighted with this response, Croesus sought an alliance first with Athens, and when his overtures failed there, with Sparta, and began to prosecute war against Cyrus, ignoring the counsel of a renowned wise man of Lydia, Sandanis, that the enterprise was not only risky but also no benefits could accrue from success in it, for the Persians were a poor and hardy people.

In the spring of 547 B.C. Croesus led his army out to challenge Cyrus. He marched beyond the River Halys and subdued part of

Right: Croesus on his funeral pyre. Cyrus sits on horseback watching while Croesus crys out woefully, "O Solon, Solon, Solon!" According to Herodotus, Croesus was spared and became an advisor to Cyrus at his court.

Cappadocia. Cyrus brought an army of considerably greater numerical strength to oppose him. A day-long battle took place, and though heavy casualties were suffered by both sides neither came off decisively victorious. Cyrus declined to continue the struggle the next day, and Croesus, aware of his numerical inferiority, did not press the matter but withdrew to Lydia, planning to gather a bigger army, with allies from Sparta, Egypt, and Babylon, and to engage Cyrus again the following year. Back in Sardis in October, Croesus sent envoys to ask his allies to send their forces the following spring, and then disbanded those of his own forces that were not Lydians. But Cyrus had spies who brought him news of Croesus' plans and moves, and realizing that he would be at a disadvantage the following year he decided to strike while Croesus was unprepared. He descended on Sardis with his large army, and although the crack Lydian troops and cavalry acquitted themselves valiantly they were overwhelmed and Sardis fell to the Persians.

According to Herodotus, when Cyrus had made Croesus captive he had a huge pyre prepared and bound the Lydian king upon it in chains. With the flames rising around him, Croesus remembered Solon's saying that no man could be accounted happy until he had had a happy death, and he called out the name of the great Athenian. Cyrus asked him what he was saying, and Croesus said he was remembering the words of a man whose philosophy all rulers should heed. A brief discourse on the Solonian wisdom by Croesus so impressed Cyrus that he gave orders for the flames to be extinguished, but this proved impossible and Croesus' life was only saved by the intervention of the god Apollo, who sent a storm to put out the flames. Croesus, whose wisdom was now enhanced by his experiences of downfall and deliverance, thereafter became a professional wise man at the court of Cyrus and gave the founder of the Persian empire much sound advice.

An inscription on a Babylonian cylinder of this period probably gives a truer account of events than the philosophical Herodotus. It states simply that "Cyrus, King of Persia, marched into Lydia, killed its king, took its booty, and put a garrison of his own therein." So ended the glory of Sardis and the Mermnad dynasty. Its great kings receded into the enigmatic shadows of legend, and its fabulous treasures enriched the ascendant dynasty of Cyrus, the lord of central Asia.

In 1913 archaeologists from Princeton University found at Sardis a tomb in which there were two tombs. One of them contained the bones of an old man and the other those of a girl of about 17 years. The bones disintegrated as soon as they were touched, but in the girl's coffin there remained a profusion of gleaming gold jewelry: headbands about her head where her hair had been, earrings beside the head, a large ring on the finger bone of one hand, gold beads scattered about her feet, and resting on her breastbone a magnificent necklace, of intricately wrought gold and superbly fashioned precious stones, a masterpiece of the goldsmith's art. Such artifacts as these, today to be seen in the museum at Istanbul, bear mute witness to the achievements of a vanished kingdom whose rulers' names have come down to us as synonyms for fabulous wealth.

Humiliation of Croesus

Below: the tomb of Cyrus the Great, who died in 530 B.C. at Pasargadae. It is set on six steps of irregular height in the form of a house with a sharply gabled roof. A double door leads to a windowless chamber in which a gold sarcophagus once enclosed the mortal remains of the great "liberator" but it is now an empty shell. A carved inscription says: "O man, whoever you are and wherever you come from, for I know that you will come—I am Cyrus, and I won an empire for the Persians. Do not grudge me this spot of earth which covers my body."

Chapter 5
Clues in the Cuneiform

"Like bird tracks in the wet sand"—that is how Europeans first described the system of wedge-shaped symbols that is probably the world's earliest writing. The Sumerians, it seems, probably devised it some 6000 years ago in Mesopotamia, and from 3000 B.C. to the time of Christ it was used by all the peoples of the Middle East—Hittites, Assyrians, Armenians, Persians. But it was not until 1802 that a German schoolmaster named Grotefeld brilliantly cracked the code. This chapter goes on to examine the work of the men like Botta and Layard who one after another excavated the cities of Nineveh and Nimrud and other vast monuments of the Assyrians and the Babylonians.

In 1840 a remarkable Frenchman became consular agent in the small, hot, dusty town of Mosul in what is now southern Iraq, in the land known as Mesopotamia. Paul Emile Botta was not an archaeologist, but a qualified physician with a deep interest in natural science. He had already traveled once around the world. A professional diplomat with a gift for picking up languages, he soon made many friends among the local Arabs. Gradually his imagination was fired by the ancient history of this forgotten corner of the Turkish empire, and he quickly became known among the Arabs as a man interested in buying antiquities. Botta would go around from hut to hut, asking if they had any old pots or vases for sale, or where they had got the bricks they had used to build an outhouse. He was particularly interested in bricks that had strange markings on them. The news of his interest must have spread because one day an Arab came to him from Khorsabad, some 10 miles away. He said that near his village there was a mound containing thousands of the inscribed bricks and many other things that would greatly interest the Frenchman.

Botta had been in Mosul for a few years at that time, and had learned to be skeptical about the marvels promised him by well-meaning Arab informants. He didn't go himself to investigate the Khorsabad site, but sent two workmen instead. When his men returned to report that they had found not only masses of inscribed bricks but also the walls of an ancient building with carvings and pictures on them, Botta hurried over to see for

Opposite: *Jonah before Nineveh*, a 17th-century roundel in the vestry of St. Mary's church, Shrewsbury, England. Jonah was swallowed by the whale as a punishment for shirking the task of preaching to Nineveh.

Grotefend and the Cuneiform

Above: Paul Emile Botta (1802–70), a French doctor appointed consular agent in Mosul in 1842. Botta took the opportunity to excavate the sand-drifted mounds.

himself. What he saw convinced him that he had found a palace of one of the old Assyrian kings, and possibly the site of the city of Nineveh itself. He withdrew a team of workmen from Kuyunjik, a site near Mosul where he had had them digging to little avail for a year, and set them to work at Khorsabad. The year was 1843, and with Botta's find Mesopotamian archaeology was born.

The ancient history of the land between the two great rivers, the Tigris and the Euphrates, was at that time known only from references in the Bible. The exact location of the great cities of Nineveh and Babylon, on which the God of the Hebrews had visited his wrath, was quite unknown, and in the early 19th century nobody suspected that the civilization of the great cities of southern Mesopotamia, of Sumer and Ur, had developed earlier and in some aspects attained higher levels than the Egyptian. For centuries there had been nothing to see in the flat deserts of Mesopotamia except an occasional mysterious mound. In the traditions of the Arabs of the area there were no ancestral memories or legends of the time when the inhabitants of this land had been proud, prosperous, powerful, literate, and cultured. A few travelers in the past had brought back odd trophies from the rubble of the Mesopotamian mounds, but before Botta came to Mosul nobody had excavated in the area.

In Mesopotamia, as in Egypt, the key that gave access to the mysteries of its past was a language. It was a language even more mysterious and difficult, or as one traveler said "more adverse to the intellect," than hieroglyphics, because it consisted of abstract geometrical shapes in which a sort of arrow or wedge shape predominated. The language had been called *cuneiform*, from the Latin word *cuneus*, meaning wedge, and for decades before Botta went to Mosul European scholars had been poring over, comparing, and trying to interpret the strange inscriptions found on ruins, on monuments, and on pieces of pottery and clay found both in Mesopotamia and southern Persia. They had achieved a considerable degree of success, thanks largely to the pioneering efforts of a young schoolmaster from Göttingen in Germany named Georg Friedrich Grotefend.

Grotefend undertook to crack the secret of cuneiform lightly, as the result of a wager made when drinking with some friends. He was only an amateur orientalist, and was no specialist in ancient languages, but often problems that confound orthodox methods of solution will yield to the unorthodox. Grotefend's breakthrough was achieved by his trying to find a logical rather than a philological solution to the problem of the cuneiform. Working with copies of some cuneiform inscriptions from the ruins of the royal palace of the ancient Persian city of Persepolis, he noted that a certain group of signs kept being repeated. It was a known fact that the Persian rulers had always begun their proclamations with their names, followed by the words "great king, king of kings," so Grotefend deduced that the repeated signs represented the word "king." The frequency of their repetition suggested that more than one king was named, so he conjectured that the introductory formula might read: "X, great king, king of kings, son of Z, etc." If his conjecture was right, he reasoned, there must be three groups of characters that stood for the names of three rulers, who in order of appearance would be son, father, and grandfather. There were a number of such genealogies in ancient Persian history, and Grotefend tested a number of them against the groups of characters that he had isolated as the names. He was able to eliminate some of the genealogical groups for purely logical reasons: that of Cyrus—Cambyses—Cyrus, because all three names began with the same letter and there was no common symbol at the beginning of each name in the cuneiform text; that of Darius—Artaxerxes—Xerxes, because the middle name was too long. Eventually he hit upon a genealogy that fitted the text that he was working with. It was: Xerxes—Darius—Hystaspes. Grotefend was confident that he was right in this because the formula "great king, king of kings," was not found in the text after the name Hystaspes, and he knew that Hystaspes had been the founder of the royal line but never a king himself. Thus by sheer reasoning he worked out that his text read: "Xerxes, great king, king of kings, son of

Above: fragment of a vase containing part of a trilingual inscription of Xerxes, king of Persia. Xerxes was a key word that helped Grotefend to decipher the cuneiform.

Left: cast of part of an inscription in Babylonian of Darius the Great, recording the name and titles of the Persian king. Darius was another of the key words which enabled Grotefend to crack the cuneiform.

Darius, great king, king of kings, son of Hystaspes." Many contemporary scholars were skeptical and unconvinced, but Grotefend was later proved to be right.

Before Grotefend achieved his breakthrough in the 1800s, nobody had known for certain that cuneiform was a kind of writing and not just decoration. If it was assumed to be writing, there was no clue as to how it should be read (horizontally or vertically, from left to right or vice versa), or as to whether it was an abstract picture language or a method of phonetic transcription. Grotefend's achievement was not only that he translated a few words of cuneiform, but that he also reasoned out the correct answers to these questions. By establishing the phonetic values of some of the strange characters he showed the way for other scholars to proceed.

Danish, German, French, Irish, and English scholars made contributions to the deciphering of the varieties of the cuneiform in the 50 years following Grotefend's publication of his theories and translation in 1805. Of these, the outstanding contribution was that of the Englishman Henry Rawlinson. A soldier, a diplo-

Above: Sir Henry Rawlinson (1810–95) in a Spy cartoon from *Vanity Fair*, 1873. Rawlinson transliterated Darius the Great's inscription, and in 1846 he published *The Persian Cuneiform Inscriptions at Behistun.*

mat, and a member of Parliament as well as a scholar, Rawlinson brought physical courage as well as intellectual ability to the task of understanding the ancient inscriptions. In 1836, when he was 26 years old, he first became acquainted with Grotefend's work. Earlier he himself had deciphered a number of inscriptions, having tackled the problem in a manner very similar to that employed by Grotefend. Needing more inscriptions to work with, in 1837 while on military service in Persia Rawlinson undertook the hazardous task of copying the inscription of Darius from the rock face at Behistun.

In the mountains of Kurdistan there is a narrow pass through which the road from Ectabana in Persia to Babylon in Mesopotamia used to pass and which today forms part of the highway from Baghdad to Teheran. Mountains rise sheer from this pass to a height of 4000 feet, and between 200 and 500 feet above ground level there is carved in the rock face an immense relief celebrating the person, exploits, and victories of the mighty King Darius. Beside and beneath these carvings there are 14 columns of writing in three distinct variations of the cuneiform script—Old Persian, Elamite, and Assyro-Babylonian. The Darius inscriptions were therefore a kind of Rosetta stone of the cuneiform. The problem was that they couldn't be copied in sufficient detail for study unless somebody actually climbed up on to the rock face. This is precisely what Rawlinson decided to do.

The old Persian sculptors who had done the carvings had worked from platforms which had then been cut away, leaving a ledge about 18 inches below the inscriptions. Rawlinson worked from ladders that were propped up on this narrow ledge. He had to have ladders of different lengths in order to copy all the characters, and of course he needed to have his hands free for the work.

Right: mark of the royal seal of Darius the Great. This finely engraved Persian cylinder seal shows the king hunting lions from his chariot. The palm, a sacred tree, stands in the background. The trilingual inscription gives his name and title ("I, Darius, the Great King") in Old Persian, Elamite, and Assyro-Babylonian cuneiform. The seal dates from the 6th or the 5th century B.C. and is made of agate.

Rawlinson Scales the Rock Face

If we imagine him standing on the high rungs of a nearly vertical ladder with a sheer fall of hundreds of feet behind him we surely cannot but admire the man's dedication to scholarship. "In this position I copied all the upper inscriptions," he later wrote, "and the interest of the occupation entirely did away with any sense of danger."

From this ledge, however, he could only get access to the text in Old Persian. The Elamite and Assyro-Babylonian texts were even less accessible, and to get a copy of the latter he had to avail himself of the help of "a wild Kurdish boy" who climbed up the perpendicular rock face "in a manner which to a looker-on appeared quite miraculous." The work was completed without mishap, and Rawlinson was able to present to the specialist scholars of the world a parallel text in three ancient unknown languages. The Old Persian text was the key to the other two, as the Greek of the Rosetta stone was the key to the Egyptian

Above: the inscription at Behistun, Iran—the cuneiform equivalent of the Rosetta stone. Hewn 340 feet above the ground into the mountain face some 2500 years ago, it describes the military triumphs by which Darius secured his throne. The relief adjoining the message shows the Persian monarch, portrayed life size, receiving as prisoners 10 vanquished rivals.

hieroglyphics, and it was Rawlinson, working by the methods that he and Grotefend had independently established, who rendered the first complete translation of the Darius inscription, "I am Darius, the Great King, the King of Persia, the King of the Provinces, the son of Hystaspes, the grandson of Arsames, the Achaemenian. From antiquity are we descended; from antiquity hath our race been kings. . . ." Thus began a long, grandly boastful text describing how Darius had, by the grace of the god Ahura Mayda, defeated all his enemies, and particularly those who had rebelled against him at the beginning of his reign. The rebel chiefs, the text announced, had fallen captive to Darius, who had cut off their noses and ears, put out their eyes, exhibited them in public in fetters, and finally crucified them.

Even with the help of the Old Persian text and Rawlinson's

Understanding Sound Symbols

Above: bricks inscribed with the name and titles of Nebuchadnezzar II, king of Babylon. Purely phonetic spelling of his name results in a totally different word, which is one reason why Assyro-Babylonian was such a difficult language to decipher. Phonetic symbols made the language flexible. An example using English is the word "season," spelled as two pictures—one each of the sea and the sun.

Below: an Assyrian inscription of 879 B.C., an example of pure cuneiform. All traces of its predecessor, picture writing, have gone. The scribe probably wrote this using a wedge-shaped stylus as a pen.

translation, the other two languages on the Behistun rock proved difficult to crack. Elamite eventually yielded to the combined efforts of a Dane, Niels Westergaard, an Irishman, Dr. Hincks, and an Englishman, Edwin Norris. Norris developed an intriguing theory that the language of the Elamites, a people about whom scarcely anything is known, was related to Finnish! The third text, the Assyro-Babylonian, however, proved the most difficult of the three. This was particularly frustrating because it was the language of all the inscriptions on the buildings, the relics, and the curious clay bricks that had been unearthed in profusion in Mesopotamia since Paul Botta started excavating there in 1843.

The problem was that the Assyro-Babylonian cuneiform was not an alphabetical script, with each symbol representing a sound. It appeared that a single symbol could represent a variety of sounds or meanings, and when a number of symbols were brought together to make a word or phrase the pronunciation of the resultant whole might bear no relation to that of its component parts. For instance, the name of the Assyrian king known in the Bible as Nebuchadnezzar was in fact pronounced Nebukudurriussur, but if the group of characters that spelled the name were pronounced according to their individual phonetic values they rendered the quite different word An - pa - sa - du - sis. Many scholars abandoned the problem as insoluble. Then the lucky find of a batch of clay tablets that together made up part of a kind of dictionary of cuneiform signs encouraged a number of specialists to persist in their efforts. One of these was a brilliant Englishman named William Henry Fox Talbot, later remembered as a pioneer of photography. Fox Talbot carried out a clever ruse that conclusively proved to the world that the apparently impossible task of translating Assyro-Babylonian cuneiform had been accomplished.

Fox Talbot first made his own translation of an Assyrian cylinder. He then sent it in a sealed envelope to the president of the Royal Asiatic Society in London, together with the suggestion that other well-known scholars in the field should be asked to make their translations of the same text. Rawlinson, Dr. Hincks, and a French scholar, Jules Oppert, were invited to do so. Each unaware of the others' efforts, they sent their transla-

Left: tablet from Assyria, collected by Paul Botta. The upper part has four soldiers, probably vassals or prisoners, leading beautiful spirited horses. The man at the head of the procession is making a motion of submission. The lower half of the tablet shows a priest in basalt. His right hand is held up in invocation, and from his left hangs a branch of poppy.

tions to the Society in sealed envelopes. When these were simultaneously opened by a commission of independent judges, and the translations were compared, the skeptics who had been murmuring that other so-called translations were no better than guesswork were silenced for good. Although a few words and phrases were differently interpreted by the four translators, their texts were substantially the same. So the writings in the strange script which someone once said looked like the marks left by birds walking over wet sand, and which were now coming out of Mesopotamia in great numbers, could be read. At last knowledge could be gained of the ancient civilizations that were Western man's cultural ancestors and whose relics had lain for centuries buried beneath the desert sands.

Paul Botta had financed his purchases of antiquities and his archaeological digs from his own pocket, but when his discovery at Khorsabad was announced generous funds were made available from official sources in France to enable him to continue the good work. Gradually his excavations uncovered the remains of what had obviously been a very grand palace, with courtyards, public rooms, and private apartments all splendidly ornamented and decorated. Unfortunately, though, most of the decorations and sculptures quickly disintegrated when they were exposed, and if the French government had not sent out an artist, Eugene Flandin, to work with the excavators and make copies of the Assyrian reliefs as they came to light, these records of the life and achievement of a lost civilization would have disappeared. Larger artifacts, however, remained intact, and Botta repaid his sponsors by shipping back to Paris numerous fine large pieces of Assyrian sculpture. The transportation of these trophies, some of which weighed as much as 12 tons, was difficult and hazardous. Wagons with extra-strong axles and wide wheels were needed for the 10-mile journey to the Tigris, and a rough track had to be

Palace of Sargon II

laid over the route. To reach the port of Basra on the Persian Gulf, the sculptures had to be floated down the river on traditional Mesopotamian rafts buoyed up with inflated skins. A number of Assyrian kings and gods, so recently exhumed from the sand, plunged back into oblivion beneath the tempestuous waters of the Upper Tigris, but Botta continued his efforts undeterred, and the Assyrian rooms in the Louvre today testify to his success.

Transportation was only one of his problems. Another was the Turkish governor of the area, Mehmed Pasha, who believed that the Frenchman was hunting treasure and wanted a substantial portion for himself. Disappointed in this, he summarily banned excavation of the Khorsabad site and refused to allow Arab workmen to work for Botta, justifying his actions by saying that the Frenchman was building a fortress and the excavations were defense entrenchments. Botta countered by going over the pasha's head to his superiors in the Turkish capital of Constantinople and obtaining permission to continue with his work. Mehmed however remained troublesome, and Botta's vexations from this quarter were only ended by the pasha's premature death.

Botta continued to believe that he had discovered Nineveh, and in 1850 he published in five volumes, illustrated by Frandin, his *Monuments de Ninive*. When it became possible to read Assyro-Babylonian cuneiform later in that decade, it was revealed that the palace Botta had excavated was that of the

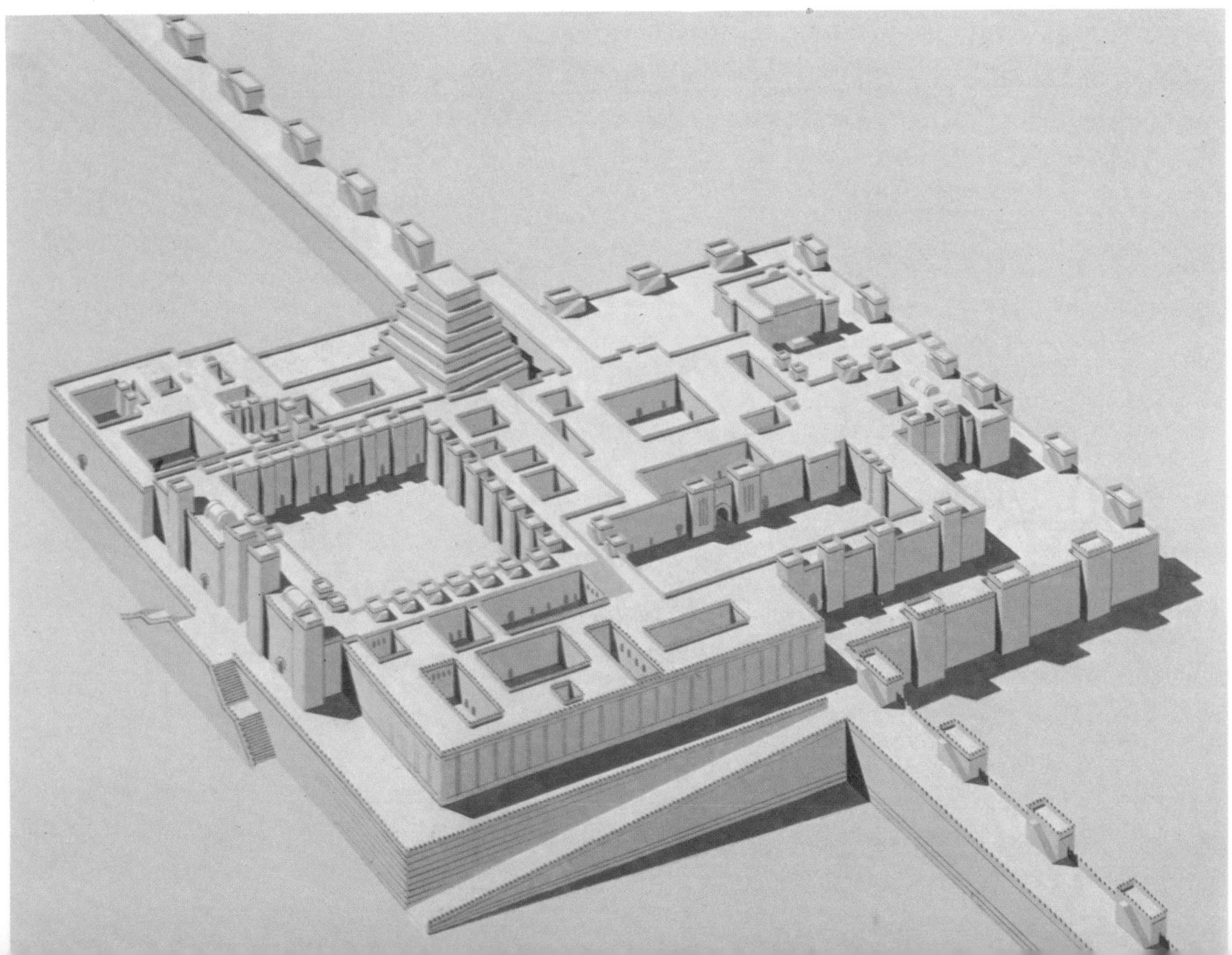

Below: reconstruction of the palace at Khorsabad of Sargon II who ruled Assyria from 722–705 B.C. Paul Botta excavated the palace believing it was Nineveh. In the halls and courtyards of the fortified town that enclosed the palace were sculptures of strong-muscled men with full, curled beards.

Assyrian king Sargon II of the 8th century B.C., and that Khorsabad had formerly been known as Dûr-Sharrukin, or Sargon's Town. It was left to a friend of Botta's, the Englishman Austen Henry Layard, to discover the actual Nineveh. He found the great city, ironically, beneath the great mound at Kuyunjik, the site that Botta had abandoned when he took his team of workmen to Khorsabad.

Layard's name is outstanding in Mesopotamian archaeology. In fact it is virtually synonymous with it just as Petrie's is with Egypt and Schliemann's with Troy. His books, *Early Adventures*, *Nineveh and its Remains*, and *Discoveries in the Ruins of Nineveh and Babylon*, are still highly readable classics of 19th-century travel and archaeological literature. He first traveled in the region at the age of 23 in 1839–40, and in *Early Adventures* he writes eloquently of the urge that inspired the most important achievements of his career in archaeology:

"I now felt an irresistible desire to penetrate to the regions beyond the Euphrates, to which history and tradition point as the birthplace of the wisdom of the West. Most travelers, after a journey through the usually frequented parts of the East, have the same longing to cross the great river, and to explore those lands which are separated on the map from the confines of Syria by a vast blank stretching over Assyria, Babylonia, and Chaldea. With these names are linked great nations and great cities dimly shadowed forth in history; mighty ruins, in the midst of deserts, defying, by their very desolation and lack of definite form, the

Above: relief of a warrior from the palace of Sargon II at Khorsabad, one of the prizes Botta took back to France. War was a very important part of Assyrian life, and it even seems to have been a religious duty of the king to undertake some sort of campaign each year. In addition to the standing army there were special units of bodyguards to the king, described as "the troops who in a place hostile or friendly never leave my feet."

Left: portrait of Austen Henry Layard painted in 1891 by Ludwig Passini. His imagination was fired when, as a child, he pored over the *Arabian Nights*. He began his work with only a £60 grant from the British ambassador to Turkey.

Austen Layard Excavates Nimrud

description of the traveler; the remnants of mighty races still roving over the land; the fulfilling and fulfillment of prophecies; the plains to which the Jew and the Gentile alike look as the cradle of their race."

Of all the "mighty ruins, in the midst of deserts" that Layard saw on his first journey the one that most fascinated him was the enormous mound known to be the site of the Biblical city of Nimrud, or Nimrod, which was named after its founder. According to the Bible he was one of the grandsons of Noah. Layard longed to excavate it, but lack of funds prevented him from undertaking any excavations on his own initiative for a further five years. Botta's successes and generous official funding made him envious, and in 1845, although he still had only £60 to finance his venture, he took a river boat down the Tigris to begin his excavations at Nimrud.

Above: outlines of the mounds of Nimrud, 20 miles south of Mosul in what is now Iraq, where Layard set to work. He was helped by the local Arabs and by a phenomenal luck. The pointed mound on the left was the site of Nimrud's Temple High.

This was not a particularly good time or place for such an expedition, for the new Turkish governor proved a tyrant and the desert tribes were in a warlike mood and inclined to vent their feelings on any foreigner. Layard was lucky, however, in gaining the friendship of a tribal sheik named Awad, whose territory included the great mound of Nimrud. Awad took an interest in the Englishman's work and was pleased to supply him with cheap labor. Layard was lucky, too, in getting his excavations off to a successful start. Faced with a virtual mountain, and helped only by six Arabs with picks and shovels, he had no idea where to begin, and when Awad pointed out a piece of yellowish stone sticking out of the ground he told the workmen to start digging there. It was hard work, for after months of drought the earth was packed hard. But Layard swung a pick, too, and his team's labors were soon rewarded. An alabaster slab was uncovered, then a second one attached to it, then eight more. The ten slabs formed a square, with a gap in one corner: the shape and proportions of a room with a door. Layard ordered the men to dig down the faces of the slabs, for these were obviously the tops of the walls of a room, and when they did so some inscriptions were soon revealed, then a finely decorated frieze. Walls so decorated and faced with alabaster could surely belong to nothing less than a royal palace.

Excited by this first find and impatient to know what other treasures the mound might contain, Layard split his team. He took half of them to dig on the other side of the mound, and again his luck, or his sense of divination, was extraordinary. The first pick swung struck stone, and more hours of exhausting labor brought to light an inscription frieze and carvings in relief. Layard declared himself "well satisfied" with his first day's work at Nimrud; as indeed he must have been, having unearthed the walls of two Assyrian palaces.

On the second day of excavation the first chamber was cleared and some interesting fragments were found among the rubble on the floor: some exquisitely carved flowers, part of a tiny sphinx, a small robed figure, some pieces of porcelain with traces of gilding. Awad, convinced that the Englishman must be looking for treasure, covertly showed Layard some flakes of gold leaf he had found, and was astonished when Layard cheerfully told him that he could keep all the gold he found. The archaeologist's interest in old carvings, inscriptions, and statues was a mystery to the desert Arab, but the lure of gold encouraged him to recruit more helpers, and at the end of five days Layard had excavated a maze of chambers with interestingly decorated and inscribed walls. He had also investigated the most conspicuous feature of the site, the pyramidlike mound that the ancient Greek historian Xenophon had written about, which he found appeared to be only a mass of solid brick. It was in fact one of the tall stepped towers of the typical Mesopotamian temple complex, known as a *ziggurat*. Layard knew that Botta had unearthed a similar mysterious structure at Khorsabad, which had contained no sculptures, and as movable sculptures were the main object of his quest he soon abandoned the investigation and returned to the palaces, where a maze of rooms and passages was gradually excavated.

Many of the rooms boasted fine reliefs, powerful and graphic portrayals of the Assyrians engaged in their most characteristic occupations of fighting, pillaging, and hunting. The first sculptures that he found, however, were disappointingly badly damaged. One of the palaces bore signs of having been destroyed by fire. Weather and vandalism had also taken their toll. But in the other building some fine pieces were eventually found. There were a pair of perfectly preserved winged lions that stood 12 feet tall and had long cuneiform inscriptions between their legs. There were winged bulls, too, and griffin-headed human figures, and sculptured eagles and massive bearded men. And one day when Layard was temporarily away from the site two tribesmen came to him and announced excitedly that they had found Nimrud himself. Layard hurried back to the mound, where all the diggers

Below: entrance to the Temple High mound at Nimrud in a drawing of 1852. Within the temple, beyond the two colossal human figures, were sculptured fish gods. To the right of the entrance, apparently outside the walls of the temple, was found one of the finest specimens of Assyrian sculpture—an early king of Nimrud carved in high relief on a solid block of limestone.

Secret Palace Underground

Above: Layard's Arab workers discover the giant "head of Nimrud" at Nineveh, from a drawing in Layard's book *Nineveh and its Remains*.
Below: reconstruction of a hall in the palace of Assurnasirpal II at Nimrud. He reigned for about a quarter of a century from 883–859 B.C. and his wars took up about half of that time. He then rebuilt the city of Kalkhi and erected his great palace on the acropolis at Nimrud.

were gathered around a trench from the bottom of which there projected a huge head of blanched stone, crowned with a rounded turban and with triple horns. Layard knew that this superb piece would be the human head of a lion or bull colossus, and that such figures were usually to be found in pairs, flanking an entrance or gateway. He paced out the usual width of such an entrance and ordered his workmen to dig another trench, and sure enough they came upon a duplicate colossal head.

Unfortunately the news that Nimrud himself had been unearthed had reached the Turkish governor in Mosul, and he, uncertain whether Nimrud had been an infidel or one of the faithful and what observances were due to his "remains," ordered Layard to suspend digging until this theological problem could be resolved. The order, coming as it did when the work was proceeding apace and exciting discoveries were coming to light daily, meant an intolerable delay, but fortunately very soon afterward there arrived from Constantinople a permit to excavate authorized by the Sultan himself, and Layard was able to complete his first excavation, which turned out to be the palace of King Assurnasirpal II, an Assyrian ruler of the 9th century B.C., and to send to Britain a mass of magnificent reliefs and colossal sculptures to provide the British Museum with an Assyrian collection to surpass that of the Louvre in Paris.

In his book, *Nineveh and its Remains*, Layard records a marvelous speech that a reflective Arab sheik made to him one evening after an arduous day's work inching a colossal sculpture of a bull out of a trench prior to conveying it to the Tigris and thence shipping it to England.

"In the name of the Most High," said the sheik, "tell me, O Bey, what you are going to do with those stones. So many thousands of purses spent upon such things! Can it be, as you say, that your people learn wisdom from them; or is it, as his reverence the Cadi declares, that they are to go to the palace of

your Queen, who, with the rest of the unbelievers, worships these idols? As for wisdom, these figures will not teach you to make better knives, or scissors, or chintzes; and it is in the making of those things that the English show their wisdom. But God is great! God is great! Here are stones which have been buried ever since the time of the holy Noah—peace be with him! Perhaps they were under ground before the deluge. I have lived on these lands for years. My father, and the father of my father pitched their tents here before me; but they never heard of these figures. For twelve hundred years have the true believers (and, praise be to God! all true wisdom is with them alone) been settled in this country, and none of them ever heard of a palace under ground.

Above left: Layard supervising the lowering of a great winged bull of yellow limestone for transport to England.

Above: a small statue, 3.5 feet tall, of Assurnasirpal II, from Nimrud. His great achievement was the consolidation of the conquests begun by his father leading to the establishment of the New Assyrian empire.

Neither did they who went before them. But lo! here comes a Frank (European) from many days' journey off, and he walks up to the very place, and he takes a stick [illustrating the description at the same time with the point of his spear], and makes a line here, and makes a line there. Here, says he, is the palace; there, says he, is the gate; and he shows us what has been all our lives beneath our feet, without our having known anything about it. Wonderful! Wonderful! Is it by books, is it by magic, is it by your prophets, that you have learnt these things?"

After Nimrud, Layard decided to excavate Botta's old site at Kuyunjik. At the time some people thought that his decision must have been motivated either by sheer perversity or by a malicious hope that another success would confirm his ascendency over his French friend and rival. A more charitable view would be that he really was, as the sheik implied, a genius as an archaeologist, and had learned at Nimrud to survey the Mesopotamian mounds with an eye for surface clues that told him where to dig. Whatever his motivation, his success was again virtually immediate and one of supreme archaeological importance.

First he had his workmen dig a vertical shaft into the mound until they struck a brick platform 20 feet below the surface. He

Sennacherib the Tyrant

Right: relief from the palace of Sennacherib, showing an incident from the Chaldaean campaign. The mud brick walls were lined by stone slabs carved with scenes of the events of his reign. Here the Assyrian soldiers are cutting off the heads of some of their prisoners.

Below: Assyrian relief from the palace of Sennacherib showing an attack by archers and wielders of slingshots.

then had tunnels dug from this platform in various directions, one of which eventually revealed a wall relief and then a gate flanked by winged bulls. Within a month he had opened nine rooms of a building that later turned out, when Rawlinson and Hincks had translated the copious cuneiform inscriptions found on its walls, to be one of the greatest palaces of Nineveh, that of one of the cruelest, greediest, and most powerful of the Assyrian kings mentioned in the Bible: Sennacherib. When the great hall of this palace was cleared there were revealed all around its walls reliefs depicting Sennacherib's conquests in great and realistic detail. Background landscapes and the modes of dress of the people portrayed made possible the identification of the various campaigns recorded, and the extent of Sennacherib's dominion and the ruthlessness with which it was established were conveyed with terrible immediacy. Here was a tyrant who had shown mercy to none, and had boasted of his tyranny and cruelty, but who had also created at Nineveh the most splendid and architecturally sophisticated city of its day and age. The palace reliefs, moreover, gave an account of Sennacherib's war against the kingdom of Judah which was entirely consistent with the account in the Biblical Second Book of Kings. This was a discovery that delighted believers in the historical authenticity of the Bible.

In his book, *The Monuments of Nineveh* (1853), Layard printed some imaginary reconstructions of the city of Nineveh, with its tremendous palaces overlooking the Tigris. The Assyrian kings had built on a colossal scale, and surely could not have conceived that all the buildings they had constructed, and even the very language they spoke and wrote in, would be utterly forgotten and lost to the world for more than 2000 years before curious scholars

Above: the palaces of Nimrud restored. Sennacherib, well aware that his palace might not long outlast his reign, left the following request: "In days to come, when these walls become old and begin to decay, let the ruins be restored by whichever of my descendants has been chosen by Ashur as shepherd of the land and people. Let him find the inscriptions which record my name, anoint them with oil, offer a sacrifice, and restore each of them to its place."

brought them to light again. The total eclipse of Assyria after it had fallen and the conditions to which its great cities and palaces were reduced were an uncanny fulfillment of the terrible promise recorded in the Biblical Book of Zephaniah that the Lord:

". . . will stretch out his hand against the north, and destroy Assyria; and he will make Nineveh a desolation, a dry waste like the desert.

"Herds shall lie down in the midst of her, all the beasts of the field; the vulture and the hedgehog shall lodge in her capitals; the owl shall hoot in the window, the raven croak on the threshold; for her cedar work will be laid bare.

"This is the exultant city that dwelt secure, that said to herself, 'I am and there is none else.' What a desolation she has become, a lair for wild beasts!"

The Hebrew prophet has it that the utter destruction of Nineveh was the work of the Lord. If so, the Lord employed for his purpose the combined forces of the Babylonians, the Elamites, and the Syrians, but oddly enough not the Hebrews themselves. The Second Book of Kings records how the king of Judea, Hezekiah, was invited by the king of Babylon to join the coalition against Assyria, and how, on the advice of his chief minister, Isaiah, he declined: an unwise decision, as it turned out, because when Assyria was overthrown Judea became one of the spoils of war and the Jews became vassals of the Babylonians.

Sennacherib himself did not live to see his palace sacked and the wrath of the Lord visited upon his city of Nineveh. He was murdered by his brothers in 680 B.C., and succeeded by a son, Esarhaddon, who kept up the family tradition of waging total war. He extended the Assyrian empire into Egypt. A typical

Above: *The Death of Sardanapalus* by the 19th-century French painter Eugène Delacroix. Sardanapalus is another name for Assurbanipal, who according to legend died amidst the ruins of his burning city after first having his slaves, horses, and concubines put to death. This is actually a description of the death of Sin-shar-ishkun, the king at the time the entire kingdom of Assyria fell in 607 B.C. Assurbanipal's renown in the modern world rests not on his military exploits but upon his patronage of literature and the library he founded at Nineveh.

inscription of his reads: "I surrounded Memphis and captured it in half a day with the aid of breaches in the walls, devastating fire, and scaling ladders. I despoiled and ravaged it and caused it to be consumed by fire. The pharaoh Tarku, his queen, the ladies of his harem, Ushanahuru his legitimate son and heir, and his other sons and daughters, his goods and possessions, his horses, his cattle, his sheep, I carried away as spoil to Assyria."

It was the Assyrian practice to parade a captive king through the streets of Nineveh with a ring through his nose or lips, like a bull. All the male inhabitants of a conquered city were massacred, and often a pyramid of their heads was built, while the young females were first raped and then burnt alive with the children. And these ruthless acts of war were graphically recorded on the walls of the palaces of Nineveh and boasted about in the cuneiform inscriptions. The Assyrians could hardly have expected anything less than total destruction when at last their empire fell to an alliance of their enemies.

It fell in 626 B.C., when Assurbanipal was king. This ruler is the most interesting of all the Assyrian kings and one to whom history owes a great debt. He waged a few wars in the early part of his reign, but was basically a peace-loving man and a scholar. His chief fame rests on his having built up, in his palace at Nineveh, a library of 30,000 inscribed clay tablets, a veritable encyclopedia of all the knowledge of his day. The most important result of Layard's excavation of the mound at Kuyunjik was the discovery of this library.

The actual find was made by one of Layard's assistants, Hormuzd Rassan, a native of Mosul who had become a Christian and had an Oxford education. In the palace that Sennacherib had built, Rassan found two rooms which had apparently been added at a later date, and where, miraculously, the scholar-king's library had survived the devastation. The fire that had destroyed the palace had helped preserve many of the tablets by baking them until they were very hard.

Assurbanipal had sent agents all over the immense empire that he ruled on missions to collect or copy ancient texts, and a text of his own records his motive: "I wrote on tablets, both wrote and read them, and when I had finished with them, I placed them

The Library of Assurbanipal

Below: Assurbanipal, king of Assyria, is shown full face with arms raised to support a basket. This is for rebuilding the temple of Esagila in Babylon.

Left: the library of cuneiform tablets founded by Assurbanipal at Nineveh. He sent his scribes to every city in his kingdom to make copies of ancient texts and inscriptions. These were then stored on shelves set into the thick walls of the storerooms. Assurbanipal was unique among Assyrian kings in that he found pleasure in reading these ancient records.

The Epic of Gilgamesh

in my library so that I can peruse them for myself or read them aloud to my guests." There were texts on medicine, on philosophy, on astronomy, on mathematics, and many on magical arts such as divination and exorcism. As the tablets and copies of them were made available to scholars, the cuneiform experts had the time of their lives. One of them, George Smith of London's British Museum, discovered among the tablets that Rassan had sent to the Museum a number that recounted the deeds of an epic hero named Gilgamesh. Smith found the story that he gradually decoded from the cuneiform and assembled into order utterly enthralling, and when he found that the end was missing he went to Kuyunjik to seek among the rubble for the missing tablets—and miraculously found them. The find was doubly sensational, for the tablets that concluded the great Gilgamesh epic contained an account of a great flood very similar to that given in the Old Testament of the Christian Bible, including a prototype Noah named Utnapishtim.

Gilgamesh is great as a work of literature and fascinating as a counterpart of the Genesis Flood story. But arguably the most important discovery to emerge from the library of Assurbanipal was that centuries before the Assyrians and Babylonians there had existed in Mesopotamia another great civilization from which these later ones had derived. These precursors had apparently

Below: terracotta plaque showing the hero of the *Epic of Gilgamesh*, from around 2000 B.C. The writer is not known, but whoever it was integrated several Sumerian stories into a single tragic account.

Above left: Hormuzd Rassan (1826–1910), an assistant to Austen Layard. Below: Assurbanipal engaged in the royal sport of hunting lions. The king stands majestically in his chariot from which he drives a spear into the animal. Aside from the sporting aspect the king was also symbolically fulfilling his royal duty to rid the land of dangerous wild animals.

been non-Semitic, and also it seemed that they had been the originators of cuneiform writing. In Assurbanipal's day their language had already been defunct, and he had found it "curious and obscure," just as European scholars were later to find Assyro-Babylonian to be. It was the Irish scholar Edward Hincks who first observed that the baffling discrepancies between the symbols of cuneiform and the sounds they represented could be explained on the hypothesis that the Assyro-Babylonians had inherited a script and the method of syllabic transcription from another people and roughly adapted it to their own language. The "dictionaries" found in Assurbanipal's library afforded evidence of the existence of this earlier, non-Semitic, highly literate people, but who they were, where they had originated, and where they had settled were mysteries.

The French cuneiform expert Jules Oppert discovered that the title "King of Sumer" occurred frequently in their texts, and it was he who called the people of this lost civilization the Sumerians. At the time the only clue to their existence was in the cuneiform tablets, and not a single ruin or artifact was known to exist. No one suspected that when the skills of the archaeologist and the cryptologist had brought to light the lost world of Sumer it would prove to be older than Egypt and the originator of most of the arts and crafts that go to make up the activities and contributions characterizing what we consider civilization.

Above: the ruined walls of Nineveh as they appear today in southern Iraq. The royal library found when the city was excavated has proved the only clue to the mysterious civilization of Sumer which preceded that of the Assyrians. Assurbanipal felt the same interest in ancient cultures that Layard and George Smith did: "I have read the artistic script of Sumer, and the obscure Akkadian, hard to master; sometimes I had the satisfaction of reading inscriptions made before the Flood, but sometimes I was furious at my own stupidity and frustrated by the beautiful script."

Chapter 6
Babylon–or Babel?

"And they said go to, let us build us a city and a tower, whose top may reach unto heaven." This quotation from the Book of Genesis describing the legendary tower of Babel for centuries provided writers and artists with a splendid subject for imaginative works. But was there ever such a tower? This chapter traces the long and exciting search for the truth behind the legend. It tells the stories of men like Loftus and Churchill, Wooley and Rich, and finally the German architect Robert Koldeway who were all intrigued by the riddle of the legendary tower and of the equally fabulous Hanging Gardens of Babylon. The result is a fascinating piece of archaeological detective work.

In 1850 two Englishmen, Henry Loftus and Harry Churchill, rode out into the desert of southern Mesopotamia in search of the land of Shinar. Their expedition was inspired by half a sentence in the Book of Genesis: ". . . as they journeyed from the east, they found a plain in the land of Shinar; and they dwelt there." The vast desert plain of southern Mesopotamia had not attracted many European explorers. The temperature often exceeded 100°F, many of the Arab tribes were far from friendly, and the occasional low mounds of sand and rubble that were the only indications that this land had once been inhabited had never been known to yield anything of value. It took a man led by a dream to venture out into this inhospitable desert, and Henry Loftus was such a man. He dreamed of finding the lost land of Shinar.

Fortunately some of the desert Arabs were friendly and co-operative. As Loftus and Churchill slowly traveled southward they heard rumors that near a place named Warka on the Persian Gulf was the site of an ancient city called Erech, which was another place mentioned in the Bible. When the Englishmen eventually reached the spot they found a huge heap of rubble covering an area some six miles in circumference. They spent three months on the site, and as well as tracing out the contours of the city they collected some clay tablets and pieces of pottery covered with cuneiform inscriptions. Loftus' prize find was a large, unbroken burial urn covered with writing. To carry it back to civilization

Opposite: Nebuchadnezzar in the Hanging Gardens of Babylon, from the painting by E. Wallcousins. To the Greeks Babylon was famous for the terraced gardens of its "new palace," erected by Nebuchadnezzar II after he ascended the throne in 604 B.C. They occupied a square more than a quarter mile in circumference. Great stone terraces resting on arches rose up like a giant stairway to a height of about 350 feet. Fruit trees grew among the luxuriant foliage and brilliant flowers, and water for irrigation was raised from the river by a mechanical device to a great cistern on the highest terrace.

Right: the ruins of Warka in modern Iraq —descendant of Erech, an ancient Mesopotamian city about 35 miles northwest of Ur. Occupied by a succession of civilizations, the city has been systematically excavated from 1912 on by a series of German archaeological expeditions.

Below: a jug excavated at Warka, dating from around 3000 B.C. Its decoration is by intaglio printing.

he had to hire Arab bearers, who carried it slung between two long poles and insisted on making the journey a funeral march. Nomads they met along the route wailed and threw dust into their hair in mourning for the remains of one who must have departed this world some time between 3000 and 5000 years ago.

Loftus was not a cuneiform scholar, and he did not know what his random collection of inscriptions would mean to scholars. Only when he got back to England did he learn that the name "Erech" was inscribed on several of his clay tablets and that he had discovered the first of the old Biblical cities that lay beneath the sand of the plains of Shinar, a name which scholars soon found was synonymous with the land of Sumer. In the next 50 years other great cities, now reduced to rubble, were identified: Ur, which the Bible said was the birthplace of Abraham; Eridu, Fara, Lagash, Larsa, Nippur, and Babylon; and as the sands gave up their secrets Europe gradually came to realize that it was not the Greeks or the Egyptians, but the Sumerians who had attained the earliest and highest prehistoric civilization and who were the original inventors of many of the institutions of Western cultures. On the now arid plains at the head of the Persian Gulf there had flourished from about 6000 years ago a great civilization of highly organized independent city states; a civilization that evolved the arts of writing, of building with brick and constructing arches, of mathematics and engineering, of mining, refining, and working metals, and which established codes of justice, principles of democracy, and institutions of administration and government that were all completely new in the world. The suddenness of the great cultural change was and remains a mystery. The historian Thorkild Jacobsen writes: "Overnight, as it were, Mesopotamian civilization crystallizes. The fundamental pattern, the controlling framework within which Mesopotamia is to live its life, formulate its deepest questions, evaluate itself and evaluate the universe, for ages to come, flashes into being, complete in its main features."

A Babylonian priest-historian of the 5th century B.C. named Berassus preserved a very curious tradition that explained this phenomenon. He said that there had come out of the sea that we call the Persian Gulf "an animal endowed with reason, who was called Oannes" and who appeared to be part-human and part-fish, and that this Oannes had taught men "to construct houses, to found temples, to compile laws, and explained to them the principles of geometrical knowledge." Agriculture, letters, and science—"in short . . . everything which could tend to soften manners and humanize mankind"—were taught by this strange being, who at sunset "would plunge again into the sea, and abide all night in the deep; for he was amphibious." Berossus said that other beings like Oannes appeared after him and continued the work of instruction. It sounds a very tall tale, but interestingly one of the finds at Nimrud was a representation of this amphibious creature, Oannes, which conforms with Berossus' description of him. Some 20th-century scholars have interpreted this tradition as a record of a contact with beings of extraterrestrial origin who in this way brought civilization to our planet, and

Oannes' Gift to the Sumerians

Above: a close-up view of the relief of the mythical Oannes found at Nimrud. Berossus wrote: "His whole body was that of a fish. Under the fish's head he had another head, and joined to the fish's tail were feet like those of man."

Left: discovery of the fish-god relief at Kuyunjik. Oannes was considered to have created the world order and to have brought technology to humankind.

The Art of the Scribe

have pointed to similar traditions in other cultures, for example among the Dogon tribe of Central Africa, as evidence that the tale was not the invention of some imaginative Sumerian. That is a fascinating conjecture, but unprovable. What is certain is that in Sumer civilization as we know it was born.

It was skillful engineering that made fertile the land between and around the estuaries of the two great rivers, the Tigris and Euphrates. By means of irrigation the land was made to yield abundant crops, but stone, metals, and hard wood suitable for building were not to be had in the vicinity of the Sumerian cities, and to obtain these commodities, essential to the settled and civilized life, the Sumerians had to become travelers and traders. They built long boats with big square-shaped sails which sailed the Mediterranean to the north and ventured southward down the Gulf and around to the coasts of Africa. A hierarchical society developed, with a ruling class, a priesthood, a merchant class, a class of scholars, and a class of artisans. The profession of scribe was highly honored and was the gateway to important posts in the administration. There also existed special schools for teaching the craft of the scribe, which was not only well remunerated but also tended to become a family profession. "Among all mankind's craftsmen," reads one clay tablet, "no work is as difficult as the scribal art. It is in accordance with the fate decreed by the god Enlil that a son follow the work of his father."

The profusion of clay tablets with identical texts that archaeol-

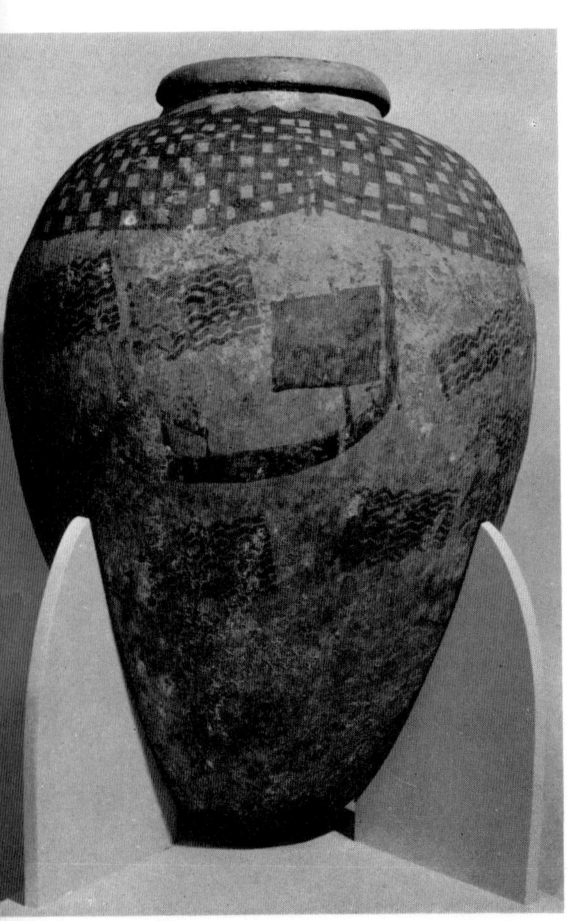

Below: the first drawn representation of a square sail, showing the kind of ship the Sumerians would have used, on a jar dating from 3000 B.C. The royal cemetery at Ur produced a rich collection of furniture, jewelery, weapons, and musical instruments, all of which showed the Sumerians were prosperous and well-traveled.

Below right: the Euphrates estuary. It was on the plains around the river that Sumerian civilization was founded. Having no stone or timber they built with marsh reeds and river mud.

ogists have found, obviously produced by trainees practicing their skills, are the products of such schools. That it was only the sons of the wealthy and privileged who were able to have such training is implied by the text of a paternal admonition which has a familiar ring and which also gives an insight into the lives of the working class. The father scolds his son for truancy, and reminds him of his privileged position: "I, never in my life, did I make you carry reeds to the canebrake. The reed rushes which the young and the little carry, you, never in your life did you carry them. I never said to you, follow my caravans. I never sent you to work to plow my field. I never sent you to work to dig up my field. . . . Go, work and support me, I never in my life said to you." In this text, inscribed on a clay tablet found at Erech, a father's disappointment thunders across 4000 years—a marvel the Sumerians made possible with their invention of writing.

Left: Babylonian astrological tablet found at Erech. Astrology was important in the sense of its application to state affairs, and reports were made regularly to the king.

Below: photograph showing how the stylus was held to make the wedge-shaped marks of cuneiform. The most crucial step the Sumerians took was to realize that a sign could be used to denote a sound rather than just the object it resembled.

They wrote on clay tablets because clay was readily available and a handful of it could quickly be slapped into a flat square, written on while still damp, and then baked in the sun. Great expertise and versatility were achieved in the craft, and all aspects of Sumerian life were put on record, from commercial transactions to poetic epics. A tablet unearthed at Nippur, for instance, comprised a physician's prescription for an unknown ailment: "Sift and knead together, all in one: turtle shell, the sprouting naga-plant, salt (and) mustard; wash (the sick part) with quality beer (and) hot water; scrub (the sick spot) with all of it (the kneaded mixture): after scrubbing, rub with vegetable oil (and) cover with pulverized fir." The ingredients of the medication may seem strange, but the tone is practical, there is no pseudomagical mumbo jumbo, and the physician clearly has a conception of antiseptic procedure which many European physicians lacked as late in our era as the 19th century. And this was some 2000 years before the Greek, Hippocrates, who is generally credited with being "the father of medicine."

There are many surviving tablets that testify to the fact that a

The Case of the Silent Wife

system of law was highly developed in Sumer. Several have been found recounting a murder trial known as "The Case of the Silent Wife." A temple official named Lu-Inanna had been murdered by a gardener, a barber, and a third, unidentified man. The killers had told the victim's wife, Nin-dada, what they had done, and she had not betrayed them to the authorities. When they were apprehended and brought to trial, Nin-dada was summoned to court, but she declined to testify and remained silent. The case was referred to a higher court, the Citizens' Assembly at Nippur, where a nine-man team of prosecutors demanded that the wife's silence should be construed as complicity in the crime and that she should pay for it with her life. But two assemblymen protested, brought up evidence that the dead man had not provided adequately for his household, and asked: "A woman whose husband did not support her, after she heard that her husband had been killed, why should she not remain silent? Is it she who killed her husband? The punishment of those who actually killed should suffice." This plea for justice and clemency prevailed with the Citizens' Assembly and Nin-dada was acquitted. The Sumerians were certainly more enlightened and humane than the later Assyrians, according to whose laws a wife was a man's property and could have her ears, her nose, her nipples, or her breasts cut off for marital offenses.

As a source of information about life in ancient Sumer, we have in addition to the inscribed clay tablets a large number of decorated cylinder seals. These were small stone cylinders with designs carved on them, which when rolled over a piece of wet

Right: neo-Assyrian cylinder seals of 900–700 B.C. and their impressions. These were perhaps the Sumerians' most original contribution to the graphic arts. A stone cylinder with a carved design was impressed in clay by rolling the cylinder over it. The designs, or seals, appear on clay tablets, jar covers, and so on, depicting various scenes. Eventually the Sumerians settled on one particular seal design which became almost their trademark—a scene showing a worshiper being presented to a god by his personal guardian angel.

clay made a mark that served to identify the person whose text was inscribed thereon. The seals were personalized, and generally depict something particularly relevant to the owner. Collectively they afford us a fascinating picture of Sumerian domestic, social, economic, and religious life.

The archaeologists who recovered these artifacts from the sands of southern Mesopotamia had to adopt quite different work methods from those employed by men like Botta and Layard. The vigorous wielding of pick and shovel that had achieved sensational results at Khorsabad, Nimrud, and Kuyunjik would only have destroyed the Sumerian artifacts wholesale. The archaeologists who excavated the Sumerian cities had to be more careful and scientific in their approach. There was no rush to this inhospitable area after the announcement of the discovery of Erech by Loftus and Churchill, and it was only toward the end of the 19th century and in the first half of the 20th that the cities of Sumer were systematically investigated. In this work the contributions of two archaeologists were outstanding: the German Robert Koldeway, who excavated Babylon between 1898 and 1917, and the Englishman Leonard Woolley, who excavated Ur between 1922 and 1932. As Ur was the older city and an integral part of Sumerian civilization in its heyday, whereas Babylon flourished later, we will consider Woolley's find first.

Near the mound of rubble that was Ur there was a smaller mound at Ubaid, and it was here that Woolley began his excavations. With luck comparable to Layard's, he almost immediately found the ruins of a temple dating from the First Dynasty of Ur, and within it a tablet with an inscription which when translated read: "A-anni-pad-da, King of Ur, son of Mes-anni-pad-da, King of Ur, has built this for his lady, Ninhursag." This tablet enabled Woolley to date the temple and its contents at about 2700 B.C., for these kings' names tallied with information on other king lists which had been dated. Ninhursag was known to be a mother goddess. On a frieze found in the temple she was represented by sacred cows that were depicted being milked by priests of the temple.

Woolley's first excavations of the mound of Ur turned up some gold beads, which made him suspect that he might find greater treasures deeper down. With admirable restraint, he deferred serious excavation until he had trained his work force of Arab tribesmen to use tools with care and not to damage their finds.

Below: Sir Leonard Woolley, excavator of Ur. He discovered the oldest royal graves in the world there.

Above: priests milking the sacred cows of the goddess Ninhursag from the frieze found and restored by Woolley. The figures are of limestone set against a black shale background with copper borders. To a primitive pastoral folk depending wholly upon its livestock, milk is the sustenance of life, and dairy cattle may be associated with and protected by a deity.

He then tackled a site that he had identified as a cemetery lying within the walls of a temple. Some 1800 graves were investigated, and found to contain nothing but bones; but among them were some deep tunnels, indicating that grave robbers had been at work and that there were other graves deeper down.

Woolley's finding the Royal Tombs of Ur has been compared with Carter's discovery of Tutankhamen's tomb. Although the treasures he unearthed were not so fabulous as the pharaoh's they were magnificent and of even greater interest to historians and archaeologists. They were more than 1000 years older than the Egyptian artifacts. The first find was the tomb of a man whose seal identified him as Mes-kalam-dug, and on whose skull there was a helmet of beaten gold fashioned like a wig with hair that fell in curls at the side and was knotted at the back—a superb specimen of the goldsmith's craft. There were also gold-mounted daggers, a shield inlaid with gold and lapis lazuli, and bowls made of gold, copper, and silver. "Nothing like these things had ever before come from the soil of Mesopotamia," said Woolley.

This though was only the beginning. A stone pavement was uncovered, and because the stone must have been imported Woolley surmised that the pavement must lead to a royal tomb. He excavated the length of it and came to a sloping trench where lay five skeletons with headdresses of gold, lapis lazuli, and elaborate bead necklaces. At the end of the row were the remains of a harp across which lay the bones of the gold-crowned harpist, as if she had expired while still playing. All around this area were scattered tumblers and chalices of gold, silver, and copper, and there were the remains of a chariot that had been decorated with gold lions and colored stones, and also the bones of the animal that had been harnessed to it.

Above: golden wig-helmet found at Ur. The ears are modeled in relief and the details engraved. When worn, the inside of the helmet was lined with cloth held in place through holes along the lower edge.

Below: headdress of a woman from Ur. It consists of leaves and flowers made in gold in a setting of semiprecious stones such as carnelian.

Below right: the Great Death Pit at Ur as reconstructed. The king's attendants, mainly women, were sacrificed at his funeral some 5000 years ago.

As more of the Royal Tombs were discovered the evidence built up that it had been customary for the royalty of early Sumer to be interred accompanied by a host of attendants, and that these had not been slaves but people (mostly women) of rank who had gone to their deaths bedecked in all their finery and jewelry. In one grave the remains of 63 men and women and 6 oxen were found, in another the skeletons of 68 women and 6 men, and in a third, known as the "Great Death Pit," there were 74 bodies laid out in tidy rows. The treasures recovered from these graves were not only the personal adornments of the dead, but also some exquisite works of art, mostly animal portraiture, such as the well-known figure of a ram standing with its front feet in the branches of a tree, which Woolley conjectured might be a Sumerian version of Abraham's sacrifice of "the ram caught in a thicket," for of course Abraham was associated with Ur.

A wealth of information about life in Sumer 5000 years ago was provided by the so-called "Standard" of Ur, a mosaic panel that was found in one of the tombs. Worked in mother of pearl and mussel shell against a background of lapis lazuli, the mosaic depicts several scenes of everyday life, such as a banquet scene, a procession of soldiers and of fettered prisoners, and a gathering of sacrificial animals. It is not so detailed as the wall paintings in the tomb of the Egyptian landowner, Ti, but it provides some vivid pictures of life in the earliest known era of civilization.

The Biblical association of Abraham with Ur is problematical. Abraham is supposed to have been the progenitor of both the Jewish and the Arab races but the early Sumerians were not a Semitic people. Nobody knows for certain where they originally came from, although there is some suggestive evidence that they were associated with another ancient culture which has recently

The "Standard," Mosaic of Ur

Above: the Great Death Pit at Ur at the time of Woolley's excavation. The clearing of the 25-foot-square pit had to be done piecemeal in order not to disturb the remains.

Below: the "Standard" of Ur, showing the victory feast. In the top register the king and his officers are seated drinking. In the two lower registers booty, including captured teams of asses, is paraded before them. The function of the "Standard" is not known.

Above: reconstruction of Babylon. At the time of Nebuchadnezzar the city spread out over both banks of the Euphrates. Close to the east bank and in the center of the city stood Etemenanki, the great several-storied ziggurat or temple-tower, already very old but splendidly rebuilt at this time.

been discovered, that of the Indus valley in India. But by about 1500 B.C. the Sumerians no longer existed as a people, for their cities had fallen to Semitic conquerors. Their culture and institutions, though, had remained alive and civilized the invaders, who adopted their method of writing and learned their engineering and building techniques and much of their science and lore. Humane Sumerian principles of law were preserved and elaborated by the great Babylonian king, Hammurabi, who reigned from 1792 to 1750 B.C. Under Hammurabi the city of Babylon became established as the cultural and political capital of Mesopotamia, eclipsing the Sumerian cities of the southern plain where civilization had been born.

The sight that most impressed the Greek historian Herodotus when he visited the ancient city of Babylon in about 450 B.C. was the great Ziggurat. It was, he said, eight stories high, and there was a path winding around the outside of it by which visitors could ascend to the temple at the top. Within the temple all there was for the visitor to see was a huge and opulently decorated couch with a golden table beside it. It was part of the religion of the Babylonians, Herodotus explained, to have women always recumbent on this couch for the enjoyment of the god Marduk, who would from time to time descend from heaven to have intercourse with her. Furthermore, it was the religious duty of every woman of Babylon to prostitute herself at the temple at least once in her life. Dressed in her finest clothes, she had to sit in the holy enclosure and wait until a man chose her by tossing a silver coin into her lap and uttering the words, "The goddess Ishtar prosper thee." It was the woman's religious duty to submit herself, and Herodotus drily remarked that tall and beautiful women invariably performed their duty within hours, whereas some of the ugly ones had to wait years for the opportunity to do so. And the rich, he noted, surrounded themselves with a host of attendants in order to keep away strangers, having made prior arrangements for a suitable partner to accost them.

No other ancient source of historical evidence exists to confirm Herodotus' account of the goings-on at the Babylonian temple. There is, however, ample evidence that the great Ziggurat existed and was one of the wonders of the ancient world. And there are traditions that identify the structure as the tower of Babel mentioned in the Bible.

The story of the building of the tower, as related in the Book

Marduk and the Great Ziggurat

Above: the god Marduk as depicted on a boundary stone dating from 1120 B.C. As part of the New Year festival, the principal religious event of the year, various ceremonies of purification and preparation were performed. These culminated in the High Priest taking the king in before Marduk, to whom he surrendered his royal insignia. The High Priest then hit the king in the face; the king, forced to his knees, uttered a formula in which he claimed to be innocent of various offenses against Marduk's city. His insignia were then restored to him.

Left: the tower of Babel as a great ziggurat. With a small temple on its summit the great tower rose to a height of almost 300 feet and dominated the view across the plain for many miles around. A staircase about 30 feet wide led up to the first and second stages.

A Tower to Rival Heaven

Right: "Building the Tower of Babel," a 17th-century Dutch roundel in Bishopsbourne church, Kent. The work of building called for considerable resources of labor for which Nebuchadnezzar conscripted foreign workers.

Below: Nebuchadnezzar recorded: "All the peoples of many nations I constrained to work on the building of Etemenanki. . . . The high dwelling of my lord Marduk I established on its summit."

of Genesis, goes: "And they said one to another, go to, let us make bricks and burn them thoroughly. And they had brick for stone, and lime they had for mortar. And they said, go to, let us build a city and a tower, whose top may reach into heaven; and let us make us a name, lest we be scattered abroad upon the face of the whole earth." As there is no natural stone in southern Mesopotamia, where Babylon was located, the detail about the tower being made of brick argues in favor of the idea that the Babylonian Ziggurat was the tower of Babel. And both the detail about the bricks, and specific mention of the aspiration to reach the heavens, are found in a cuneiform inscription of the Babylonian king Nabopolassar: "The lord Marduk commanded me concerning Etemenanki, the staged tower of Babylon, which before my time had become dilapidated and ruinous, that I should make its foundations secure in the bosom of the nether world and make its summit like the heavens. I caused bricks to be made . . . I caused streams of bitumen to be brought by the canal Arahtu . . . I deposited in the foundations under the bricks gold, silver, and precious stones from the mountains and from the sea. . . . For my Lord Marduk I bowed my neck, I took off my robe—the sign of my royal blood—and on my head I bore bricks and earth. As for Nebuchadnezzar, my first-born son, the beloved of my heart, I made him bear the mortar, the offering of wine and oil, in company with my subjects." Confirming this account, and the Biblical tradition of the overweening ambition of the builders that incurred God's wrath, there is an inscription of Nebuchadnezzar's which says: "To raise up the top of Etemenanki that it might rival heaven, I laid to my hand."

Nebopolassar, who ruled from 626 to 605 B.C., stated that in his day the tower was dilapidated and ruinous. It is possible that the original tower went back to the age of the great Sumerian law-giver Hammurabi and had been destroyed by Sennacherib. We know from cuneiform and graphic records that the Assyrian despot turned his wrath on the city of Babylon in the year 689 B.C. His army attacked and took the city, slaughtered every one of its inhabitants, razed its buildings, and finally diverted the waters of the Euphrates to flood the ruins and wash away much of the rubble. But after Nineveh itself suffered a similar fate Babylon rose again to power and splendor. Nebopolassar and Nebuchadnezzar not only re-built the Ziggurat, but also built around Babylon the most impregnable defensive walls ever seen in the world at that time, the most splendid royal palace, and, according to some ancient historians, an architectural masterpiece worthy to be ranked with the pyramids as one of the seven wonders of the world: the famous Hanging Gardens of Babylon.

By the beginning of the Christian era, however, Babylon was once again a ruined and almost abandoned city, and its architectural and engineering marvels had largely been destroyed. Alexander the Great had conquered it in the 4th century B.C., but had died in 323 B.C. there at the age of 33 as the result of a drinking bout. The Greek general under whose rule it then fell, Seleucus Nicator, decided to build a new city some 40 miles to the north, which he called Seleucia and built partly with materials taken

Below: the fall of Babylon. Babylon was the target of Sennacherib's revenge for being the center of a coalition against him. He gave the order to sack the city.

Above: *The Fall of Babylon* by the 19th-century British painter John Martin. The fall of the city is here represented as an apocalyptic event as foretold in the Bible—in Isaiah, Chapters 13 and 14, and Jeremiah, Chapters 50 and 51. Legend has it that the ageing Nebuchadnezzar had a presentiment of what would come to pass. According to Cyrus the Great of Persia, Marduk himself, the god of Babylon, had directed his footsteps toward the city, "going as a friend by his side." Cyrus took Babylon in 539 B.C.

from Babylon. For some time Babylon remained of religious importance, and the festival and the shrine of Marduk were preserved, but by the year 50 B.C. the Roman historian Diodorus Siculus wrote that "only a small part of the city is now inhabited, and most of the area within its walls is given over to agriculture," and his contemporary the Greek geographer Strabo wrote that the Ziggurat was destroyed and that only the walls stood as evidence of the former greatness of Babylon.

Brick, of course, does not last as well as stone. By modern times the ravages of weathering had combined with the destruction of ancient conquerors to reduce Babylon to rubble. But after Layard had achieved his spectacular success at Nineveh, for archaeologists the lure of the other great city of the Assyro-Babylon empire was greatly enhanced.

A pioneer English archaeologist, Claudius Rich, had in fact made a preliminary study of the Babylon site in 1811. He only spent 10 days there and employed a small party of workmen, so he could do little more than make a few sketches and measurements, collect some inscribed bricks, and probe about a bit in the rubble. He noted that there was a great square mound which the Arabs called the tower of Babel, but his investigation of it was inevitably cursory and yielded no interesting discoveries. A coffin excavated from it gave off such a stench when it was opened that it was obvious that the mortal remains in it were of no great antiquity. Layard, too, had this unpleasant experience when he briefly investigated the site in 1851, and in a report he wrote that the chances of finding anything of importance in the vast

Sifting through the Rubble

sprawling brick heap did not justify the cost of a thorough excavation which he estimated at £25,000. The excavation of Babylon was therefore left to the German archaeologist Robert Koldewey, who devoted 15 years, from 1898 to 1917, to the work.

By the 1890s the situation in Mesopotamia was very different from the situation in the days of Botta and Layard. Both the Turkish authorities and the local inhabitants had become aware of the value of the artifacts to be found and excavated in the historic sites. This meant that it was no longer possible to ship masses of sculptures to the museums of Europe, and also that there was a brisk covert trade in antiquities. Many Arab tribesmen had adopted their procurement and sale as a means of livelihood. This situation, combined with the nature of the Babylon site, required a different type of archaeologist from Layard—that is, a man more concerned with the acquisition of knowledge than of treasure, and one not impatient for quick and sensational results but content to work carefully and systematically over a long period of time. Robert Koldewey was just such a man. And as well as possessing the personal qualities and motives for his task, Koldewey also had the advantage of being generously funded. Although the Germans had made great contributions to Assyro-Babylonian scholarship, they had not shared in the early archaeological bonanza. The Koldewey expedition was therefore intended to some extent to make good the omission for the sake of German national prestige. So Koldewey was enabled to engage a work force of more than 200 men to shift and sift the mountains of rubble that were the remains of Babylon.

Left: the Ishtar Gate, an overall view from the north, from Robert Koldewey's book published in 1918. One of the most impressive monuments rediscovered in Mesopotamia, the gate formed one of the principal entrances into Babylon.

His first great find was the legendary defensive walls of the city. Everybody had thought that the description of the walls of Babylon given by Herodotus must be exaggerated. The Greek historian had said that one wall was broad enough for two chariots each drawn by four horses to pass each other. Koldewey's excavations showed that this was no exaggeration. To expose the

Above: a cuneiform inscription found in Mesopotamia in the Tigris-Euphrates delta. Through such finds the archaeologist has learned the early history of such previously forgotten civilizations as Sumer.

walls was a gargantuan task. At some points rubble as deep as 75 feet or more had to be removed, but when at last a section of the walls was laid bare Koldewey found that the defensive system of Babylon comprised a series of three walls, all made of fired brick. The first wall was 24 feet thick, the second 25 feet thick, and between them was a space of more than 38 feet, which had apparently originally been filled with earth. This would have provided more than enough room for the passage of the two large chariots of Herodotus' description. The space between the middle and the inner walls had been a moat, and the inner wall had been fortified with towers spaced every 160 feet. Koldewey estimated that there had been some 360 such towers and that the circumference of these fortifications had been 10 miles. This latter estimate seemed to contradict Herodotus' statement that Babylon had been some 15 miles square, or a circuit of 60 miles, but if he had included the suburbs, farms, and villages clustered around the city outside the walls he may not have been far wrong. The 10-mile extent of the walls was certainly a phenomenal feat of engineering and a clear testimony to the power and genius of Nebuchadnezzar, who had built them.

Nebuchadnezzar's own account of the fortification of Babylon, found inscribed on a cuneiform tablet, corresponded with Koldewey's findings. "I caused a mighty wall to circumscribe Babylon," the king had written. "I dug its moat; and its escarpments I built out of bitumen and kiln brick. At the edge of the moat I built a powerful wall as high as a hill. I gave it wide gates and set in doors of cedar wood sheathed with copper. So that the enemy, who would [wished] evil, should not threaten the sides of Babylon, I surrounded them with mighty floods as the billows of the sea flood the land. . . . I heaped up a heap of earth beside it, and surrounded it with quay walls of brick. This bastion I strengthened cunningly, and of the city of Babylon made a fortress."

Robert Koldewey was an architect by training, and his primary interest was in the architecture of ancient Babylon. One day his

Below: model of the city of Babylon, constructed by W. Struck and now in Baghdad. In the back corner of this model (of a section of Babylon along the Euphrates) Etemenanki, the tower of Babylon, can be seen. To the left is the principal temple of Marduk, the Esagila.

workmen unearthed a curious arched structure at a part of the site identified with the oldest part of the city. This find intrigued him as an architect. It was not only the unique shape, but also the fact that it was made partly of stone and that in the midst of the ruins there was a well with three shafts, that interested Koldewey. Here, he surmised, had stood some very unusual and cunningly contrived artifact. He studied all the ancient descriptions of the city for clues and came to the conclusion that it must have been the elevated park known as the Hanging Gardens of Babylon.

The account that confirmed him in this belief was that of the Roman Diodorus Siculus, and specifically mentioned both the arched, or vaulted, structure that supported the gardens, and the fact that stone was used in the construction. The relevant part of Diodorus' description went: "The Garden was 100 feet long by 100 wide and built up in tiers so that it resembled a theater. Vaults had been constructed under the ascending terraces which carried the entire weight of the planted garden; the uppermost vault, which was 75 feet high, was the highest part of the garden, which, at this point, was on the same level as the city walls. The roofs of the vaults which supported the garden were constructed of stone beams some 15 feet long . . ." As according to Diodorus stone was only used at one other place in Babylon Koldewey felt certain that the structure he had found must be the supports of the fabled Hanging Gardens. The presence of the triple-shafted well also supported the hypothesis. There could have been a chain of leather buckets that passed empty down one shaft and full up the

Hanging Gardens of Babylon

Below: the Hanging Gardens of Babylon. A legend claims they were built to please a Persian concubine who was depressed by the unbroken flatness of the country. It is said to have risen in a series of terraces to a height of 75 feet. The whole structure was then waterproofed with bitumen, baked brick, and lead in order to keep the vaults underneath it dry.

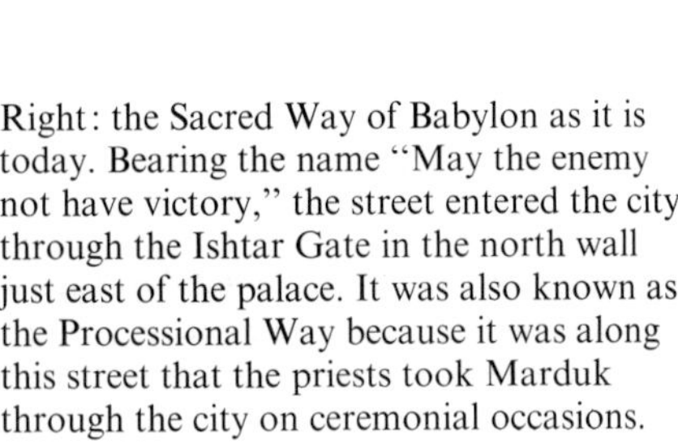

Right: the Sacred Way of Babylon as it is today. Bearing the name "May the enemy not have victory," the street entered the city through the Ishtar Gate in the north wall just east of the palace. It was also known as the Processional Way because it was along this street that the priests took Marduk through the city on ceremonial occasions.

other, carrying water to the highest level where it would be channeled to supply all the gardens. The middle shaft could have been constructed for maintenance purposes.

If Koldewey was right in his conjectures, the Hanging Gardens had been nothing magical, as their traditional name suggested, but rather a kind of terraced park laid out on the roof of a specially designed building. A description by the Jewish historian Josephus appeared to confirm this. Writing about the "prodigiously large and magnificent palace" that Nebuchadnezzar had built, Josephus said: "In this palace he erected very high walks, supported by stone pillars; and by planting what was called a pensile (hanging) paradise, and replenishing it with all sorts of trees, he rendered the prospect an exact resemblance of a mountainous country. This he did to please his queen, because she had been brought up in Media, and was fond of a mountainous situation." There was no doubt that the construction of the Hanging Gardens of Babylon had been an engineering tour de force at the time, but the plausible reality unearthed by the German archaeologist did rather diminish the romance and the mystery of that particular wonder of the world.

In bringing to light the Processional Way of the god Marduk and the Ishtar Gate which spanned it, Koldewey compensated for his revelation of the down-to-earth reality of the Hanging Gardens by giving the world a glimpse of the former grandeur and splendor of Babylon.

The Processional Way was a broad thoroughfare leading from the outer wall of the city to the Gate of Ishtar, which was the main entrance to the inner citadel of Babylon. One of Nebuchadnezzar's inscriptions described it: "Aibur-shabu, the street of Babylon, I filled with a high fill for the procession of the great lord Marduk, and with Turminabanda stones and Shadu stones,

I made this Aibur-shabu, from 'the holy gate' to Ishtar-saki-patebisha, fit for the procession of his godliness, and linked it with those parts which my father had built, and made the way a shining one." Koldewey's excavation brought to light the street whose construction was so magnificently described. It was nearly 74 feet wide and on each side there were walls 22 feet high, which made the street a kind of gully running into the heart of the city from the perimeter, and therefore a death trap for an invader who tried to enter by that way. Spaced along the walls were enameled reliefs of lions in bright colors—120 of them in all. The foundations of the street itself were of brick covered with bitumen and then limestone paving slabs on the underside of each of which was the inscription: "Nebuchadnezzar, King of Babylon, son of Nabopolassar, King of Babylon, am I. The Bale street I paved with Shadu slabs for the procession of the great lord Marduk. Marduk, lord, grant eternal life."

Processional gates and triumphal archways were of course common in later Roman and European civic architecture, but the Gate of Ishtar was earlier than any of them and was the best preserved of all Babylonian remains that Koldewey unearthed. Buried beneath tons of rubble, the colorful decorations on the Gate had remained intact for more than 2000 years. And in this

Gate of Ishtar to Shining Way

Below: "Is not this great Babylon, that I have built . . ." The great Ishtar Gate, dedicated to the goddess Ishtar, was one of the splendid works of Nebuchadnezzar II in the beautification of his capital. The Gate was the starting point for processions, which assembled in front of it.

Foundations of Heaven and Earth

Right: the dragon of Babylon, sacred to Marduk, a relief on the Gate of Ishtar. A fabulous monster that can scarcely be identified with any living animal, it has a scaly body, serpentlike neck, and a hairy mane. From the horned head a forked tongue darts forth. The forefeet are those of a feline, the hind feet are griffon's claws.

bleak and barren waste of clay and brick, the colors of the decorations adorning both the Gate of Ishtar and the Processional Way were a welcome contrast and exciting find. Nebuchadnezzar had inscribed that he had ordered that the gate should be "made glorious for the amazement of the people" and had had it decorated with enameled reliefs of nearly 600 bulls and dragons on the brick walls. Koldewey found that many of these reliefs were in a very good state of preservation. Of particular interest were the many representations of the dragon of Babylon, a curious creature with a scaly body, a long neck supporting a horned serpent's head from which projected a split tongue, and with paws on its forelegs and talons on its hind legs. This dragon, known as Sirrush, was known from the Bible to have been a creature sacred to the god Marduk. The multitudes of them enameled in silver and bronze against a bright blue background on the Gate of Ishtar must have been an impressive sight for the worshipers of Marduk. It is still impressive to the visitor to the ruins of Babylon, although rather fewer than a third of the original number remain. Others have been taken away to museums, particularly to the Berlin Museum, where a reconstruction of the Gate of Ishtar is one of the principal sights.

Bright blue, too, according to Herodotus, was the upper temple of Marduk which crowned the great Ziggurat. There was also a lower temple, he tells us, in which there was a statue of the god seated on a throne with a large table beside him and a footstool in front—all this made of pure gold and weighing 800 talents, that is to say about 26 tons. The name of the temple-tower, Etemenanki, meant "The House of the Foundations of Heaven and Earth." In its day it must have been one of the most awesome structures in the world. Standing on the flat plain of Babylon and rising to a height of 300 feet, it was said to be visible from a distance of 60 miles. No less than 58 million bricks had gone into its construction. There could have been no contemporary building comparable to it, and this fact, combined with the fact that ancient descriptions of it tallied with Biblical descriptions of the tower of Babel, indicated that it was indeed the fabled tower that in the Judeo-Christian tradition symbolized man's extreme and

Opposite: reconstruction in Berlin of the Ishtar Gate. The gateway, flanked by twin towers and ornamented with pinnacles, is completely covered with colored enamel bricks. Dragons and bulls are molded in relief, the animals symbolizing the gods Marduk and Adad. The bright yellow and brown beasts are surrounded by tiles tinted with lapis lazuli dust. The Gate of Ishtar was reconstructed with material excavated by Robert Koldewey.

culpable ambition. But before Koldewey excavated at Babylon nobody knew for certain whether the great pile of rubble that the Arabs called the tower of Babel really was the Bibilical structure.

Of course Koldewey was only able to excavate the foundations, but these proved to be both compatible with the descriptions in the Bible and in Herodotus and consistent with a description of the dimensions of the tower of Babel given on a Babylonian tablet. This tablet was discovered by the English Assyriologist George Smith, disappeared after his premature death in 1876, and turned up mysteriously years later in the Oriental collection of the Louvre in Paris. It stated that the dimensions of the base of the tower of Babel were 300 feet by 300 feet and the height was also 300 feet, and that there had been seven different stages with given distances between them; the top one, the actual temple of Marduk, being 80 feet long, 70 feet wide, and 50 feet high. Koldewey's excavation was of course only able to confirm the dimensions of the base, but that was enough to convince him that here indeed had stood the terraced tower that was sacred to the Babylonians and an object of ridicule and self-righteous indignation to the Jews.

The entire 15 years' work of the German archaeologists, with their 200-strong labor force, did not succeed in producing for the tourist any overwhelming impression of the grandeur of ancient Babylon. On the rubble-strewn site that they left the only impressive structure is the remaining part of the Gate of Ishtar, and the visitor has to use his own imagination to envisage what this great walled city with its magnificent palaces and temples must originally have been like. Koldewey's work, however, is accounted one of the triumphs of archaeology. After Babylon had been ransacked for centuries, first by conquerors and then by opportunist builders for its bricks, and had been reduced to a waste land of debris and dust, he patiently unearthed what remained of it, which was enough to show that in

Below: massive remains of a once-great ziggurat at Aqar-Quf near Baghdad. Almost 200 feet high, these ruins resemble other huge brick temple-towers in the "land of Shinar."

its age it must have been an architectural phenomenon of a complexity and sophistication unequaled in the world.

Some decades before Koldewey began his work the poet Wordsworth had written: "Babylon, Learned and wise, hath perished utterly, Nor leaves her speech one word to aid the sigh, That would lament her." But the archaeologist and the scholars proved the poet wrong; the first by laying bare the lineaments of the vanished city, and the second by translating the many cuneiform inscriptions found among the rubble, including those of the proud and gifted rulers, Nabopolassar and Nebuchadnezzar, under whose sway Babylon, which even then had a history going back nearly 2000 years, enjoyed a last brief but splendid period of glory before the prophecies of Jeremiah were fulfilled. Babylon, declared Jeremiah, "shall become a heap, a dwelling-place for dragons, an astonishment and a hissing, without an inhabitant;" and "the wild beasts of the desert with the wild beasts of the islands shall dwell there, and the owls shall dwell therein; and it shall be no more inhabited for ever." Strangely enough, in the light of this latter prophecy, when Babylon fell to the Persians in the 4th century B.C. it was used as a royal game park by the Persian kings.

"An Astonishment and a Hissing"

Below: the site of ancient Babylon as it is today. In the center front of the picture the tall, straight column is the Gate of Ishtar. Much of what we know about the city in Nebuchadnezzar's time is due to the magnificent work of Robert Koldewey, who spent nearly 20 years excavating Babylon.

Chapter 7
The Martyrs of Masada

For centuries the story of Masada and of the defiant band of Jewish martyrs known as Zealots who killed one another rather than fall into the hands of their Roman conquerors was familiar to all educated men from Josephus' contemporary account. But was it the true story? After all, wasn't Josephus himself a Roman collaborator, a traitor to the Jewish cause? It was an exciting and inspiring story to all patriots bitterly defending their homeland against hopeless odds, but was it true? The very inaccessibility of Masada prevented early travelers from solving the mystery. It was not until the 1960s that the astonishing truth was laid bare. This chapter tells the intriguing story of Masada and its excavation.

For two years the 960 men, women, and children occupying the hill fortress of Masada had defied the might of Rome. The situation was intolerable for the Romans. They had circulated coins boasting "Judaea Capta," they had destroyed the Jerusalem Temple two years before, and yet here was this pocket of defiance, this focus for smoldering Jewish nationalist hopes, this pimple on the face of the Roman empire. It had to be subdued at any cost. The Zealots, the last of the Jewish rebels, had to be put down. So Flavius Silva, the Roman governor, led the Tenth Legion out into the desert to lay siege to the outpost. Augmented by auxiliary troops and a labor force of thousands of prisoners, the Tenth Legion would account for the embattled Zealots if it took them months to do so.

Which no doubt it would. Masada was a natural fortress, an immense rock surmounted by a plateau with sheer sides of over 1000 feet. A century before King Herod the Great had chosen the site as a pleasure resort and a retreat in case of emergency. He had built palaces there and formidable defensive fortifications, including a double casement wall some 1400 yards in length which ran around the entire top of the hill. At the beginning of the Jewish Revolt against the Roman occupation in A.D. 66 a group of Zealots had taken the Roman garrison by surprise and seized Masada. After the fall of Jerusalem in A.D. 70 they had been joined by Zealot refugees from the capital, and under the leadership of Eleazar ben Yair they fought a guerrilla war

Opposite: aerial view of Masada from the northwest, showing Herod's summer palace. There were terraces on three levels looking out over the Dead Sea coast, and at the top were his administrative buildings, storerooms, and baths.

The Siege of Masada

Above: Roman coin proclaiming "Judaea Capta" issued after the victory over (most of) the Jews in 70 A.D. It bears the picture of a Roman legionary and a captive Jewish woman under a palm tree. Masada alone held out after that date.

Above right: the siege of Masada by the Romans. Flavius Silva could not afford to wait out the Masada defenders because they were too well supplied. The Romans wanted the last of the rebels stamped out to prevent them from sparking off further rebellion in the empire.

against the Romans from their outpost for two years before Flavius Silva mobilized the Tenth Legion and pinned them down.

To prevent anyone escaping from Masada, Silva began his offensive by building a wall right around the fortress and establishing Roman camps on all sides of it. But he was not content to sit tight and wait for the Zealots to starve or surrender. He knew that they might have ample provisions for a long siege, and that Herod's ingenious engineers had contrived a system of conduits and cisterns which enabled Masada to collect and store water from the rare but heavy storms that occurred in the area. No, the Zealots would have to be driven from their fortress, or exterminated there. So Silva chose a rocky site near the western approach to Masada and set his work force the task of building, with stones and earth, a broad ramp that would enable the legionaries to assault the wall in force at one spot.

The work took months, but as the ramp gradually rose the Zealots must have realized that their days were numbered. When the ramp was completed, the Romans built a siege tower on it and soldiers gave covering fire from the top while others used a battering ram to make a breach in the wall. They succeeded, and at the end of a day's desperate fighting with the defenders Silva withdrew his troops to prepare for the final massive assault the next morning. On Masada that night Eleazar ben Yair reviewed the situation and came to a terrible decision. There was no chance of escaping, or of beating the vastly more numerous Roman soldiers. If their community were all men, they could fight to the very last and go down in glory, but if every Zealot warrior fought to the death the next day their wives and children would fall captive to the Romans. "Let our wives die before they are abused," Eleazar urged, "and our children before they have tasted of slavery; and after we have slain them, let us bestow that glorious benefit upon one another mutually, and preserve ourselves in freedom, as an excellent funeral monument for us. But first let us destroy our money and the fortress by fire; for I am well assured that this will be a great grief to the Romans, that they shall not be able to seize upon our bodies, and shall fail of our wealth also: and let us spare nothing but our provisions for they will be a testimonial when we are dead that we were not subdued for want of necessaries; but that, according to our original resolution, we have preferred death before slavery."

Not all the Zealots were convinced at first that mass suicide was preferable to putting up a fight, but Eleazar argued his case at length and eloquently and inspired every one of his men with ardor to kill and be killed instead of surrendering his loved ones to the unthinkable ignominies of captivity. From the ensuing carnage two women and five children escaped by hiding in an underground cavern, and from them the pro-Roman Jewish historian Josephus later learned what had been said and what had happened on the summit of Masada on that fateful night. Here is part of his account of the events after Eleazar had finished his speech:

"The husbands tenderly embraced their wives and took their children into their arms, and gave the longest parting kisses to them, with tears in their eyes. Yet at the same time did they complete what they had resolved on. . . . Nor was there at length any one of these men found that scrupled to act their part in this terrible execution, but every one of them despatched his dearest relations. . . . So they, not being able to bear the grief they were under for what they had done any longer, and esteeming it an injury to those they had slain, to live even the shortest space of time after them—they presently laid all they had in a heap, and set fire to it. They then chose ten men by lot out of them, to slay

Left: view from Masada of the Roman camp. It has remained well preserved due partly to the dry climate but also to the remoteness of the site. Flavius Silva's own command headquarters were located in a camp slightly north of and close to the assault ramp. From there he could not only follow the course of battle but also, because of the acoustics, could speak directly to Eleazar if he wished.

End of the First Revolt

all the rest; every one of whom laid himself down by his wife and children on the ground and threw his arms about them, and they offered their necks to the stroke of those who by lot executed that melancholy office; and when these ten had, without fear, slain them all, they made the same rule for casting lots for themselves, that he whose lot it was should first kill the other nine, and after all, should kill himself . . . so, for a conclusion the nine offered their necks to the executioner, and he who was the last of all, took a view of all the other bodies, lest perchance some or other among so many that were slain should want his assistance to be quite despatched; and when he perceived that they were all slain, he set fire to the palace, and with the great force of his hand ran his sword entirely through himself, and fell down dead near to his own relations."

When the Romans launched their assault the next day they were bewildered to meet no opposition and to find the buildings on the summit ablaze, and when they found the multitude of the dead, they "could take no pleasure in the fact, though it were done to their enemies: Nor could they do other than wonder at the courage of their resolution, and at the immovable contempt of death which so great a number of them had shown, when they went through with such an action as that was."

Thus ended the First Jewish Revolt. The Second Revolt, 60 years later, which began successfully with the recapture of Jeru-

Below: Titus besieging Jerusalem in 70 A.D. The First Revolt began in 66 A.D. and was suppressed when Titus sacked Jerusalem, destroyed the Temple, and expelled most of the Jewish survivors from the country. He left only Herod's palace to be used as an administrative center.

salem, ended with the elimination of the Jewish state and the dispersion of the Jewish people. For centuries thereafter Jews all over the world kept alive the story of the martyrs of Masada. Throughout those centuries a few relics of the Zealots' last stand remained on the site, but Josephus' story became a legend and even the whereabouts of the historic fortress were forgotten. To the nomadic Arabs who were the only inhabitants of the Judaean desert the rock was known as Sebbeh. Although the ruins of the Herodian buildings were just visible on its summit, this was nothing remarkable in a land plentifully scattered with ruins, and Masada remained virtually undisturbed until 1963, when the Israeli archaeologist Yigael Yadin led an expedition to explore and excavate it.

As well as being a professor of archaeology, Yadin had served as a general in the Israeli army, and he applied methods of large-scale military organization to his archaeological field work. Three years before he embarked on the Masada expedition he had made some important finds associated with the Second Revolt and its leader, Simeon Bar-Kokhba. The Second Revolt had, in fact, ended in a rather similar manner to the first, with the last group of survivors seeking refuge in the Judaean desert and being hunted down and annihilated by the Romans. In the 1950s some documents associated with Bar-Kokhba had been offered for sale by Bedouin Arabs, who after the sensational and profitable discovery of the Dead Sea Scrolls at Qumran had taken up scroll-hunting in the desert caves as a profession. The appearance of these documents prompted the Israeli government to organize a thorough search of caves in the area where they had been found. The area was divided into four sectors, each of which was allocated to a senior archaeologist, who was provided with an Air Force helicopter in order to survey his sector and military help in gaining access to the caves he wished to investigate. Yadin had been appointed head of one of the sectors and it happened that in one of the caves that he excavated there were found many artifacts and manuscripts associated with the Bar-Kokhba revolt, including some letters written by the legendary leader himself. One clue that prompted Yadin to explore this particular cave was that he noticed the remains of a Roman camp situated on the plateau immediately above it. If the Romans had besieged the cave, he reasoned, its occupants must have been important. His reasoning was rewarded with the most prolific and varied find ever made of objects and manuscripts associated with the Second Revolt. So when the project arose of excavating the most important site associated with the First Revolt, Yadin was the obvious man to be appointed to lead the expedition.

The rock that the Arabs called Sebbeh had first been identified as Masada in 1838, when an American scholar, Edward Robinson, on a visit to the Dead Sea area, scrutinized the ruins from below by means of a telescope and recognized some of the features from Josephus' description. He did not attempt to climb up to the plateau; in fact he wrote that it was "apparently inaccessible." It was another American, a missionary named S. W. Walcott, who in 1842 became the first Westerner to do so in modern times. He made the ascent by scrambling up the remains of the Roman ramp, and when he was on the plateau he correctly

Above: Yigael Yadin. Aside from being a professor of archaeology, Yadin also became Deputy Prime Minister of Israel in 1978. He led two excavations of Masada in 1963–5 which were staffed by volunteers from 28 different countries.

Excavation of the Great Ship

Right: aerial view of Masada from the southwest, showing the Romans' ramp and some storage rooms. The ramp, rising toward the casemate wall just north of the west gate, is one of the most remarkable siege structures of the Roman army in existence today. Its length is some 215 yards as is its width at its broadest part near the fortress.

identified the ruins of Herod's wall, of the storerooms, and of one of the palaces. He also located two of the water storage cisterns. He noted the outlines of the Roman camps below, "as complete as if they had been but recently abandoned," and traced the surrounding Roman wall. He found everything just as Josephus had described it, and wrote that "in few instances where topographical identity is in question, have modern researches better sustained the testimony of an ancient writer than they do in this instance."

Over the years other travelers visited Masada and wrote descriptions of it, and in 1932 a German archaeologist, Adolf Schulter, spent a month on the site and drew plans which laid the foundations for the future study of the ruins. But for proper and thorough excavation heavy machinery and a large work force were needed, and these did not become available until the 1960s when a group of private sponsors helped by the Israeli government financed Yadin's expedition and the technical assistance of the Israeli Army engineers was made available to the archaeologist. An eager volunteer work force from many countries was recruited by a mention of the expedition's requirements in the London *Observer*. The response of the thousands of applicants for the arduous and unpaid work under harsh conditions astonished Yadin, who regarded it as indicative of the "enchantment and attraction of Masada" both on account of its scenic splendor and its significance both for the Jews and for all mankind as the symbol of defiance by a group of passionate patriots pitting their all against the assembled military might of an aggressive occupying power. By allowing volunteers to participate for a minimum period of two weeks, Yadin was able to keep a constant labor force of about 300 and accomplish not only a thorough excavation of Masada but also a reconstruction of the

Left: water cistern at the top of the rock of Masada. It has three tiers, and at the top (at the left of picture) an opening allowed excess water to drain off. The cisterns had been scooped out of the rock and each had a capacity of up to 140,000 cubic feet.

Below: aerial view from the north of Herod's palace-villa after excavation by the Yadin team. The supporting wall is visible below the lower terrace. The "hanging villa" is constructed at the narrowest part of Masada on the very edge of the escarpment.

foundations of its buildings. Before the expedition began its work, the plateau was strewn with rubble and mounds of stone, and as Yadin wrote, "we could not see the buildings for the stones." Although there are no complete buildings left on Masada, today's visitor can get a powerful sense of history and of the layout of the fortress thanks to the expedition's work in the two seasons between 1963 and 1965.

The emotional appeal of the Masada site lies, of course, in its association with the Zealots' last stand, but its architecture and archaeological interest belong to the earlier Herodian period. Herod had obviously spared no effort or expense to create a retreat provided with the luxurious amenities and the splendor befitting his royal rank, but the Zealots had been desperate refugees crowded into an area not designed to accommodate so many. As it turned out, the excavations produced many relics of the Zealots' occupation of the fortress; certainly a richer haul than Yadin would have dared hope for before he began.

Seen from above, Masada is shaped rather like a great ship, broad in the middle and narrowing to a point at each end. Yadin decided to excavate systematically, starting from the northern end, where most of the buildings had been, and working gradually southward. His first efforts were concentrated on ruins on three terraces below the level of the plateau at the north end. These were the remains of a marvelous palace-villa that Herod had built, a magnificent pleasure palace set on a steep incline which led down to a sheer precipice. Josephus had described the structure with awe, and written about its opulent decorations and furnishings and the elaborate contrivances for supplying water for various uses, "as if there had been fountains there." To view a modern aerial photograph of the ruins and imagine what the original structure must have looked like is to share his

Right: inner row of columns on the lowest terrace of Herod's hanging villa, showing the walls painted to resemble marble. The artists also succeeded in convincing observers, including Josephus, that each pillar was made of a single stone. They were actually constructed of several drums of soft stone which were plastered and then grooved to look like giant sculptured monolithic columns.

awe of the Herodian engineers' achievement. The situation of the palace was ideal, for it was the only spot on Masada that was sheltered from the burning sun and also from the strong wind that sometimes blew from the south. But the conception was incredibly bold, and as Yadin wrote, "Only Herod, the great and ambitious builder, could have conceived the project of erecting a three-tiered hanging palace-villa for himself on this spot."

Initial archaeological work on the lower terrace involved the clearing of piles of debris, and when this was done the excavation revealed stone pillars and colorful frescoed walls. The walls had been painted to look like marble, and the colors had lasted remarkably well for 2000 years. This was obviously a terrace used only for leisure. Annexed at one side of it were some rooms on two levels which were at first thought to be storerooms but on further investigation turned out to comprise a small bathhouse with a cold pool, a tepid room, and a hot room with facilities for heating the air—in fact, a kind of sauna bath. On this terrace, probably, Herod would have taken his relaxation with a few favored companions, enjoying privacy, refreshment, and the magnificent view over the Dead Sea 1000 feet below and in the distance to the oasis of Ein Gedi.

Below: the plaited hair found in the bathhouse by Yadin. The scalp had been preserved due to the extreme dryness of the atmosphere. Beside the skeleton the plaster was stained with what looked like blood. The young woman may have been the wife of the last defender at Masada.

It was in the small bathhouse on this lower terrace of Herod's palace that Yadin found unmistakable evidence of the Zealots' occupation and tragic end. When the debris was cleared the remains of three skeletons were found on the steps leading to the coldwater pool and on the ground nearby. They were the skeletons of a man, a woman, and a child. Next to the man's skeleton there were hundreds of silvered scales of armor, the garment they had been sewn to having rotted away, and also scores of arrows. Of the woman there remained an intact scalp and attached to it and marvelously preserved, a full head of hair, beautifully plaited. The young woman's sandals, strikingly modern in design, were nearby too, as was the skeleton of the child. Contemplating these remains, Yadin recalled Josephus' account of how the last Zealot had set fire to the palace before taking his own life and falling where his family lay. This lowest level of the palace could have been the last part the survivor had set fire to, and Yadin wondered, "Could it be that we had discovered the bones of that very fighter and his kith?" There was no way of knowing, of course, but the find did give the excavators a poignant sense of physical contact with the martyrs of nearly 2000 years ago. "As we gazed," wrote Yadin, "we relived the final and most tragic moments of the drama of Masada."

On the middle terrace of the palace there had been a circular roofed building, and this area, too, had been decorated with wall paintings and used for purposes of pleasure and relaxation. The upper terrace had been the residential area, though the actual living quarters consisted of only four rooms, which implied that this entire palace had been built not with any motive of ostentation but for the private enjoyment of King Herod and perhaps one of his nine wives. When the floors of the living quarters were excavated mosaic patterns were found on them, and fragments of the walls and the collapsed ceilings showed

Skeletons in the Bathhouse

Left: colored mosaic fragments from the floor of the western palace, very little of which remains. The design contains motifs popular in Jewish art of the period—pomegranates, vine and fig leaves, and a geometrical pattern of circles in the center. The damaged floor provided insights into the technique of the mosaic artists: lines incised on the plaster beneath guided the artist along the borders of the pattern.

that the quarters had originally been ornately decorated. If this was the prodigal king's love nest, he had certainly spared no effort to make it as luxurious as anyone could desire.

Josephus wrote that when the Zealots occupied Masada they found storehouses where there was laid up "corn in large quantities, and such as would subsist men for a long time . . . wine and oil in abundance with all kinds of pulse and dates heaped up together . . . fresh and full ripe, and in no way inferior to such fruits newly laid in, although they were little short of a hundred years from the laying in of these provisions." The buildings where these provisions had been stored stood out clearly in an aerial photograph of the site. They were not far from the upper terrace of the palace-villa, and were easily identifiable because

Above: the storerooms, laid out as long narrow halls. They were built in two groups—the southern group, the larger of the two, was separated from the other by a road running east to west.
Below: a cooking stove in the casemate wall. The Zealots made minor architectural alterations in order to house the families living in Masada, and the resulting units provided archaeologists with some of their most exciting finds.

they were laid out as a series of long narrow halls with stone walls. At ground level the walls were not at first so clearly identifiable because the upper part of them and the roof they supported had fallen in and the area was one mass of rubble. To clear the rubble was a formidable task, and for this purpose cranes had to be hauled up to the summit of Masada. Simple manual cranes, consisting of a tripod, pulley, and chain, were used—machines in fact rather similar to those that the Romans, and probably Herod's builders, had employed. Tractors, too, were needed for the work, and these were transported to the summit by overhead cable rail part by part and reassembled on arrival.

It was decided that before the storerooms were excavated their walls should be reconstructed from the rubble. A mason who was expert in restoring historical sites was engaged, and most of the walls were rebuilt with their original stones, while others were left to show what the site had looked like before restoration.

In a number of the storerooms, when the rubble had been cleared nearly down to the level of the original floor, there was found a thick layer of ashes and charred beams, with fragments of hundreds of smashed pots scattered among them. Here again was evidence of the events of the Zealots' last desperate hours. They had obviously deliberately smashed their storage vessels in order to prevent their contents falling into the hands of the Romans. Archaeologists were able to reconstruct several specimen vessels from the fragments, and some were found to bear the Hebrew names of their owners. This finding, however, posed a problem, for, according to Josephus, Eleazar had said that the Zealots should not destroy their provisions in order to show the Romans that they had not died for lack of necessities, but here was evidence of systematic and deliberate destruction. A few of the storerooms, on the other hand, were found to be empty of broken fragments and to show no signs of fire, and Yadin conjectured that the Zealots had destroyed most of their provisions and left just a few rooms intact to demonstrate Eleazar's point.

The Zealots' leader had also urged that the Jews should destroy their money, but this was obviously more difficult than disposing of things that would easily burn. In the entrance to one of the storerooms nearly a hundred bronze coins were found strewn on the floor within a small area. "It seemed," wrote Yadin, "as though the person in charge of the stores, in the final bitter moment, had taken his stock of coins from the treasury and flung them on the floor as useless objects."

The most exciting find of coins in the course of the dig was made in the next building to be excavated, a building which consisted of a number of apartments grouped around a central courtyard. These had probably been the dwellings of administrators or officials in the Herodian period. Many alabaster vessels and expensive cosmetic items found there indicated that the occupants had been wealthy. The apartments had later been used by the leaders of the Zealots. In one of the rooms, beneath the level of the original floor, one of the volunteer workers one day turned up a heap of coins. They were congealed together with mold and there were bits of cloth stuck to parts of the heap, which showed that they had originally been put in a bag and hidden under the floor. When the coins were treated in a laboratory and cleaned they proved to be valuable silver shekels and half-shekels in superb condition. They had Hebrew inscriptions, such as "For the freedom of Zion," "Jerusalem the Holy," and "Shekel of Israel." The earliest of them had been struck in the first year of the Revolt, A.D. 66, and the latest, which was extremely rare, in the fifth year, the year when the Temple was demolished. Here, then, was another definite physical link with the martyrs of Masada.

The biggest building on the plateau, situated on the western side overlooking the Roman camp and ramp, had been Herod's ceremonial and administrative palace. Occupying an area of 36,000 square feet, and comprising a central court, royal dwelling quarters, a throne room, an administrative building, a service wing, and a storeroom wing, the palace had obviously been a great and impressive building. The amount of rubble covering the site showed that parts of it had been of two stories. The work of excavation was arduous and occupied a substantial proportion of the work force throughout the two seasons of the dig. The most interesting find from the archaeological point of view was a substantial area of colored mosaic floor in a good state of preservation in which designs typical of Greek and Jewish decorative art of the 1st century B.C. were to be seen. This, Yadin thought, was probably the oldest colored mosaic floor ever found in Israel, and certainly the most beautiful one of its period.

There was a mosaic floor, too, in the private bathhouse in what had been Herod's living quarters in the residential wing of the palace, and also in the narrow corridor leading to the bathhouse. And built right on this floor, with no regard for its beauty, was the rough stone base of a cupboard, or possibly a stove, that had been built by the Zealots. Yadin wondered whether this structure should be removed in order to bring to light more of

Silver Shekels of Israel

Above: a shekel of the First Revolt (66–70 A.D.) found in the administrative apartments at Masada. The inscription reads "Shekel of Egypt." The finding of the coins helped to date true shekels to the very years they were struck—the last was in 70 A.D. when the Temple in Jerusalem was destroyed.

Burning their Belongings

Right: Herod's private bathhouse with its frescoes. Impressions of the black and white tiles which once decorated the room's upper floor are also visible. In a corner of the room a few pipes were still stuck to the wall.

the mosaic floor, but decided against doing so. "We left the remains as we found them," he wrote, "to serve as an illustration of the two main contrasting periods of occupation on the summit of Masada . . . of the contrast between the splendor of Masada in Herod's time and the poverty in the time of the revolt."

The royal storerooms in the western wing of the palace had enabled the occupants to live independently of the large public storerooms at the northern end of the plateau. One of these royal storerooms was 210 feet long, and among the ashes that lay beneath the rubble thousands of fragments of smashed jars were found. Some had inscriptions in still legible Hebrew, for instance "crushed pressed figs" and "dried figs," and the finders were reminded of Josephus' description of preserved fruits in excellent condition though nearly 100 years old. There were also fragments of delicate vessels, such as flasks used for cosmetic oil, which indicated that some of the contents of the royal storerooms had been more sophisticated than those of the public storerooms.

Clustered in the neighborhood of the main palace there had been five smaller palace-villas, which had probably been the homes of members of Herod's family. Amid this complex of palaces a massive swimming pool with plastered steps at one end was discovered and restored. There was evidence that the small palaces had been ornately decorated. In several of them frescoed walls like those on the lower terrace of Herod's northern palace were found. Zealot families had obviously lived in the palaces at the time of the revolt and had built additional walls and partitions to enable a number of families to occupy one building.

The problem of accommodating nearly 1000 people at Masada had been solved by adapting the wall that ran around the entire summit for dwelling purposes. This was a *casemate* wall—that is, a double one with partitioning walls dividing the space between into chambers. There had been about 110 rooms of varying sizes between the walls and in the towers. The larger ones had been divided by the Zealots into smaller dwelling units. In these "homes" the occupants had built cupboards and mud ovens, and the excavation of the casemate wall revealed a wealth of artifacts providing evidence of the daily life of the Zealots. In contrast to the palaces and public buildings, these humble dwellings had not been burned down in the rebels' last desperate hours, for they would not have contained much that would prove of value to the conquerors. In many of them, however, there was a corner with a little heap of ashes, which were the remains of clothing, sandals, domestic utensils, and personal items that each Zealot family had burned before the end. Josephus had written that before they were killed each family had laid all their belongings in a heap and set fire to them. These heaps of ashes, Yadin wrote, "were perhaps the sights that moved us most during our excavation."

The rooms of the casemate wall yielded more relics of the martyrs of Masada than any other site. Many domestic vessels were scattered about the floors, and there were cosmetic items,

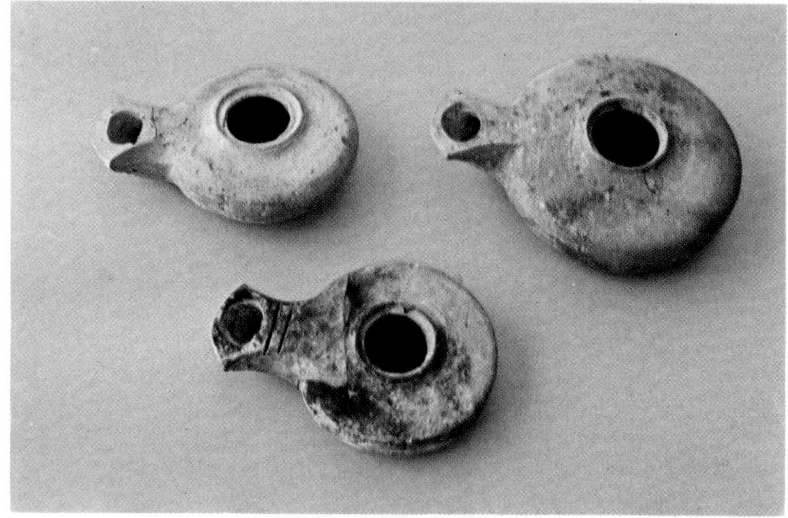

Left: clay oil lamps typical of the 1st century A.D. Scores of these were found in various rooms belonging to the Zealots in the casemate wall, which were not burned before they committed suicide.

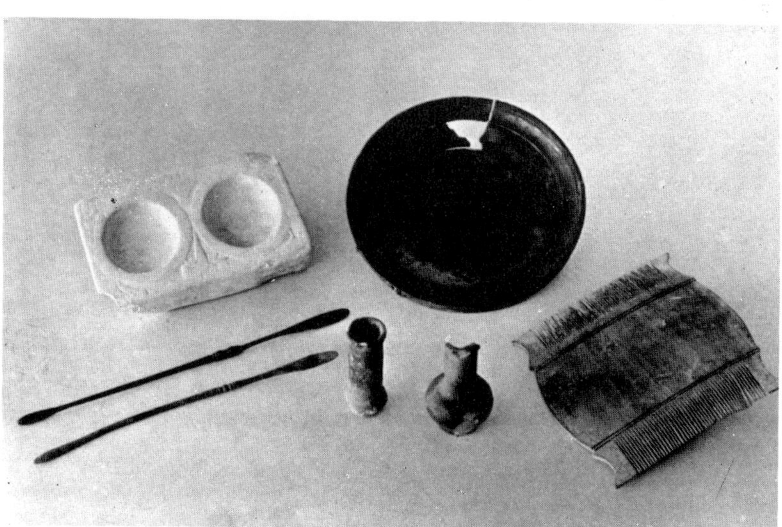

Left: cosmetic items found in the Zealots' dwellings. They would have been in daily use and would not have been considered worthy of burning. From left to right: twin palette; two bronze eye shadow sticks; clay perfume vials; bronze mirror case; and a wooden comb.

Above: Gamala, an ancient city east of the Sea of Galilee. A natural stronghold, it was fortified by Josephus in 66 A.D. and taken by storm by Vespasian the following year. The situation bore a striking resemblance to that of Masada, and in the foreground are missiles similar to those found at Masada.

oil lamps, signet rings, and bronze buckles, and also remains of cloth and sacking. When assembled these last proved to be the most complete collection of textile material from the Roman period in existence. Hundreds of coins from the period of the revolt were found on the floors of the rooms, and several hoards of coins buried beneath the floors were unearthed. In many of the casemate rooms on the western side hundreds of stone balls about the size of grapefruits were found—missiles with which the Roman catapults had bombarded the fortress before they breached its wall.

One of Yigael Yadin's dreams before he started the Masada excavation was that he might find some ancient scrolls there. "Had the Zealots hidden their writings before committing suicide?" he asked. "And if they had, would any of them still be preserved? And would we find them?" To his delight, there were no less than 14 discoveries of fragments of manuscript scrolls

Discovering the Book of Psalms

Left: the tenseness of archaeological work. Here fragments of papyrus are detached from the remains of baskets in the room of the scrolls. Not only was this the first time scrolls had been found preserved outside a cave, but it was also possible to date the finds without the slightest doubt, since they could not have been produced any later than 73 A.D. when Masada fell.

made in the course of the excavation of Masada, most of them in the rooms of the casemate wall.

The first was made just a few weeks after digging had begun. One afternoon a colleague rushed to where Yadin was working, brandishing a piece of black and creased parchment. There was clear writing on it, and a cursory examination revealed that it was a part of the Book of Psalms. Another part of the same book was later found nearby. The importance of the find to scholars was that these scrolls, and all the others unearthed at Masada, were known to belong to a very specific period, not later than A.D. 73, and their chief interest was that when compared with modern Biblical texts they were found to be almost exactly identical, whereas in the Biblical scrolls found in caves at nearby Qumran in 1947 there had been significant departures from modern texts. The Masada finds showed that the traditional accepted texts were authentic and that the Essene community at

Casting of Lots

Qumran had made changes probably for doctrinal reasons. Other important scroll finds made at the site included fragments of the Books of Leviticus and Ezekiel, and parts of known texts which had not made the Old Testament canon, the Book of Jubilees and the Wisdom of Ben Sira. Both of the latter books were only known in Greek translations, and the discovery at Masada of versions in the original Hebrew was of supreme importance.

The most intriguing of the scroll finds, however, was a fragment of a sectarian scroll with a text that Yadin recognized as identical with that of a scroll that had been found in one of the caves at Qumran. The discovery of this text at Masada had interesting implications. The Essene community at Qumran was thought by many scholars to have been pacifist and not to have participated in the revolt. Yadin disputed this and suggested that the Essenes had indeed fought the Romans, and when Qumran was overrun some of them had escaped to Masada, taking some of their own writings with them.

Just below the casemate wall on the southern cliff of Masada there were a number of caves. When these were explored one was found to contain a mass of human skulls and bones scattered about in disorder. When these remains were studied by experts at the Hebrew University Medical School they were found to be of 15 males, 6 females, and 4 children, which suggested that they must be the bones of some of the Zealots. Apart from the skeletons of the man, woman, and child found on the lower terrace of the north palace, these were the only human remains found at Masada. As a Roman garrison had been posted there for some years after the conquest, the Byzantine monks had lived there for a period from about 400 on, it could hardly be expected that

Above: the cave in which a mass of human skeletons were found. Accessible only by rope on the southern side, the cave had protected the human remains for 2000 years.

Right: an excavated cave at Qumran. It was called the "cave of the dead" because several human skeletons were found there, believed to be the bones of people who died in Bar-Kokhba's anti-Roman revolt 1800 years ago. Qumran was also the site of the discovery of Essene texts.

the site would be strewn by skeletons of the Zealots. The few in the cave were probably of bodies that had been unceremoniously dumped there when the Romans cleared up the holocaust preparatory to occupying Masada themselves.

Yadin has often been asked what he considered the most important discovery made during the Masada excavations. He answers that many of the discoveries are of equal importance from different archaeological and scholarly points of view, but there was one find that he personally considered the most spectacular of the entire dig. At one of the most strategic spots on Masada 11 small *ostraca*, or fragments of pottery, with names inscribed on them in Hebrew were turned up by volunteer workers when they cleared the debris. Workers familiar with Josephus' account of the Zealots' last stand remembered the passage: "They then chose ten men by lot out of them, to slay all the rest . . . and when these ten had, without fear, slain them all, they made the same rule for casting lots for themselves. . . ." Could these pieces of pottery with the names on them have been the very ones used in the casting of the lots? The probability of this was strengthened by the fact that one of the fragments bore the name of the leader of the Zealots, Eleazar ben Yair. It was plausible that after the 10 men had completed their bloody task, Eleazar would have put his name with theirs in the lottery to decide which one of them should despatch the last 10; which would explain why there were 11 ostraca and not 10 as Josephus had described. If this conjecture was right, the 11 fragments were certainly the most spectacular find of the excavations, the most moving link between the heroes and martyrs of Masada of A.D. 73 and the descendants of their people who 1900 years later came to the forbidding desert fortress to reconstruct a legend.

Below: ostraca found at Masada with the Hebrew name "Ben Ya'ir" written on it. It could well mean Eleazar ben Yair, commander of the Zealots at Masada.

Left: excavations at the storeroom complex at Masada. Special manually operated cranes with tripods, pulleys, and chains were required, and expert builders and masons lovingly restored the site. The walls of the storeroom were rebuilt with the stones found strewn over the ground, layer by layer, on the sections of ruined walls that remained.

Chapter 8
Secrets of the Seabed

In 1900 Greek sponge-divers wearing primitive equipment discovered a 2000-year-old treasure ship in the shallow waters of the eastern Mediterranean. The Greek authorities launched what was probably the first example of systematic underwater archaeology. It was an important beginning, and nowhere has this work proved more profitable and exciting than in the shallow coastal waters of the tideless Mediterranean. This chapter examines some of the most intriguing finds, from Carthaginian warships to the exploration of the harbor at Tyre. Here is an absorbing introduction to underwater archaeology and how it sets out to solve the mysteries of the seabed.

"Horses . . . naked women . . . people . . . a city!" The diver could scarcely wait to surface and free his head from its "fishbowl" helmet before babbling about the wonders he had just glimpsed lying 200 feet below the surface.

It was early in 1900. A Greek sponge boat had been sailing home from a stint off North Africa when a storm broke. The crew sought shelter off Antikythera—a small island between the southern Greek mainland and Crete. Deciding to try his luck for sponges, one of the divers put on his lead-soled shoes and rubberized canvas suit, weighed down by lumps of lead on back and chest to stop him bobbing up like a cork. He screwed on his glass-fronted metal helmet and checked that enough air to breathe was flowing into the helmet through a hose from the vessel's compressor. Then he sank to the sea floor. At best he hoped to find sponges, the plant-like animal colonies whose skeletons in those days were so much in demand for bathrooms. What he saw banished all thought of the dangerous drudgery of this everyday task.

Through the dim blue gloom ahead a murky mass lay on the seabed some 60 feet off the coast of the island. As the diver trudged nearer, the mass resolved itself into a jumble of bronze and marble statues, like a crowd of drowned people half buried in sand and mud. He wrenched free a giant bronze arm and tugged urgently on a line for his shipmates to haul him up.

Demetrios Kondos, the ship's captain, himself dived to con-

Opposite: amphora, once filled with wine, found at the wreck of a 1300-year-old Byzantine merchant ship near the island of Yassi Ada off the southwestern coast of Turkey. In all, the wreck held about 900 of the large jars, whose contents had long been supplanted by octopuses and moray eels. The team of underwater archaeologists under the direction of George Bass was the first to use a submarine and aerial survey techniques.

Above: the Youth of Antikythera, found in Marathon Bay in 1925. It is just over 4 feet high and is thought by some to be an original work by Lysippos, a sculptor of the 4th century B.C. It is the only surviving large-scale bronze from the first quarter of the 4th century.

firm the unbelievable discovery. Then the ship sailed for home. Back in port at Syme the captain produced the arm and details of the find to the Greek authorities. They were so impressed that they decided to sponsor a salvage expedition by Syme's divers.

At this time there was no such thing as planned underwater archaeology. Lacking tools designed for the job, men constricted by cumbersome gear ambled awkwardly over the sea floor groping for finds. Each could work only for two five-minute spells a day before beginning the slow ascent that safety demanded. If divers came up too fast, nitrogen gas forced by water pressure from lungs into the bloodstream expanded as the pressure lessened. Expanding nitrogen formed bubbles in the blood that set it fizzing like champagne. The result was that excruciating divers' disorder known as the "bends." For rising too swiftly, two of the Antikythera divers suffered permanent paralysis. Another died.

But the team did solve the mystery surrounding the drowned statues. One by one, these were tied to ropes and pulled from the sea. Sometimes a rope snapped and its valuable load sank into water too deep for recovery. Sea creatures had badly gnawed and deformed most of the marble figures. But among these 36 statues, 4 horses, and 33 fragments of legs and arms was a huge, intact figure recognizably depicting the legendary Greek hero Heracles, and another of the goddess Aphrodite. Bronze pieces included a bronze bed, statuettes, a bearded head, and the so-called "Youth of Antikythera"—one of the finest bronzes of the 4th century B.C. ever found.

Besides all this, the divers brought up pottery lamps and storage jars; glass containers; a gold earring; and a corroded metal astronomical instrument designed to find the positions of sun, stars, planets, and moon. The expert who identified this calculator described it as the "only truly scientific instrument surviving from Classical times"—apart, that is, from simple tools for everyday measuring.

The whole collection plainly formed the contents of an ancient ship that had sunk just off the island.

By studying these objects, experts were able to decide broadly where the ship was bound for and when it foundered. Most of the

Right: the mechanical parts of the astronomical computer or clock found at Antikythera. They were badly corroded when discovered, but when reconstructed an upper scale could be seen to pertain to the months and a lower one to the zodiac. The various dials show the annual motion of the sun and the main risings and settings of bright stars and constellations throughout the year.

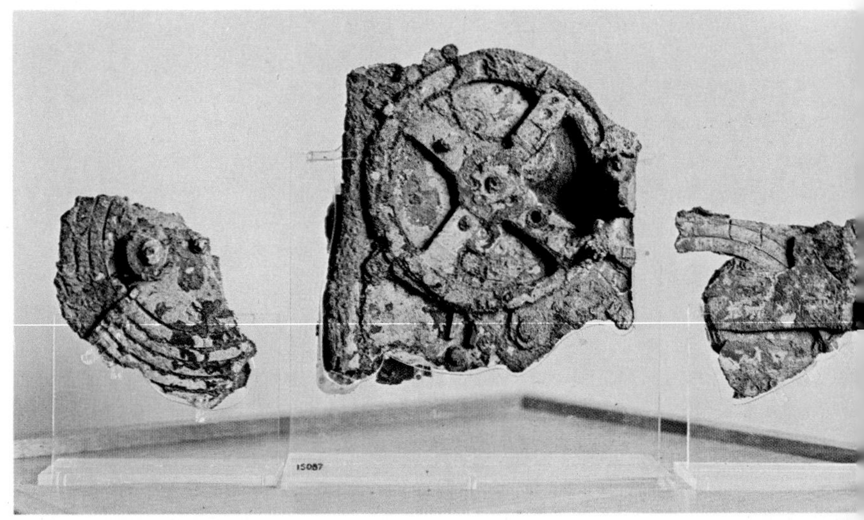

marbles proved to be copies of Greek sculptures evidently on their way from Greece to Italy where ancient Roman connoisseurs collected Greek art objects. The name of a month shown on the astronomical calculator had been introduced only in 30 B.C. Together with the type of pottery aboard the vessel, this clue would make the wreck about 2000 years old.

The sponge divers' find at Antikythera gave a tantalizing glimpse of the lost heritage of ancient civilizations preserved beneath the Mediterranean Sea. More glimpses followed. In 1907 sponge divers stumbled on another underwater treasury of Hellenistic art—this time including more than five dozen marble statues, together with stone and bronze sculptures. Like the Antikythera wreck, the ship that bore this cargo had foundered in the 1st century B.C., this time off Mahdia in Tunisia. In the 1920s the sea at Cape Artemision off the Greek island of Euboea yielded a sculptured jockey, part of a sculptured horse, and a superb 5th-century B.C. statue of the god Zeus—all part of an

otherwise unknown sunken cargo. The same decade revealed the submarine wreck of a 2000-year-old ship near Albenga in Italy. It was now plain that beneath the Mediterranean lay hitherto untapped archaeological sites rich in clues to the past, if only men could—and would—explore them carefully.

But their first efforts were mere treasure hunting. At Antikythera no one had photographed or drawn a plan of the site. No archaeologist even dived. Men never probed the ship's structure or the way in which its cargo had been distributed. Efforts to recover the Albenga wreck half a century later were even cruder. In 1950 a giant grab let down from a surface salvage ship chewed into the wreck, and dragged up a mangled mess of wood, wine jars, and old metal in a way that offered no insight into how the ship had been fashioned and laden.

The first use of tools devised for the job came only two years later, at Grand Congloué Island just off Marseilles in the south of

Jockey of Euboea

Below: sailors of the salvage ship *Artiglio II* watch as amphorae are brought up from the Albenga wreck in the Gulf of Genoa in 1950. This was the third salvage attempt to be made since the 2000-year-old ship was discovered.

Below left: Hellenistic jockey sculpture found at Cape Artemision in 1928. Parts of a galloping horse were also found, and pottery from the site dates the shipwreck at around the time of Christ. Pieces of the ship's wooden hull have been found, which indicate that the rest of the vessel and its cargo probably remain beneath the mud.

Bronze Age Merchantmen

Right: diver holding an amphora from the wreck off Grand Congloué Island. It was probably discovered by divers working on the construction of the great Marseilles sewer whose outlet is nearly opposite the island. An airlift was used to extract mud and sand from the ship's remains.

France. Here, a team of free-swimming aqualung divers led by Frenchman Jacques-Yves Cousteau employed a suction tube known as an air lift to clear sand and mud from the cargo of a Roman wineship more than 2100 years old. What they found added much to our knowledge of the trans-Mediterranean wine trade 200 years before Christ, threw new light on the dating of ancient pottery, and supplied the first evidence of how a Roman ship was built and loaded. However, the project's lack of detailed measurements still left unanswered questions about the tubby, square-sailed merchantman. Only when archaeologists themselves learned to dive and direct operations from under the water would the Mediterranean's old wrecks begin to reveal their full story under the knowledgeable eye of experts

Below: a Roman wineship like the one wrecked at Grand Congloué. The ship was a 100-ton freighter, and while investigating it Cousteau developed the tool of underwater television.

For several reasons this story has unfolded largely off the Mediterranean's northeastern coasts. Fragile ships and lack of navigation equipment forced early Mediterranean seafarers to hug the shores—especially those with clear landmarks such as tall headlands. The north Egyptian coast is low and featureless. But the rugged south coast of Turkey abounds in rocky peninsulas. This made it the preferred route for ships plying between the east Mediterranean and ports farther west. The same coast also teems with offshore pinnacles, many hidden just below the water, so that this sea highway was also a ships' graveyard.

By the same token, the waters that lap Turkey's southern flank are now perhaps the Mediterranean's richest hunting ground for underwater archaeologists. Active among these, in the late 1950s, was an amateur, the American photo-journalist Peter Throckmorton. In 1958 and 1959 Throckmorton spent months listing scores of wreck sites in the northeastern Mediterranean, largely by gleaning information from a Turkish sponge-diver, Kemal Aras. Among other valuable information, Aras told Throckmorton of a corroded mass of bronze slabs and spearheads at a wreck off Cape Gelidonya on Turkey's southern coast. The Turk himself half-hoped to dynamite the mass to salvage it for scrap. But Throckmorton suspected that the metal had a value far above its commercial worth. He guessed that it had formed the cargo of a Bronze Age ship—a ship perhaps 1000 years older than the oldest wreck so far discovered. If fragments of the ship itself survived beneath its cargo, archaeologists might learn how men had built some of the first cargo ships that sailed the sea off Asia Minor. Accordingly Throckmorton earmarked this as the site above all others on his list most worth investigating.

Above: the rocky coast of Turkey, its offshore pinnacles hidden by the high tide, at Antalya Bay near Cape Gelidonya. The treacherous current running around the cape can reverse its direction without warning, and there are jagged rocks just beneath the waves.

Finding it proved far from easy. In 1959 the steel ketch *Vigilant* hovered for two days above the wreck's supposed location, while teams of divers equipped with aqualungs scoured the seabed. Each time they came up empty-handed. Then, on the last planned search, two divers glimpsed a shimmering, overgrown mound. It lay some 100 yards deep on a ridge between two islands. The Turkish diver Mustafa Kapkin quickly sketched the area of the mound. Sample finds brought to the surface revealed a late Bronze Age date of roughly 1200 B.C. Here, indeed, lay the oldest shipwreck known.

Next year the American archaeologist George Bass helped to launch a University of Pennsylvania Museum expedition to retrieve the cargo. The team lived largely on a narrow, cliff-foot base. There, scientists cleaned and identified recovered objects in uncomfortable and even dangerous conditions. Voracious flies forced work to take place under netting. Temperatures soared above blood heat. Rocks dropped from above. At times waves pounded the shore and landslides threatened the scientists.

There were underwater problems too. The eight divers working from an offshore vessel had to toil against the tug of currents. For reasons of safety none could spend much more than an hour a day down on the wreck. At first their work appeared abominably difficult. Stone-hard coralline concretions over eight inches thick masked the outline of pots and metal objects. To prise these individually free proved impossible.

Instead, Frédéric Dumas, the chief diver, had a brainwave. He

suggested lifting great chunks of fused cargo at a time. First, though, each chunk was marked in such a way that the whole cargo could be reassembled once ashore. It took weeks of chiseling to free the lumps—some almost as weighty as two men. Heavily undercut bolders would refuse to budge until dislodged from the seabed by a jeep's hydraulic jack. The next step was to lift the bulky masses. This was accomplished with a winch aboard a small Turkish vessel designed to drag for sponges. Once the masses had been brought ashore, archaeologists set to work with hammers, chisels, and a kind of dentist's drill to free the cargo from its stony mold.

The largest single group of objects comprised nearly three dozen copper ingots, shaped for handling purposes like ox-hides. This was the form in which such metal had been shipped from nearby Cyprus—an island, incidentally, whose very name means "copper." Some ingots had retained their form remarkably, but sea-water acting on copper ingots lying close to tin bars had caused severe corrosion.

Tin and copper are the raw materials for making bronze. Thus it seemed that the vessel had been shipping processed raw materials from one port to a landfall where these would be

Above: Dr. George Bass on a diving ladder. As Assistant Curator of the University of Pennsylvania's division for underwater archaeology Bass has been influential in several underwater digs, especially in the Mediterranean.

Right: using plastic salvage balloons to raise lumps of concreted cargo off Cape Gelidonya. The diver is equipped with a "hookah" through which he draws his air from a compressor on the surface. Another tool used was an underwater metal detector to locate hidden deposits.

fashioned into weapons, tools, or ornaments. Other finds backed up this theory, among them broken pins, picks, axheads, and spearheads deposited in wicker baskets—one of the richest ever hoards of Bronze Age scrap. All told the ship had held more than a ton of metal.

Intriguingly, the merchantman had metal worker's tools aboard. Polishers and whetstones turned up at one end of the ship where the cabin may have been. Other implements included smooth-surfaced stone hammer heads suitable for beating out metal sheets. A large hard stone, flattened on one side, may have been an early type of anvil. Probably a traveling metalworker had been among the passengers.

Personal objects recovered from the cabin area included stone sets of merchant's weights for a balance pan, an oil lamp, and a seal for authorizing documents. Analysis of the entire contents suggests that ship and cargo were Phoenician in origin, and thus that the sea trade of the ancient world's greatest seafaring peoples was well advanced by 1200 B.C.—much earlier than many prehistorians had thought.

Because the ship had landed on an underwater ridge, no thick protective coating of sand had covered it to save its wood from dissolution, but bits of wood survived beneath one great concretion. Among the fragments divers discovered the remains of planks pierced by bored holes containing nails—a Bronze Age shipbuilding feature accurately described in Homer's writings. Another find was brushwood lining for the hull's interior—again just as recorded in the Homeric epics. Enough of the 35-foot-long merchant ship survived to prove that the seagoing Phoenicians had reinforced their ships with ribs, while the nearby powerful Egyptians still had only flimsy, largely frameless vessels.

By 1960 underwater excavation had added much to archaeologists' knowledge of how men had gone to sea in ancient days. Yet undersea recoveries so far accomplished had told the experts far more about the cargoes carried in the early ships than about the ships themselves. For in almost all the wrecks discovered, little of their ancient timbers had survived. This point is easily explained. Wooden ships that ran aground in shallow seas were quickly smashed to pulp because a wave's destructive work penetrates beneath the sea five times deeper than the wave is high. Bombarded by the sea's artillery of stones and pebbles, old ships off shallow rock or shingle coasts stood no chance of escape. Then, too, their timbers suffered from attack by underwater currents and the gnawing inroads of the shipworm and other small invertebrates whose tunneling turns planks to sieves that soon disintegrate. Generally speaking, ships' timbers stood a better chance of enduring if they sank into a soft thick bed of mud or silt too far beneath the sea's surface for the mightiest of storms to jostle them.

Even here, though, as metal fastenings corroded, ships' sides bulged outward and collapsed beneath their own weight and that of the cargo they contained. Such vessels ended up flattened on the seabed. Moreover unless overlying cargo or a gentle rain of sand, silt, or mud enveloped them, these timbers, too, were liable to rot.

What made the first full excavation and reconstruction of an

Copper Ingots Like Ox Hides

Below: copper ingots recovered from the Cape Gelidonya wreck. Comprising the largest part of the cargo, 40 of them were shaped like ox hides as here. They varied in weight from 35 to 60 pounds and so may not have been used as currency as was previously assumed.

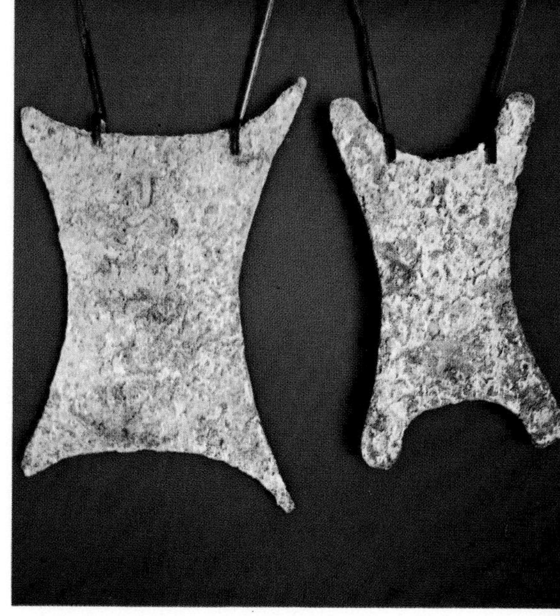

Investigation at Yassi Ada

Right: a Roman corn ship or merchantman like that found off Yassi Ada. A reef had torn a hole in the underside of the hull. The ship as reconstructed would have been about 60 to 70 feet long and 17 feet wide.

ancient vessel so remarkable was the fact that not much of the ship survived. George Bass, who led the team involved, declared the ship to be preserved no better than some other ancient wrecks. Only the divers' imagination, innovation, and dogged, meticulous recording and recovery of each fragment of its structure ensured what proved to be a triumph of underwater archaeology.

The wreck selected for this task was that of a Byzantine merchantman of the 7th century A.D. Its fragments lay 120 feet down like scattered pieces of a jigsaw puzzle, almost obliterated by the mound of wine jars that once comprised its cargo. Above was Yassi Ada (Flat Island), a low, barren, rat-infested rock just off the southwest coast of Turkey, considerably west of Gelidonya. Prospecting off Yassi Ada late in the 1950s, Peter Throckmorton had glimpsed this merchantman and others close together on the seabed—all evidently victims of an underwater reef that jutted from the island.

Building on the knowledge won at Gelidonya and other underwater sites, George Bass tackled the Yassi Ada excavation like any major dig on land. He reversed the system used in pioneer underwater digs, and gave the key role of excavation to archaeologists turned divers. Supporting and interpreting their work were photographers, draftsmen, architects, an art historian, and a classicist. A geologist, a mechanic, and a doctor brought other necessary skills to the task. Work began in 1961. Before it ended there had been more than 5000 dives spread over four summer seasons.

Scared off by hordes of biting island rats, the archaeologists at first lived and worked from a barge tethered just above the site. Teams of two or three would dive together. First, with wire brushes, they scrubbed seaweed off the wreck. They then fixed a numbered plastic label to every item they could see. Thus experts could readily identify each object on photographs and drawings of the cargo. Aided by light, easily assembled wire grids, underwater artists "drawing by numbers" recorded tagged objects by pencil on plastic sheets depicting miniature versions of the metal grids.

Once drawings or photographs had fixed the positions of a batch of objects, divers with a check list of their numbers began raising these objects to the surface. To lift an amphora, a diver simply held it upside down and poured air into the jar, which

Left: diver with amphora and the grid used for mapping the location of the finds at Yassi Ada. A composite blueprint of the ship and its cargo emerged from the painstaking photographic and plotting techniques used by the expedition.

Below: an amphora recovered from the Yassi Ada wreck, originally used for water and wine. Shells and pebbles had sifted down through their broken seals to replace the wine.

then ballooned up to bob upon the waves until collected. All told the wreck proved to hold about 900 of the big, bulbous pots.

It also contained concreted lumps of sand and shells forming molds around the spaces left by rusted iron articles. Using a jeweler's diamond-edged saw, the archaeologists sliced open these molds. By pouring liquid synthetic rubber in the hollows they found that they could make accurate casts of the vanished iron objects. In this fashion they reconstructed implements including billhooks, axheads, pickaxes, a shovel and a pruning hook, files, a caulking knife, and barnacle scrapers—proof of the vessel's self-sufficiency when out of reach of port facilities.

Men worked methodically downward through the wreck by layers, an air lift hosing sand and other debris to the surface to be gathered and explored for tiny articles.

Reconstructing Ancient Ships

Now began the daunting task of trying to discover how the ship was built. The man who tackled this conundrum was an American archaeology graduate, Frederick van Doorninck. Most thought he faced a super-human problem. A coat of silt had saved the stern part of the vessel but, grounded on a rocky bed, the bow had vanished totally. Moreover the remains of stern-end ribs were so scattered and scanty that people had almost failed to recognize them.

However, each scrap of timber had been tagged and photographed before removal. Van Doorninck was therefore able to obtain a complete drawing of fragments as they lay, together with a record of joints, holes left by rusted nails, and other clues to show how shipbuilders of 13 centuries ago had worked.

Van Doorninck discovered that the shipwrights had begun building up an outer shell from planks held in place by interlocking mortise and tenon joints. Reinforcing ribs came later. This was how the ancient Greeks and Romans had worked. But Byzantine builders had reversed the sequence for the upper hull: first fashioning supporting frames, then facing them with planks. This is a modern building method. Van Doorninck's detective work had apparently revealed a shipbuilding revolution in the making. His other studies pinpointed the exact position of the cabin, and showed that tiles found in that area had roofed it over. This solved the mystery of heaps of tiles already found with many ancient Roman ships.

From further studies of the 60-foot-long wreck came a new understanding of how ancient merchantmen were loaded, sailed, and anchored. No other underwater excavation of a wreck so old had been so detailed or had yielded so much information.

Below: the Isola Lunga wreck on first discovery, looking toward the stern post. In the foreground some of the ribs show through the sand and ballast stones still lie between them.

So far we have mentioned only wrecks of cargo vessels. Before the 1970s the Mediterranean had yielded no trace of a warship from classical times. From old writings, seals, coins, and sculptures people knew that such ships had been relatively long, slim vessels, armed with rams and powered for battle by many oars—sea greyhounds compared with those workhorses, the slow, sailing merchantmen. But much remained disputed—for instance, did the names bireme, trireme, quinquereme refer respectively to ships with two, three, and five banks of oars or to ships with two, three, and five rowers to each oar? Either interpretation raises huge problems of design.

Because they lacked a heavy cargo to weigh them down, breached or capsized warships were likelier to drift and break up than to sink and be preserved in mud and sand. Archaeologists were therefore astounded in the early 1970s when sand dredging off western Sicily bared the bones of a warship more than 2000 years old. The wreck had been preserved by a covering of sand under water only three feet deep, off the small Sicilian island of Isola Lunga.

The British aqualung archaeologist Honor Frost began its excavation in 1971. From early on she was convinced that she had stumbled on a unique find. Moreover the vessel was among the best preserved of all old ships so far discovered. She managed to recover over 30 feet of the keel; ribs; flooring; one-third of the port side's planks below the water line; part of the *wale* (that is, the timbers reinforcing the upper hull); and even scraps of superstructure. She also found the stern post—a rare survival for an ancient wreck and a vital clue to the ship's length.

Three years later she capped all this by finding the stern and some of the prow (including two of the ram's so-called "tusks") of a sister ship about 50 yards away from the first. Armed with these relics, Honor Frost was able broadly to determine the ships' lengths, outlines, age, and other vital details. She visualized both as long, slim vessels some 100 feet from end to end and 14 feet at their widest. This placed them, she considered, in the Libornian class of warship—an invention by Adriatic pirates adopted by Mediterranean sea powers and used for 600 years.

By carefully examining the wale for its supporting fixtures she worked out that there had been 17 oars each side—spaced about four feet apart. She reckoned that two oarsmen would have had to pull each oar. Honor Frost thus put the rowing crew at 68. But she knew from writings of the time that a warship bore as many fighting men as rowers. The crew and soldiers combined

Above top: oak, maple, and pine ribs of the Isola Lunga ship as they were at the start of the second season of excavation when the port side of the wreck was uncovered.

Above: the planking of the inside of the Punic ship's hull seen when the ribs had been removed. Honor Frost's excavation team nicknamed this part of the ship the "ballroom floor" because the joinery had remained in such excellent condition.

Left: ram of an ancient warship found lying about 40 yards south of the first wreck, assumed to have sunk at around the same time. The sign resembling a figure "7" painted on the ram is the letter *waw*, one of the Phoenicians' 22 consonants.

Above: sea battle of the First Punic War (264–41 B.C.) between Rome and Carthage during which the Isola Lunga wreck was probably sunk. In 260 the Romans built their first large fleet of 120 standard battleships, supposedly in the incredibly short time of two months. One reason for this series of three wars in the 3rd and 2nd centuries B.C. was that Rome wanted to break the hold of Carthage on several important islands of the western Mediterranean and particularly to prevent Sicily from being overrun.

would therefore have totaled as many as 136 men.

Radiocarbon dating suggested that both ships sank about 260–250 B.C. At this time the First Punic War between Rome and Carthage was raging around Sicily.

The ships' shapes, date, and location off Motya—an old Carthaginian artificial harbor—and between Trapani and Marsala (the Carthaginian ports Depana and Lilybaeum) hint strongly that these warships had been embroiled in a struggle that left Rome master of the western Mediterranean.

But for which warring side had they been built—the old established sea power of the Carthaginians, or the upstart Romans, whose first fleet only took to sea in 260 B.C., not long before these vessels foundered? In 241 B.C. Drepana and Lilybaeum suffered surprise attacks by Roman ships. Soon afterward Rome sank 50 Carthaginian ships and seized another 70 off western Sicily in a victory that closed the First Punic War and drove the Carthaginians from Sicily. Both powers had therefore had ships in the area where these two went down.

Conclusive proof that they were Carthaginian and not Roman came from carpenters' marks painted on the woodwork. These marks included not only ticks and crosses but most of the 22 letters of the now long-extinct Phoenician alphabet used by the Carthaginians. Seven of these letters stood out plainly. Ten others were more worn and deciphered with less certainty by the scholar who examined them.

But the most startling implication of the 200 marks and letters

Carthaginian Prefabrication

Left: the keel of the Punic warship with the carpenters' marks painted on it. The long, elegant ship was shell-built—the planking was erected before the skeleton was placed on it. Here the line painted down the center of the top inner face of the keel is shown, and to one side is another shipwright's sign like a bird's foot.

painted on the sunken ship is the light they throw upon the way in which the ships were made. Some carpenters' marks appeared below the floor timbers. Also, spilled paint had slopped across three planks in a way that shows that planks for the upper sides had been joined while lying flat, then added to the structure. Moreover, the planks' sides were straight, not curved to fit their neighbors like those of wooden ships in later times. Historians of shipbuilding suggest this may have influenced the design of the high prows and sterns of such early vessels as represented on old coins and sculptures.

A further fascinating detail is the beveled or slanting outer sides of those prefabricated planks that just cleared the sea's surface. Shaped in this way, they deflected spray away from the ship's armed passengers. No other ancient ships hitherto discovered had had this subtle feature.

Proof that the Carthaginians prefabricated vessels makes credible the fantastic rate of shipbuilding claimed by the ancient Roman writer Pliny and the Greek historian Polybius. Pliny claimed that it took 16 Romans only two months to build 100 warships in the First Punic War. According to Polybius, Romans subsequently took a mere three months to build more than twice that many vessels. Significantly, he described the Roman ship designs as based on Carthaginian models. No doubt both sides relied on similar techniques of mass production, largely based on huge warehouse stocks of planks and frames of standard shapes and sizes.

Honor Frost found that special care had gone into protecting the wooden hull. The ship's stern still bore bits of the lead sheath that had helped to ward off wood-boring mollusks and crustaceans. Between the lead and wood were fragments of cloth padding. Copper tacks driven into the wood had held the lead and cloth in place.

Inside the hull were twigs, branches, nutshells, and chips of wood used as *dunnage*—a cushion to protect the hull from the ballast stones inside. Some of the twigs still had leaves, and some of these had stuck into them soft, new putty used to seal up gaps in the woodwork. This shows that the ship had sunk soon after completion—maybe even on its maiden voyage.

The dunnage represented many kinds of plant including maple, oak, olive, bracken, and pistachio. The acid soil that bracken likes is not found at Marsala (Lilybaeum) where the vessel foun-

Below: Pliny the Younger (ca. 62–ca. 114), Roman author and administrator who claimed that a handful of Romans built over 100 warships in the space of two months. His *Letters* give an account of contemporary aristocratic life.

Above: dunnage or cushioning found under the ribs of the ship, which were made mostly of oak or maple. The planking was built of pine. When newly cleared of sand by Honor Frost's team of archaeologists, the colors of the wood were as they must have looked when new, although later they darkened through oxidation.

dered. Similarly pistachio is only found growing in certain places around the Sicilian coast. The volcanic ballast stones match a type from Pantelleria, a once Carthaginian-controlled island off Sicily. Between them, then, dunnage and ballast may hold clues to where the ship was built.

Mixed with pork bones, olive stones, and other garbage just above the keel were two small baskets. These proved to hold the most surprising find of all. Both contained pale, bamboolike stalks of a plant identified by analysts as *Cannabis sativa*. Honor Frost thinks that Carthaginian troops and oarsmen would have steeped the stalks in water, then drunk the drugged liquid as later sailors gulped down rum to help them beat fatigue or build up courage.

Underwater excavations of ancient merchantmen and warships have answered many questions about the ships on which the Mediterranean peoples sailed in ancient times. But the same sea that had concealed these secrets held others. Among these were many of the ports and harbors between which those ancient vessels plied. From 3000 B.C. to the collapse of the West Roman Empire in the 5th century A.D., ancient records and land-based archaeology reveal that civilized peoples built a chain of about 300 sizeable ports and cities around the Mediterranean. Thousands of lesser harbors, villages, and private villas lay strung

Searching for Submerged Ports

along the coasts between these centers. All told, these settlements enshrined the successive cultures of Semitic, Egyptian, Aegean, Greek, and Roman peoples.

In time, war, neglect, or earth movements wrecked roughly half the settlements where they stood. The rest subsided underneath the waves. Some slumped dramatically through earthquake: the Mediterranean is notoriously earthquake prone. Others sank imperceptibly as sea levels rose in relation to the land.

Tremors, modern harbor works, or other factors destroyed or concealed half the sunken ports and cities. But this left maybe 70 sites surviving under water. Archaeologists guessed that large parts of some of these remained intact beneath the waves. By probing their remains, the experts hoped to learn new information about the bases where the old seafaring peoples had built and sent forth ships.

Clues to the sites of underwater ports abounded in the works of classical historians and geographers—men like Herodotus, Thucydides, and Strabo. Among sites easily located, an obvious early choice for exploration was the old Phoenician port of Tyre, on what is now the coast of southern Lebanon. No ancient Mediterranean seaport had a more romantic history. Dating from at least the 15th century B.C., Tyre outstripped its parent city Sidon to become the Mediterranean's greatest trading center. Hiram, King of Tyre (970–936 B.C.), enormously enhanced the city's maritime position. He linked the port's three offshore islands and built a southern or "Egyptian" harbor. Tyre was then the chief Phoenician center for trade and starting point for exploration and colonization of the western Mediterranean. From Tyre in about 900 B.C. Phoenician sailors first ventured out into the

Below: yellow stalks identified as *cannabis sativa* were found in two baskets in the keel of the ship with the kitchen waste. Honor Frost thinks it likely that the soldiers and sailors on board infused the stalks in water and drank it to counteract fatigue or fear.

Left: Hiram I, king of Tyre, receiving a messenger. Son of Abi-baal, he is linked by some accounts in a close relationship with the Israelites under Solomon.

Above: the siege of Tyre by the soldiers of Alexander the Great. Most of Phoenicia yielded to Alexander, but Tyre, which had been besieged in vain for 13 years by the Babylonian King Nebuchadnezzar, resisted and underwent seven months of siege in 332 B.C. Alexander was forced to equip a fleet of ships for a blockade of the harbor before the city could be taken. It was then totally destroyed and its inhabitants were slaughtered or sold into slavery.

Right: the ruins of Tyre, now the site of an insignificant cotton and tobacco town called Sur in Lebanon. After Alexander had brought an end to Tyre's predominance the action of the sea added silt to his artificial mole so that the island-fortress was robbed of its strongest defense.

Atlantic. Soon afterward, Tyre founded Carthage—which for centuries controlled the western Mediterranean. Tyre lost importance later, but flourished until 332 B.C. when Alexander the Great captured and destroyed the port, spanning the sea gap to the island by building a massive mole or causeway over 1000 yards wide. Later, sand piled up along the mole, and the decayed port became a peninsula. Meanwhile, its harbor works were lost beneath the waves.

The man whose work rediscovered Tyre's ancient underwater structures was a French Jesuit priest, Père Antoine Poidebard. Surprisingly, he carried out his work between 1935 and 1937—

that is, before the aqualung had brought that freedom of movement we now consider indispensable to underwater archaeology. Nevertheless, Poidebard made the most of the technology available. By means of aerial photographs he traced the outline of submerged harbor works. Then he sent down helmeted divers to measure the underwater masonry and to take archaeology's first underwater photographs. Because their heavy gear made the men slow and clumsy, Poidebard had local skin divers help by pointing out features of special interest. These divers proved capable of plunging more than 40 feet below the surface and laboring for 90 seconds before they rose to take breath. Such feats led archaeologists to guess that similarly durable Phoenician divers must have helped to build the underwater structures in the first place.

Because the water was nowhere very deep, men could place buoys above key underwater points. Poidebard could then survey the site. He also even made three-dimensional camera studies of submerged walls by photographing them from the surface through a glass-bottomed bucket half thrust beneath the water. Poidebard learned that the harbor walls' foundations comprised precisely positioned blocks supporting concrete faced with stone. Some blocks had lead packing and were joined by iron dowels. A major find was an immense concrete wharf bisecting one harbor basin to create an area for building and repairing vessels. Moreover there were signs that the Phoenicians had ingeniously capped Tyre's northern and southern offshore reefs with massive walls in order to save harbor approaches from the erosive effect of storms.

Thanks to Poidebard's pioneering work we now have a pretty clear idea of exactly where the famous port of Tyre extends, and how it was constructed.

Since the 1930s we have discovered much about drowned wrecks and ports. Year by year, underwater archaeology lays bare the seabed's secrets. But we still don't know just how those quinqueremes were built, or precisely what Minoan vessels looked like. Many of the Mediterranean's mysteries will continue to intrigue and baffle us, and maybe future generations.

The Ancient Port of Tyre

Above: stone Phoenician anchor found by divers working with Père Poidebard at the sunken harbor of Tyre. He found that the harbor itself consisted of two basins enclosed by moles constructed of large blocks set on the existing rock. Substantial quays bordered the shore, and the entrance was on the south side.

Left: over 20 years later a team of young marine archaeologists leaves Nice, France to follow in Poidebard's footsteps. The Jesuit priest had also made a pioneering survey of Sidon, a port on the same flat coastline north of Tyre; the team's itinerary included the ancient Phoenician ports of Tripoli, Tyre, and Sidon.

Chapter 9
Who Really Discovered America?

Every schoolboy knows that Christopher Columbus first discovered America for the Spanish in 1492. But did he? Scholars and archaeologists argue fiercely that Columbus was almost certainly not the first European to sail across the Atlantic and step ashore on the North American continent. English merchants from Bristol may well have been the first. Many believe that Bjarni Herjolfsson, a Norwegian Viking, may have stepped ashore as early as A.D. 985. Others argue that Irish monks were the real pioneers. Another faction maintains that the Welsh prince Madoc was the first. The claims are numerous, and this chapter examines the evidence.

For weeks the three Spanish ships had been sailing with no glimpse of land. Hour by hour, day by day, a persistent wind pushed them westward, away from the Canary Islands where they had stocked up with provisions.

It was late September in 1492 and the 90 seamen aboard the *Niña*, the *Pinta*, and the *Santa María* grew understandably scared. They believed no one had ever sailed for so long in one direction without sighting land. Scholars had long before established the idea that the world was round. But no one had actually circled the globe or shown that land indeed rimmed the western Atlantic. For all the crews knew, nothing but trackless ocean lay ahead. They wondered how long their Italian-born admiral Christopher Columbus would persist in his plan to reach the Indies from the east, in order to bypass the Moslems controlling the Asian route to this rich trading region. Already, the seamen surmised, they might have sailed too far to return in the teeth of a wind that was chasing them ever farther from home.

Unrest was fueled by the discomfort of shipboard life. Few had bunks to sleep on. The dull, inadequate food began to run low. Faults showed up in their frail wooden craft—none as large as many a modern seagoing yacht.

Men began secretly grumbling. Complaints led to plots to oust a commander evidently bent on sacrificing his crew to what now seemed a monomaniac's fantasy. It took all of Columbus' skills as a commander to prevent discontent erupting in mutiny. He

Opposite: painting by Jerry Lazare of Leif Eriksson's landing at Vinland. The scene is based on L'anse Aux Meadows, a remote fishing village on the northern tip of Newfoundland, Canada. This painting is based on Helge Ingstad's expeditions.

kept control by a judicious mixture of threat and promise—threat of punishment for dissidents, and promise of a big cash reward for the first man to sight land.

After more than a fortnight at sea, one of the two Pinzón brothers captaining the *Niña* and the *Pinta* suddenly cried "Land, land!" to Columbus aboard the nearby *Santa María*. Pinzón had glimpsed an islandlike shape in the distance. Night fell as the ships set course for his haven. But morning revealed no more than storm clouds mimicking land. This was just one of several false sightings.

Below: Christopher Columbus in 1519 in a portrait by Sebastiano de Piombo. Born in Genoa in 1451 the son of a weaver, Columbus went to sea at an early age.

After more than three weeks, Columbus knew he had spanned more than 2000 miles, but he kept this great distance a secret to avoid scaring his men. However, seagulls began to show up, and after nearly four weeks on the ocean the crews glimpsed flocks of land birds. The birds were probably on their southward autumn migration from North America to the Caribbean area. Columbus took heart and steered southwest after the birds, judging that they would be unlikely to stray far from land. By October 8 the numbers of birds increased and the air grew fresh and fragrant, reminding the men of Seville in the spring. Three days later came the first clear proofs that land lay at hand. The crew of the flagship *Santa María* noticed a green branch. Next, men from the *Pinta* fished up a carved stick. People on board the *Niña* discovered a thorn branch with berries on it. That night Columbus thought he glimpsed a light in the distance, and claimed and later received the reward. But it was 2 a.m. on October 12 before Rodrigo de Triana aboard the *Pinta* glimpsed land in the moonlight. It proved no more than a small green island, peopled by black-haired, olive-skinned natives, whom Columbus mistakenly took to be Asian Indians. Later that day Columbus set foot here on San Salvador (Watlings Island) in the Bahamas.

In spite of his subsequent landfalls in Central and South

Right: allegory of Columbus discovering America with fanciful figures gazing up at him from the unfamiliar waters. On the morning of October 12, 1492 Columbus went ashore on what he believed to be Asia. It was actually the island of San Salvador in the Bahamas, 500 miles southeast of Florida.

America, Columbus always believed he had reached the fringe of East Asia. It was only when Spanish and other voyagers had mapped and colonized the Americas that Columbus gained fame as the discoverer of a brand new continent.

But did he really discover it? He was plainly not the first man in the Americas. The Amerindians' ancestors had peopled both continents long before. How far back is disputed. Some prehistorians put their arrival about 30,000 years ago; others even earlier. All agree, however, that these Stone Age explorers came in on foot across a land bridge once linking Siberia with Alaska. From North America's northwestern tip, hunters probed south, and when the Europeans arrived they found Amerindians in every habitable corner of the Americas. But the inflow of people from Asia was stemmed as ice caps melted some 10,000 years ago and meltwater raised ocean levels, submerging the Bering Land Bridge between Asia and North America. Archaeological evidence shows that the Bering Strait thus created proved no barrier to the Eskimos' maritime ancestors. But the civilized world once thought no one had made the long sea crossing from the east, until Columbus anchored off the Bahamas. However, old records, recent research, and voyages made in reconstructions of early ships now suggest that Columbus was only the last of a long line of European voyagers who sailed west across the Atlantic, discovering and rediscovering America.

In the late 1970s close study of old Bristol customs records revealed that ships from this west British port may have been secretly fishing off Newfoundland and even trading with the local Indians as early as 1479—that is, 13 years before Columbus discovered the Bahamas. Officially the ships were trading with Ireland. But they took too long about it. One of the ships, for instance, completed a return voyage in 115 days, during which time another vessel completed three round trips to Ireland.

Thorn Branch of Columbus

Below: an Eskimo village. The first inhabitants of the New World were Stone Age explorers who crossed the then-existing land bridge across the Bering Strait from Siberia in Asia to Alaska. The Eskimos of North America are the most direct descendants of these early colonizers.

Bristol Seamen or Welsh Prince

Below: John Cabot leaving Bristol in 1497 in the ship *Matthew* carrying letters from Henry VII of England. These granted John and his three sons "full and free authority . . . upon theyr own proper costs and charges, to seeke out . . . whatsoever isles, countries, regions or provinces . . . unknown to all Christians."

These vessels officially plied at a loss persistently enough to make their trading figures suspect. Above all the nature of their cargoes changed. Before 1479 many exported cloths, iron, salt, wine, and vinegar. From 1479 they switched to cloth and dyeing substances, condemned wine (used for pickling fish), and honey. Their imports altered strikingly, too. Instead of linen, Irish oak, salmon, and other articles of obviously Irish origin, the ships brought back salted and pickled fish, and timber. It seems unlikely that these could have come from mainland Europe, for almost anywhere there the Bristol seamen would have met hostile monopolies. The historian who analyzed these figures suggested

that the Bristol shipmen were really taking stores to a depot in Newfoundland where they caught fish in the rich offshore waters, then landed to mend damaged ships, and also to trade cloth for furs with local Indians. Naturally enough, they would have kept their commercially valuable discovery a closely guarded secret. Unfortunately for this theory, no traces of any such depot have so far turned up.

Intriguingly enough, though, the chief sponsor of John Cabot's voyage to mainland North America in 1497 was a leading Bristol citizen, called Richard Amerycke. In 1896 a local antiquary, Alfred Hudd, claimed that America had been named in Amerycke's honor and not, as customarily believed, for the contemporary Italian explorer Amerigo Vespucci. But America's "Amerigo" origin is much the better authenticated.

Standing at the eastern threshold of the North Atlantic, the British Isles have produced several rivals to Columbus. Some have had support from unexpected quarters. In 1962 the Russian geographer Samuel Varshavsky suggested that the adventurous Carmelite friar Nicholas of Lynne had anticipated Columbus by more than a century, arriving in America soon after 1360. The evidence is slim indeed.

The Welsh advance claims for their own Prince Madoc, who predated Nicholas by almost two centuries. Old writings depict

Above: Amerigo Vespucci, a middleaged Florentine businessman who sailed with Alonso de Ojeda to South America in 1499. Vespucci probably gave his name to the continents of the New World.

Left: Prince Madoc leaving Wales on his voyage to America in the 12th century. There is a memorial at Fort Morgan near Mobile Bay, Alabama that asserts: "In memory of Prince Madoc, a Welsh explorer, who landed on the shores of Mobile Bay in 1170 and left behind with the Indians the Welsh language."

Madoc as a son of Owain Gwynedd, a powerful ruler of North Wales. Not much is known about him. Indeed, only considerable study has separated Madoc the voyager from nine other Madocs. He emerges from legend as a big, bold, handsome, landless, sea-loving adventurer. The chance find in an English sale-room of old port records dating from 1166–1183 links his name with the ship *Gwennan Gorn* (Horn Gwennan) which also figures in the Madoc legend.

Early accounts suggest that Madoc set forth with about 30 men in one or two ships—presumably tubby, square-sailed vessels with single masts, such as appear on old ports' seals. Among fanciful references to Madoc's "magic unsinkable ship," we find more credible references to his use of a lodestone as a primitive ship's compass and the fact that he fastened his ship's

Above: the stone pier from which it is claimed that Prince Madoc left for his voyage to the New World. The pier is at Rhos-on-Sea, a suburb of Colwyn Bay described in contemporary accounts as Aber-Kerric.

Above right: painting of a Mandan Indian village. Boats like Welsh coracles can be seen in the foreground. Legend has it that the Mandans were visited by Welshmen, who were familiar with these small, broad boats made of wickerwork and covered with a waterproof layer of skin, canvas, or tarred or oiled cloth.

timbers with horn nails rather than iron nails which would have produced false compass readings.

The port record discovered in England gives Madoc's point of departure as Aber-Kerric-Guignon. Tradition identifies this with Rhos-on-Sea in North Wales, where a rocky beach seemingly marks the remains of the old stone pier on the former river-mouth from which Madoc allegedly set forth on the first of two long westward voyages. His motive for travel seemed twofold: civil disturbance at home and the urge to seek land rumored to lie in the west. Where he sailed and what he saw are clouded by fantasy and distorted by British post-Columbian writers seeking to prove their country's prior claim to have discovered America. However, a significant early account, evidently written before 1240, was produced by someone called Willem the Minstrel. Willem tells how Madoc discovered a "treacherous garden in the sea"—perhaps the great weedy tract of the Sargasso Sea met by Columbus. Some have supposed that "one of the isles of Llion" that Willem describes was Bermuda or somewhere in the Bahamas. According to Willem, Madoc returned from his first voyage to fit out another, which some authors believe set out from the island of Lundy in the Bristol Channel.

Proof that Madoc indeed founded at least one colony in North America apparently came to light after Welshmen began settling there in the 17th century. A Welsh clergyman wrote that he was traveling overland from Carolina to Virginia in 1666 when he was captured by Welsh-speaking Indians. Later came various reports of Welsh-speaking Indians claiming Welsh ancestry. Then explorers allegedly discovered white-skinned, fair-haired Indians deep inside North America. These were the Mandans of the Missouri River area. They reputedly made Welsh-type coracles, and people claimed that their words for coracle, paddle, and many other objects strikingly resembled the Welsh equivalents. In 1837 smallpox effectively destroyed the tribe and its traditions were lost.

Meanwhile, more hints on its "Welsh" origin emerged, notably a letter written in 1810 by John Sevier, "founder of Tennessee." Sevier claimed that an old Cherokee chief had told him of indianized whites descended from Welsh colonists. These had landed at Mobile Bay near the mouth of the Alabama River, then traveled north, the chief had declared. This could have happened long after Columbus discovered America. But a Spanish chart of 1519 labels the Mobile Bay area *Tierra de los Gales* (Land of the Welsh), linking the Welsh with America before they had any business to be there—unless perhaps the Madoc tradition is true. Borne by the winds and currents, Madoc could well have fetched up on this northern shore of the Gulf of Mexico about the year 1170. But there is no indisputable proof that he did.

One thing is certain: Madoc lived long after Europe's first undoubted voyagers to set foot in North America. In about 1070 the German monk Adam of Bremen wrote an ecclesiastical history. In it he describes the Norse discovery of Vinland—a distant isle where grapes and wheat grew wild. Adam had obtained his information in Denmark, but the discoverers of what we now know to have been part of North America were actually of Norwegian origin. Proof largely lies in the old Icelandic *sagas*—family histories at first passed on by word of mouth, but eventually written down. Many scholars dismissed these ancient tales as mere folklore until in 1837 a Danish historian showed that they had a factual basis.

Norse Emigrants in Iceland

Coupled with archaeological finds, the sagas give us amazing insight into exploration of the North Atlantic 1000 years ago. At that time most ships were frail and largely lacked effective navigation aids. No wonder most seamen seldom sailed far out of sight of land. Norse adventurers, though, were made of sterner stuff than most. Roving in their long, lean, sharp-prowed, square-sailed Viking ships, Norse emigrants had settled Iceland before A.D. 900. Briefly outlawed from Iceland, in 981 Erik the Red sailed west to Greenland, where he soon set up a colony upon the south-

Below: Erik the Red arriving in 982 at Greenland where he set up a colony. He stayed for the three years of his banishment from Iceland and then returned later with about 450 settlers. The colony lasted for more than 400 years, and in 1261 Greenland became the farthest outpost of the Norwegian empire.

Above: Leif Eriksson sights land in America in a painting by Christian Krohg. He first reached land at the third of Bjarni Herjolfsson's sighted lands where he anchored and rowed ashore. Then he sailed on to the other two, finally building a house for winter in what he called Vinland.

west coast. In about 986 the Norwegian merchant Bjarni Herjolfsson sailed off to join the colonists, but rough weather blew him off course and into dense fog where he drifted for days. At last the fog lifted and he glimpsed an unfamiliar, wooded coast ahead. Bjarni reckoned he had overshot Greenland and found land to the south. Rather than risk attack by natives, he altered course to the north. Days later another stretch of tree-clad shore appeared. Later still, Bjarni reached a harsh, rocky, icy landfall. He sailed on, eventually reaching the very fjord in Greenland where the original Norwegian colonists had landed.

Norse colonists flourished for centuries in Greenland, but in that treeless land they always lacked wood. Thus Bjarni's story of forests to the southeast excited speculation. About the year 1001, Leif Eriksson (Leif, son of Erik the Red) hired Bjarni's vessel and took 25 men on what proved a successful voyage of rediscovery. Bjarni's rocky shore Leif christened Helluland (Flat Rock Land); the next, Markland (Forest Land); and the third and southernmost, Vinland (Wineland), from the grapes he found there.

The sagas describe this last landfall in astonishing detail. We learn that Leif sailed his ship between an offshore island and a cape jutting northward from the nearby mainland. He landed where a river flowed from a lake. Salmon teemed in both. Wild wheat and "grapes" flourished nearby, and grass grew through

Leif Eriksson Finds Vinland

Left: Danish map of the North Atlantic dated 1570 showing the British Isles, the Shetlands, Orkneys, Faeroes, and Iceland. Greenland is linked to the North American mainland which includes Vinland, Markland, and Helluland. They had long been deserted by this time.

Above: painting by an unknown 17th-century artist of two American Indians, called *Skraelings* (foreigners) by the Vikings. The Skraelings attacked Leif Eriksson's Norse settlements, and after his men left Vinland no white man set foot on Indian territory until the 1500s.

the frost-free winter, which had longer days than in Greenland or Iceland. Leif and his crew built sturdy houses and wintered there.

Next spring Leif sailed back to Greenland, but then his fellow Norsemen took up the challenge. Thorvald reached Vinland but died in a fight with Indians, whom the Norsemen called "Skraelings." However, Thorvald's followers spent two years ashore before retracing their journey.

About A.D. 1006 Thorfinn Karlsefni took people and cattle, meaning to colonize Vinland. They too built houses and Thorfinn's wife bore him a son—the first recorded European child to start life in the New World. The first winter proved harsh, and only a stranded whale saved the pioneers from starving. However, the local Indians seemed friendly, bartering furs for milk and red cloth. Then quarrels erupted. Two Norsemen died in the fighting. Outnumbered, Karlsefni pulled out.

Leif's sister Freydis led a separate bid to colonize Vinland. There were other attempts, but all foundered. By about 1400 worsening climate destroyed the Greenland colony too, removing a vital stepping stone on the Norsemen's northern route to America. Only their sagas survived to tell how a New World had been found and lost.

But what part of this continent had the Vikings actually discovered? They vividly described the places they saw, but lacked the navigation tools needed to pinpoint their position. For

Above: the Kensington Rune Stone, supposedly a pre-Columbian document. Found in Kensington, Douglas County, Minnesota in 1898 by a Swedish immigrant farmer called Olof Ohman, the stone was said to describe an expedition by 30 Norwegians and "Goths" traveling west from Vinland. Most scholars believe the stone is a 19th-century fake. The stone is about 2.5 feet high and 3 to 6 inches thick.

decades archaeologists searched unsuccessfully for traces of Norse settlements in North America. Such evidence was essential to prove the sagas' story. In 1898 the so-called Kensington Rune Stone turned up in Minnesota, but its "old" Scandinavian inscriptions proved fakes. In 1965 Yale University disclosed a map depicting Vinland, supposedly drawn in about 1440. For years even experts were fooled. Then ink tests unmasked the Vinland Map as a modern hoax.

Meanwhile, a Norwegian archaeologist had made a meaningful find. With the old sagas as his chief travel guides, Helge Ingstad set out in 1960 to look for signs of lost Norse settlement along the northeast coast of North America. Walking, flying, traveling by bus, he scoured the seaboard from Rhode Island northward. Ingstad knew that two days' northward sailing had separated Bjarni's glimpses of two wooded shores and that three more had brought Bjarni to a glaciated coast. In all, Bjarni had spent nine days sailing to Greenland from what had probably been Vinland. Ingstad knew, too, the time Leif Eriksson had required to retrace Bjarni's voyage in the opposite direction. By marrying this information with the pattern of ocean winds and currents in the area and by calculating the likely rates of sail for

Right: Helge Ingstad and his wife Anne, who led expeditions to discover where on the northeast coast of America Leif Eriksson had landed at Vinland. After a great deal of scrutiny he decided that Vinland was probably situated in northern Newfoundland, the most easterly territory in North America. Eventually he reached L'Anse aux Meadows where remains of a Norse settlement were found in 1960 and excavated over the following eight years.

The Hunt for Vinland

Viking craft, Ingstad believed that he could find the places so clearly described in the sagas. His travels convinced him that cold Baffin Island had been Bjarni's Helluland. He thought Labrador's white beaches backed by forests matched Leif Eriksson's account of Markland. From there Leif Eriksson had needed a mere two days to get to Vinland. Ingstad felt that the Norseman's destination must have been Newfoundland—fish-rich, grassy, forested, and mild in winter.

Because Newfoundland's climate is unsuitable for grapes, many archaeologists have refused to recognize Newfoundland as Leif's Vinland. One explorer who retraced Leif's voyage by boat in 1966 favored Massachusetts as the likely site. There, far south of Newfoundland, wild grapes abound beside Nantucket Sound. But Ingstad noticed that some Viking voyagers had reported picking grapes in winter somewhere north of Vinland. Ingstad argued that the Vikings' grapes had not been grapes at all, but the juicy red squash-berries from which Newfoundlanders make wine today. On the other hand, maybe "Vinland" could be a simple mistake, based on the misreading of one letter in an old Scandinavian word. If so, the Norsemen had christened it "Grassland"—a likely name for an island with good grazing.

Either way, Ingstad clung unshakably to his conviction that he need hunt for Vinland no farther south than Newfoundland. Accordingly he visited fishing villages there. He was searching for old ruins near a shore facing an island flanked by a cape, and backed by meadows and forest, with a river that flowed to the sea from a lake. His persistence paid off. At last he met someone who had heard of something likely at L'Anse aux Meadows ("Meadow Bay"). George Decker, a leading local personality, directed Ingstad to the site, where he found a river flowing from a small lake. It wound through low-lying land and emptied in a bay. Nearby stood an island, and a northward jutting cape. Far off lay the shore of Labrador. Inland grew grasses, berried bushes, and coniferous woodland. The waters around teemed with fish. Ingstad found he could trap fish in man-made tidal pools as the Norsemen had done. Here, too, darkness fell about 4.30 on midwinter day. It all matched the sagas' Vinland like a

Below: clusters of wild grapes of a type known to have grown in abundance on America's northeastern coast around 1000 A.D. when Leif Eriksson landed. The Vikings, having come from the frozen regions of Greenland and Iceland, found Vinland a remarkably mild and fertile place.

Left: woodcut attributed to Olaus Magnus from 1555 showing the Vikings spearing salmon. According to the sagas, the fish were plentiful and the largest they had ever seen.

Did the Irish Arrive First?

Right: the site, just west of L'Anse aux Meadows, a tiny fishing village with about 70 inhabitants. On a broad grass plateau through which Black Duck Brook runs out to Epaves Bay were the remains of Norse dwelling places.

dream. But there was more to come. Inshore a low rise bore the fuzzy outlines of old tumbled buildings. Surely here, if anywhere, lay the remains of homes fashioned by the New World's first European visitors.

Beginning in 1961, years of summer-season excavation followed. They revealed no less than eight structures. The largest had been a house 70 feet long, 55 feet broad, and subdivided into six rooms, mostly small. Floors had consisted of beaten clay, walls of turf, and grassy sods had waterproofed the roof. There were signs of ancient hearths and holes for cooking in. A separate structure turned out to be a smithy. There were also signs of a steam bath—a kind of primitive sauna.

The buildings resembled known medieval Norse houses. A brooch and part of a Norse spindle confirmed this supposition. Radiocarbon tests of wood from the ruins gave the significant date of about A.D. 1000. Only a few dozen people had lived here, and then only briefly, before fire had burned down their homes. It had been a small, poor settlement. No on-site relics linked it

Below right: a 4-inch-long, ring-headed bronze pin found close to a cooking pit. Its type is well known from other Viking studies—similar examples have been found in Norway, Iceland, the Shetland Islands, and the Isle of Man. It was probably used to fasten men's capes on one shoulder so that their sword arm would be free.

Below: a spindle whorl made of soapstone found near the doorway of one of the houses. It is similar to one found at a Norse farm in Greenland and indicates that there must have been women and wool at L'Anse aux Meadows.

directly with Leif Eriksson. But it was undeniably Norse and predated Columbus' voyage by nearly 500 years. The finds at L'Anse aux Meadows brilliantly justified Ingstad's theory and rewrote North American history.

If the Newfoundland discoveries solved one mystery, they only pointed up another. For old Norse writings suggest that white men had preceded Northmen to North America. Near Vinland supposedly lay *Hvitramannaland* ("Land of the White Men"), also called *Irland-ed-Mikla* ("Ireland the Great"). Also two Skraelings (American Indians) reportedly told Vikings they had seen men dressed in white, shouting and carrying poles with cloths attached. The Vikings believed this description fitted the Irish, whose priests dressed in white and may have carried banners in a religious procession.

This account appears to support claims that the Irish had found America before the Vikings. Such claims rest on an epic voyage narrated in the *Navigatio Brendani*, or "Voyage of St. Brendan," first written down about A.D. 870 but probably far older. More than 120 Latin versions survive, and there are many others. With surprising consistency, they describe how a 6th-century Irish saint sailed west into the Atlantic with a select band of companions, variously put at from 14 to 150. They sought a fabled Paradise. After seven years of adventures, St. Brendan arrived there to find a beautiful land luxuriantly covered in plants. The narrative left its location vague. But St. Brendan's Island, as this paradise came to be called, made a major impression upon Europe's mapmakers.

A Catalonian chart of 1375 put it just west of southern Ireland. Other mapmakers took it to be one of the "Fortunate Isles" of antiquity. Accordingly the Hereford chart of the 13th century located it among the Canary Islands. Various 14th- and 15th-century maps give its name to Madeira. But as the eastern Atlantic became better known, mapmakers began pushing the island farther west into that ocean. By the early 1800s the Atlantic was well known enough for most people to dismiss the whole story as a myth. Yet soon there were scholars suggesting that St. Brendan's landfall had been no less than America. They cited the Viking "evidence" and declared that the plants and creatures described in the *Navigatio* tallied with America's. Then, too, Brendan had reportedly guessed his "island" paradise must be a continent because he failed to reach its limits. A weedy sea that trapped Brendan's boat until his men rowed themselves clear sounded suspiciously like the Sargasso Sea. This suggested that Brendan had maybe reached the Bahamas by the southerly route that Columbus followed much later.

But would Irish monks have risked a daring exploratory voyage some 1400 years ago? They possessed only small, open, rather unmanageable sailing boats; a sketchy notion of geography; and little more than sun, stars, and birds as guides. Undoubtedly they did sail far to find secluded islands where they founded monasteries. They built beehive homes and boatlike oratories on the forbidding Great Skellig island, eight miles off the coast of western Ireland. Sailing northward, they passed the Shetlands and reached the Faroe Islands where Vikings found them living in the 8th century. In 825 an Irish monk reporting a

Below: St. Brendan the Navigator, whose popular adventures were read in nine languages during the Middle Ages. Ordained in 512, he attracted a band of followers and began founding monasteries. Two survive in the counties of Kerry and Galway in Ireland.

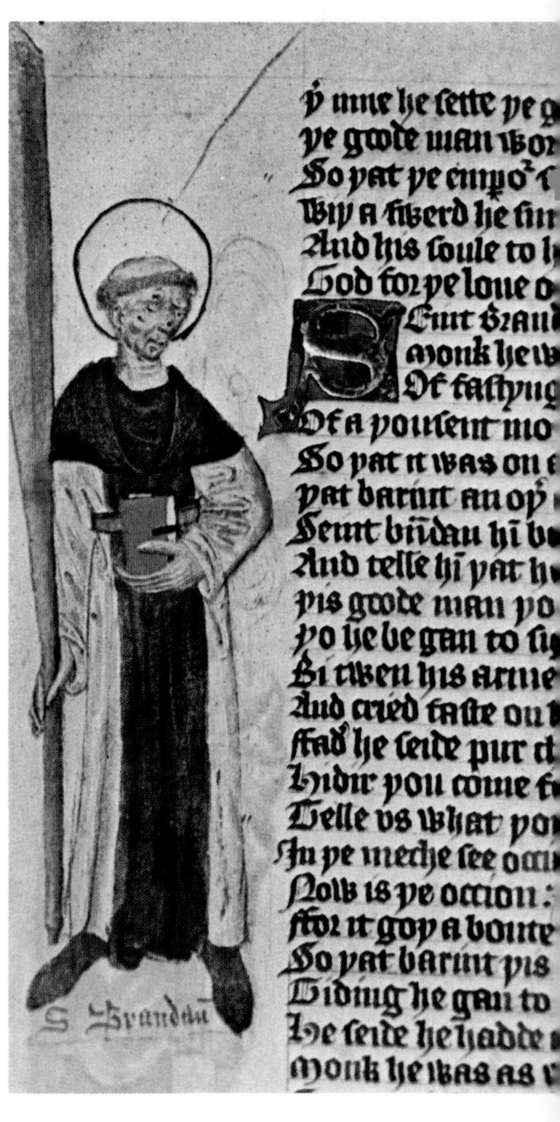

Above: hermit cells at the Skelligs, County Kerry, Ireland. Irish priests and monks seeking converts to Christianity were among the first people to travel in frail boats across uncharted seas.

30-year-old account of Iceland, mentioned the summer glow from the Arctic midnight sun, and pack ice north of Iceland. Thus Irish monks voyaged freely between North Atlantic island stepping stones before the Vikings. Could they, like the Vikings, have sailed the northern route to North America?

The British sailor-writer Tim Severin believed so, and thought this route more likely than any suggested southern crossing. To prove his point, in 1976 he set out on a voyage in what he felt must be the long-vanished wake of St. Brendan's vessel. Appropriately, Severin named his craft the *Brendan*. He built it in the image of its predecessor, basing his design on old chronicles and the living tradition of the Irish *curragh*—a long type of open boat still used by Irish fishermen. The result was a whalelike craft 36 feet long, with an outer skin of 49 tanned oxhides, joined by 20,000 flaxen threads, and drawn across a "wicker-work" ash-lath frame lashed together by two miles of leather thongs. Tarpaulins stretched between the gunwales to keep out storm waves gave *Brendan* the appearance of a giant *kayak*. Two square flaxen sails emblazoned with red Celtic crosses provided the driving power.

Right: stitching together the hull of the *Brendan* with 14-strand flax thread. Following specifications from the earliest surviving Latin text of the *Voyage of St. Brendan*, Tim Severin's crew used ox hides tanned in a solution of pungent oak bark.

Because modern curraghs are rowing boats, and have tarred canvas coverings, no one knew quite how the oxhide sailing ship *Brendan* might handle, or if she would remain afloat. Even big modern trawlers have sunk in North Atlantic storms.

Severin prudently set sail in spring, when winds were likeliest to aid an east-west transatlantic crossing via the northern island stepping stones, for he knew his square-sailed boat, unlike a modern yacht, would make no progress in a headwind. From St. Brendan's supposed starting point at Brandon Creek in southwest Ireland, Severin coasted north past the Aran Islands and Iona to the Isle of Lewis, then on to reach the Faroes. Meanwhile the crew grew hardened to their primitive mariners' conditions: cramped quarters, monotonous food, and the stench from a leather hull, waterproofed with wool grease. Incidentally, warm southern waters would have dissolved the grease and sunk the vessel, a fact that made a northern route for St. Brendan's voyage that much more likely. The men learned of both the *Brendan*'s strengths and limitations. Only six days out, the craft impressively weathered a gale. But storms and calms later meant that she spent more than a week covering the last 100 miles to the Faroes. Above all, though, her flexible hull held and kept out water. Two months after setting forth, the *Brendan* proudly sailed into the harbor of Reykjavic, the capital of Iceland.

It was now late July. Contrary winds and threatened autumn gales forced Severin's crew ashore for winter. Next May they resumed their voyage—their target, Newfoundland. This second leg proved nearly fatal. In late May mountainous seas swamped the cabin. The crew survived—thanks to pumping and an oxhide shelter hastily rigged across the gap that had let in the water. Worse followed a month later. The *Brendan* had cleared southern Greenland when she ran into a huge field of ice floes. Two vast slabs ground together, nipping the *Brendan* and punching a hole

In the Wake of St. Brendan

Below left: May 17, 1976, launch day for the *Brendan*. Blustery winds snap at her flags and pennants at Brandon Creek in southwest Ireland.

Below: the *Brendan* breathes with the waves as it nears the coast of Newfoundland.

Far left: Tim Severin navigating according to the heavens. Each day a radio report was made pinpointing their position to the nearest coastal stations in case rescue aircraft were needed.

Left: the *Brendan* sails off from Iceland, the westernmost outpost of Irish exploration then proved.

The "Great Fish Jasconius"

in the hull. Again only pumping and a leather patch sewn over the puncture saved the crew from an icewater death. At last, in July 1977, and six weeks and 3500 miles out from Iceland, the *Brendan* touched shore in Newfoundland.

This voyage by a boat of ancient design brilliantly proved that St. Brendan *could* have reached America. Moreover the *Brendan*'s route helped throw new light on some of his adventures. The *Navigatio* describes a narrow channel separating a "Paradise of Birds" from an "Island of Sheep." The word Faroe in fact means "Island of Sheep" and the *Brendan*'s journey through the Faroes took it past Mykines Island whose cliffs spewed seabirds like confetti. The *Navigatio* also vividly describes an "Island of Smiths" whose hostile savages hurled molten slag at the passing Irish vessel, and seemed to set the isle ablaze by stoking up their furnaces. The account fits Iceland, with its frequent volcanic activity.

The "Great Fish Jasconius" of the *Navigatio* could only be a whale. At different stages in their voyage the *Brendan*'s crew glimpsed no less than five species of these giant creatures, some attracted to their odoriferous, whale-shaped craft. The legend also described St. Brendan's encounter with a "thick white cloud" and a crystal column—identifiable respectively as fog and an iceberg. Vessels coasting from Greenland down to Labrador often meet these hazards. Severin saw both. At one time his crew were grabbing hold of floes to urge the *Brendan* through the pack ice—an improvised technique recalling how St. Brendan's

Below: St. Brendan at the "Isle of Smiths," described as a stony island without a leaf or blade of grass. Sailing closer St. Brendan and his companions saw a noisy party of smiths who hurled lumps of red-hot iron at the ship, and St. Brendan, identifying the place as hell, urged the monks away. It may have been an Icelandic volcano that appeared to stand at the gate of hell.

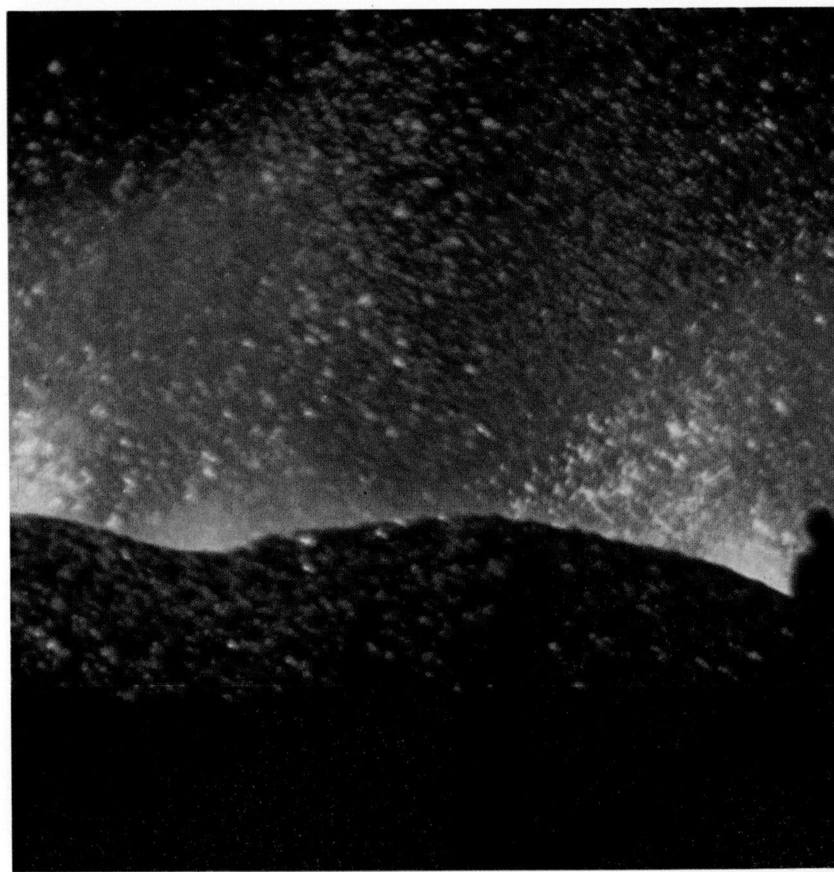

monks traditionally forced their vessel through a marble "net" to get a close glimpse of an iceberg.

Plainly the *Navigatio* is partly fiction. No one today believes its tale of fish surfacing to hear the saint say Mass. The numbers it gives are often symbolic: 3 for the Holy Trinity, 12 for Christ's Apostles, and so on. But much compels belief. Between the years A.D. 570 and A.D. 870 several Irish curraghs probably reached North America. The *Navigatio* may represent a confused compendium of the discoveries of those navigators who managed to return.

Even as Severin was sailing the *Brendan* to Newfoundland, scholars there were poring over local "proofs" that Irish or maybe other Celts had sailed in long ago. The clues were merely scratches in the rocks—but marks that some experts consider had been purposefully made. Slow-growing lichens had so well encrusted some that these at least seemed ancient. Similar scratches have turned up elsewhere in eastern North America. A casual observer would dismiss most as the random doodling of Red Indians or as furrows gouged by modern plows or rasped by stones embedded in the base of moving ice. However, certain students of old writing systems believe the scratches to be *ogam*—an ancient Celtic form of writing where straight lines differing in number, length, and angle stood for different letters. What appeared to be traces of this script convinced some scholars that early Irish priests had set their mark upon New England's rocks.

In 1976 Barry Fell in his book *America BC* went even further.

Above: a stone found at South Woodstock, Vermont, said to be carved with Runic inscriptions. According to Barry Fell, the lines are letters of the ogam alphabet.

Left: the eruption in January 1973 of Vestmannayjar volcano in Iceland. A sight similar to this may have greeted St. Brendan on his voyage to the Isle of Smiths.

Right: a root cellar in South Woodstock, Vermont. Barry Fell claims the chamber was a stone temple and dates from some time after 433 B.C.

Below: Buggibba Temple in Malta. A direct link can be deduced from the similarities between the architecture of ancient Maltese temples and the Neolithic structures of western Europe. Barry Fell has attempted to draw a similar parallel between the root cellars of Vermont and pre-Columbian Celtic mariners.

Summarizing his hypothesis, *The Times* of London declared Fell believed that New England rocks enshrined the speech of Celts who had lived in Spain and Ireland 3000 years ago. From this, Fell theorized that Celtic mariners had reached America and intermarried with Red Indians some 1500 years before St. Brendan's legendary transatlantic voyage. Among supporting evidence for this idea, Fell drew attention to New England's mysterious "root cellars"—stores for keeping root crops through the winter.

Many archaeologists dismiss Fell's theories as, to quote one critic, fruits of "the maniacal fringes of archaeology." They think that 17th-century European colonists made the stone-roofed caves that Fell refers to. But Fell argues that root cellars were unknown in the colonists' European homelands. Moreover he declared that some New England root cellars bore traces of old writings.

Admittedly the largest of such structures are not easy to explain away as food stores. Strangest of all are 22 "cells" composed of uncemented granite slabs that sprawl across Mystery Hill, a New Hampshire hillside 40 miles north of Boston. The major features include a flat-topped four-ton "Sacrificial Stone," rimmed by a rock-hewn gutter. Below the stone a passage leads into a long, Y-shaped, more than man-high chamber from which a resonant shaft rises eight feet to the Sacrificial Stone. One theory suggests this was a speaking tube that eerily conveyed the voice of a priest hidden in the chamber to devotees around the Sacrificial Stone above. These big, uncemented stone building blocks and crude roofing recall Europe's ancient megalithic structures. Yet as one scholar said, "The big things are too little, the small things so big." The site impressed him with disorder and naïveté. Maybe we have here a relatively recent fake or folly rather than an ancient monument influenced by European Bronze Age builders.

Mystery Hill is only one of many alleged circumstantial proofs of Old World voyagers that have been unearthed in North America. Some are blatant forgeries. But others merit careful study. A startling account of these appeared in 1971 in *Before Columbus* by Cyrus H. Gordon of Massachusetts' Brandeis University. Professor Gordon defends the authenticity of artifacts

Maniacal Fringe of Archaeology?

Left: the Sacrificial Stone of Mystery Hill, New Hampshire, thought by some to have a Neolithic religious significance.

Below: the Oracle Chamber at Mystery Hill.

that others have dismissed as spurious, or wrongly dated. To Gordon, evidence abounds of early Old World contacts with the New. Research convinced this specialist in the ancient cultures of the Mediterranean and Middle East that Vermont's one-roomed stone structures roofed by loaf-shaped megaliths resembled a 4000-year-old Maltese temple. He implies that both were built by Bronze Age mariners who had evolved a world-wide culture. Pottery from Japan appeared in Ecuador 5000 years ago, declares Gordon. He believes that a sculptured head recovered from within a Pre-Columbian pyramid in Mexico was a Roman work of art fashioned 1800 years ago. He cites a hoard of Roman and Arabic coins more than 1000 years old discovered off Venezuela as proof of a Moorish Pre-Columbian transatlantic voyage. Gordon also suggests that Portugal's Coimbra map of 1424 genuinely features areas of North America.

Most dramatic of all, perhaps, Professor Gordon claims genuine antiquity for two inscriptions found in North America. One involves lines and circles scratched into a stone found near Fort Benning, Georgia, in 1966. Manfred Metcalf, who discovered the stone, declared that he was looking for slabs to build

Hebrew Refugees in North America

Right: the Phaistos Disk, a relic from ancient Cretan archives. Impressed with 241 pictogram seals, this 4500-year-old clay disk holds the earliest known example of printing. Its 61 "words"—separated by lines and arranged in a spiral—may express a hymn to some god, but its hieroglyphics do not belong to any known language system. Manfred Metcalf has suggested that parallels may exist between Minoan and Mayan writings.

Above: Professor Israel Naamani of the University of Louisville, who has investigated the various Bar-Kokhba coins found in Kentucky. These may indicate Roman contact with the New World at an early date.

a barbecue pit when he found the stone in the crumbling wall of a 19th-century mill. Men had built the mill before Sir Arthur Evans found the first Minoan inscriptions at Knossos in the early 1900s. Yet the Metcalf Stone's inscriptions also seemed to be Minoan—possibly a Cretan inventory of around 1500 B.C. Professor Gordon remarks that there were also parallels between Cretan and Mayan writing. He suggests, too, that the "feathered headdress" and other objects pictured on the so-called Phaistos Disk from ancient Crete had counterparts in Aztec glyphs. Gordon suggests that back in Bronze Age times there must have been some cultural connection between seafarers of the eastern Mediterranean and the Amerindians.

Hebrew coins dating from Bar-Kokhba's anti-Roman revolt (A.D. 132–135) have reportedly turned up at three Kentucky sites since 1932. Unfortunately none of these finds resulted from methodical excavation by archaeologists. However, back in 1891 a United States Bureau of Ethnology report had actually published a Hebrew inscription found at Bat Creek in nearby Tennessee. Intriguingly, remarks Gordon, this inscription was printed upside down. The discoverer had wrongly thought the writing to be Cherokee. This is not surprising, because archaeologists found the stone lying under the skull of a dead chief buried with his wife and seven attendants in a mound that had been undisturbed for centuries. Not until 1964 did someone try to read the writing right way up. The result was no more than a cryptic Canaanite fragment. But scholars recognized the word "Judea" and the letter forms suggested a date about A.D. 100. This stone and the Bar-Kokhba coins convinced Professor Gordon that Hebrew refugees from Roman rule had somehow sailed to North America in the 2nd century A.D.

Bristol merchants, Welsh princes, Norse colonists, Irish monks, Celtic sailors—this chapter has examined the claims and evidence for most of the men and women who probably crossed the Atlantic from Europe to North America before Columbus got there. There are numerous other claims. In 1970 the Norwegian explorer Thor Heyerdahl sailed from Morocco to Barbados in a flimsy reconstruction of the reed boats of ancient Egypt. The successful voyage of his *Ra II* makes it conceivable that it was after all the Egyptians, many centuries before Christ, who first made the transatlantic crossing. Nor did all these early explorers travel from Europe. Chinese inscriptions have been found on Pre-Columbian objects, and in 1962 a Chinese claim was made that a Buddhist monk with five companions sailed across the Pacific to Mexico from China via the Kurile and Aleutian Islands in A.D. 459.

The existing transoceanic Pacific and Atlantic currents make any or all of these journeys possible. We can never know who really first discovered America. Whoever he was, it is clear that his name was not Columbus. Whoever he was, Columbus belittled his achievement, because the Italian sailed there and back and *published* his discoveries. Only then, we may believe, did Old World peoples finally impose their rule and culture upon the New World.

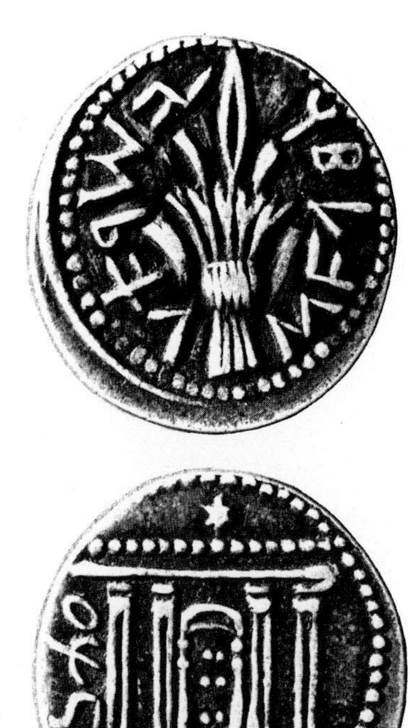

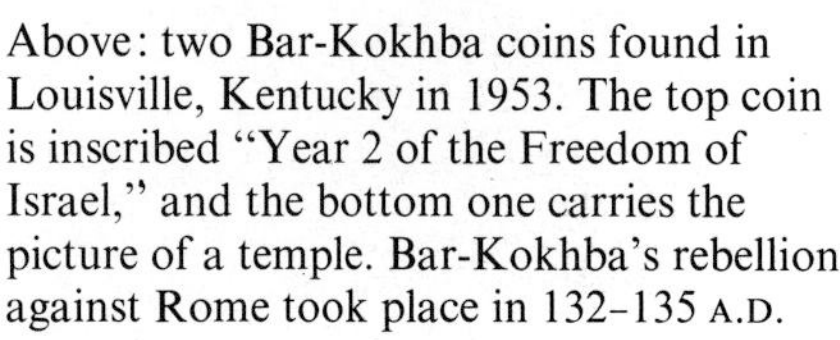

Above: two Bar-Kokhba coins found in Louisville, Kentucky in 1953. The top coin is inscribed "Year 2 of the Freedom of Israel," and the bottom one carries the picture of a temple. Bar-Kokhba's rebellion against Rome took place in 132–135 A.D.

Left: Thor Heyerdahl's boat *Ra II* at Barbados. Having made the 57-day journey from Morocco to Barbados without a reed out of place, he showed that it was possible for the Egyptians to have crossed the Atlantic in papyrus-reed boats. The original boats are more like those used by Mexican and Peruvian Indians than they are like contemporary Arab or African vessels.

Chapter 10
Bodies in the Peat Bogs

In 1952 peat cutters in Denmark dug up the well-preserved body of a man. So well preserved was the body that some local people believed it was that of "Red Christian," a peat cutter who disappeared mysteriously in the 1880s. Only scientific evidence proved conclusively that the man had been killed and thrown into the bog some 2000 years earlier. Moreover, the manner of his death and other evidence linked him with many similar finds in northern Europe—men and women, their throats cut and their bodies thrown into the peat. The riddle of these mysterious corpses and its eventual solution are the subject of this chapter.

It was a late April day in the quiet Danish countryside. Men from the nearby village of Grauballe toiled in a drained bog, cutting slabs of fibrous brown peat. For thousands of years peat had served their ancestors as a fuel for heating homes and cooking food. Suddenly one cutter's spade crunched into something hard. As he began clearing peat from the obstruction, his glance fell on a brown human head with short hair. Below the head, a neck and shoulders peeped from the peat. The horrified men stopped work and gazed at the corpse. A breeze sighing through the birches around Nebelgård Fen and the peaceful nearby hills seemed to make the apparition only more incongruously gruesome.

At first sight the men had found the victim of a recent murder—committed perhaps that same year of 1952. Or could the corpse date from a more remote past? Several feet of undisturbed peat had formed over the body since its disposal.

Someone called in the local doctor, an amateur archaeologist. He suspected the corpse to be ancient and notified the Museum of Prehistory at Aarhus, the county capital. Soon the prehistorian Dr. Peter Glob was on his way. Dr. Glob, who later set down his findings in *The Bog People*, first published in Denmark in 1965, and is today Director of the National Museum in Copenhagen, stepped down into the pit and examined the body. He judged that the Grauballe man lay in an old peat working filled in by maybe as much as 2000 years of bog deposits. He decided to

Opposite: Tollund man, who lived in the early Iron Age around the time of Christ. One of the most spectacular among the peat-preserved finds, this man's face was amazingly well preserved. He lay on his right side, and that side was in the better condition. (Silkeborg Museum/Photo Lars Bay)

Above: Grauballe man as he was excavated from the peat, which can be seen around his body. The immediate impression was of a dark-colored human head with a tuft of short-cropped hair sticking up clear of the dark brown peat. Part of the neck and shoulders were exposed. His head lay to the north and his legs to the south.

delay disinterment until he could arrange to transport the body safely back to the country museum for proper study. This proved surprisingly simple. Men drove a metal roofing sheet through the peat, under the corpse. Then they lifted the body still in its peat cocoon. Many helpers heaved the great load onto a truck which gingerly drove the 25 miles to Aarhus.

There, a small army of experts began exploring the body from the bog. They established that it had lain chest down, in a twisted posture, with left leg and arm outstretched and right leg and arm drawn upward. They found that the weight of peat pressing down upon it had somewhat flattened the body. Also, they discovered that bog chemicals had begun dissolving bones away. But the skin of head, torso, and limbs remained miraculously intact. So did some of the internal organs.

There was nothing else—no clothing, no personal possession—from which to establish the individual's identity. At least, so the archaeologists thought. But when they briefly placed the body on display, some of the spellbound public had different ideas. Among the visitors was a farmer's wife from the Grauballe area itself. The old woman claimed the corpse to be that of a peat cutter who had vanished late in the 1880s. There followed a newspaper story describing how she had even recognized "Red Christian's" face as it lay in the museum. People grew skeptical. Was this indeed the world's oldest known well-preserved body, as the scientists suggested? Could any corpse ripened by nearly two milleniums survive with hair and fingernails intact and even stubble on the chin? Surely it seemed far likelier that the Museum of Prehistory's prize exhibit was no more than a drunk drowned by falling in a bog sometime in living memory.

The scientists' belief that here lay a lifelike Iron Age man remained unshaken. They had good reasons to be confident. First, there was the dark brown color of the skin, which past experience told them had been literally tanned by soaking for centuries in bog water starved of oxygen but rich in tannin and soil-acids—a sure defense against bacterial decay. This would explain not only the skin's survival but also the signs of bone destruction—a long-

Right: Dr. Peter V. Glob, foremost among the scientists involved in the excavations of the Danish peat bog bodies. A respected archaeologist who has worked in many parts of the world, he is the author of *The Bog People*.

Grauballe Man

term effect of immersion in soil-acid that is highly concentrated.

The second proof of the bog man's antiquity came in prehistoric pollens found in peat at the level where his body lay. These pollens showed he had lived and died at a time when heather, clover, bird's foot trefoil, and other wild plants flourished nearby. They grew on old farmlands abandoned when soil exhaustion had cut crop yields. The plants were known to have thrived in Denmark in the first four centuries of the Christian era.

But what put Grauballe man's date beyond all reasonable doubt was the carbon contained in his body. Scientists took away bits of liver and muscle and measured their C14 (radioactive carbon) content with a special Geiger counter. The amount of C14 in organ tissue drops off slowly at a known rate after death. The reading for the Grauballe man showed conclusively that he had died within a century (on either side) of A.D. 310. When the press published these findings the former skeptics fell silent.

Meanwhile, the Iron Age body had been yielding other secrets. Deformed by the overlying peat and damaged by the peat cutters, head and neck nonetheless provided clear proof of how the

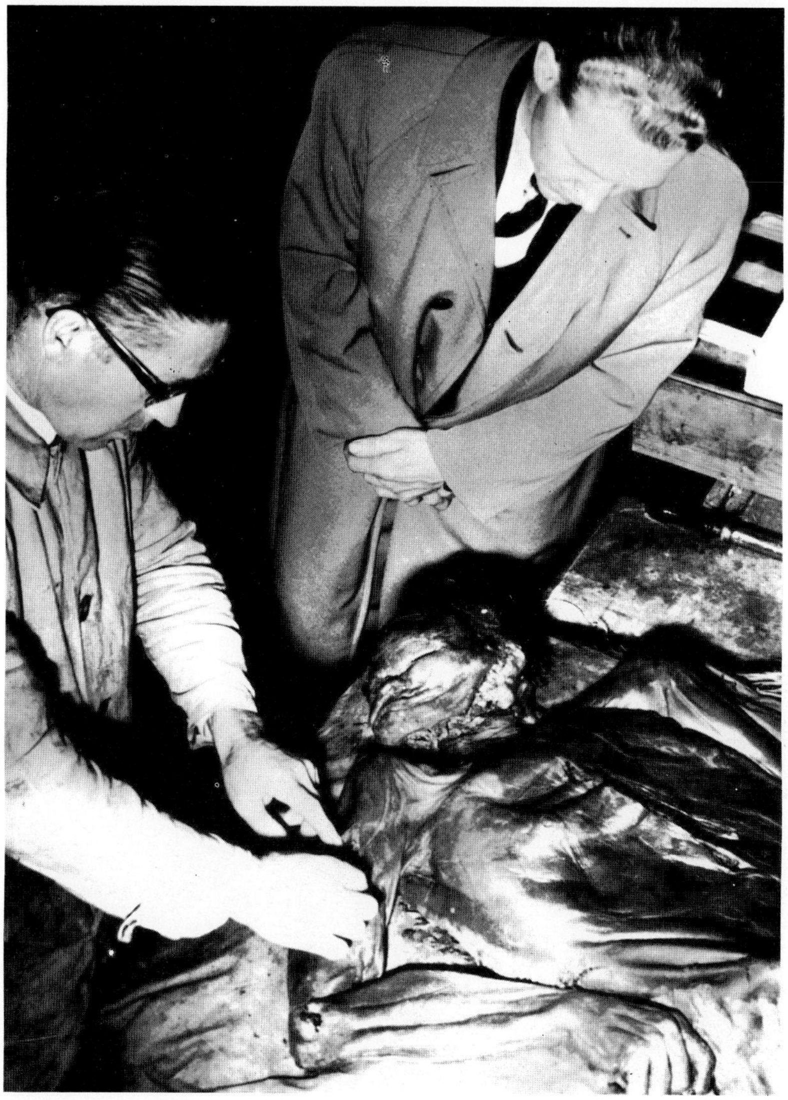

Left: scientists investigating Grauballe man. Carbon dating was performed on certain body tissues like the liver and muscles; pollen analysis was also carried out. The skin was as firm as if it had been tanned, due to the preservative qualities of the bog water.

Iron Age Victims

Below: two Aarhus policemen taking Grauballe man's fingerprints—some of the oldest patterns actually preserved in human skin. It was also possible to take prints of his right foot, the lines of which were as sharp as a baby's.

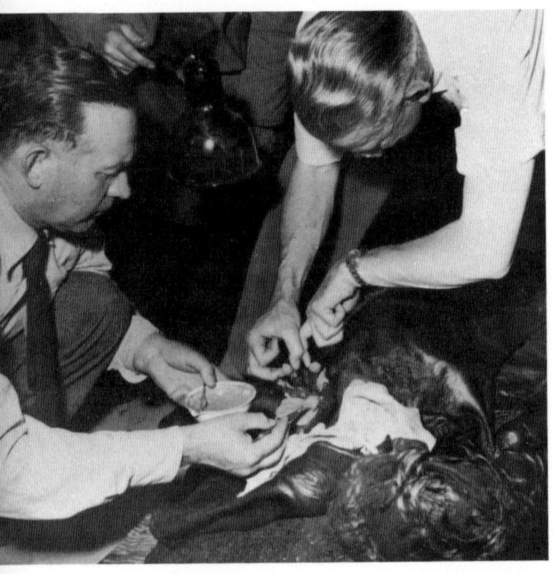

Grauballe man had died. Repeated knife blows had ripped his neck from ear to ear, severing the gullet. Puckered forehead, screwed up eyes and mouth half open in a cry spoke of the victim's fear and agony as he perished. X-rays revealed more damage, this time to bones. Two leg bones were broken, and the skull was fractured, though experts could not say whether these injuries had occurred before or after death. Early signs of rheumatoid arthritis and the condition of the teeth showed that the man had been aged at least 30 when he died.

Cause of and age at death had been determined. There was also even evidence to show at what time of year the bog man had been murdered. This came from remarkable finds in his intestines. Analysis of substances found in the digestive tract showed that just before death the man had eaten a vegetarian meal containing more than 60 kinds of food plants, chiefly seeds of uncultivated species. He had probably swallowed the mixture in some kind of gruel. There were no leaves, or fruits that ripen in summer and autumn. It seemed, then, that the Grauballe man had consumed his frugal last meal in winter or early spring.

The question of who this Danish bog man was remained open. Had he had a recent criminal record, finding his identity would have proved simple. Police laboratory tests revealed fingerprints as plain as those of most living men, and line patterns on part of the right hand plainer still. As it was, all that the fingerprints proved was that these were not a toilworn peasant's hands. Their owner had done no heavy manual work for at least some months before he died. They suggest he had held a special status in society, perhaps as priest or chieftain.

Impressive though they were, these findings left unanswered some tantalizing questions. Who was he? Why was he killed?

Right: Grauballe man on view. The solution to the problem of preservation of the find was to continue the tanning process of the peat bog. The final stage of the process took nearly two years. Some 1825 pounds of oak bark were used, and the tanning took place in a specially designed oak trough. He lies in his glass case at the Museum of Prehistory at Aarhus in exactly the posture in which he was found.

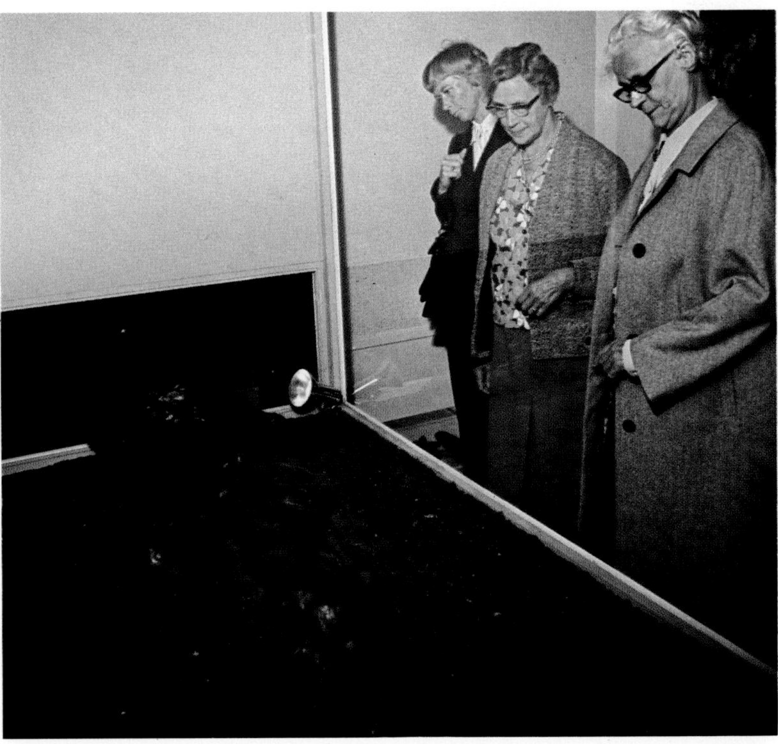

Why had his body been thrown in a bog? These mysteries surrounding the Grauballe man in fact formed just part of a much larger puzzle. For the prehistorians knew he was by no means the sole victim of an Iron Age killing to be done away with in this fashion.

Only two years before his discovery, peat cutters had found another well-preserved ancient body, this time in Tollund Fen, a few hours' walk west from the Grauballe man's bog burial. Tollund Fen is larger than Nebelgård Fen; it grew from an ancient lake slowly choked by vegetation. A steep sunken track leads down to the bog past dark firs and pale, shimmering aspens.

Out in the fen farm workers were harvesting fuel for the winter. It was spring, and around them rose the evocative, bleating love-calls of snipe. Then, as at Nebelgård Fen two years later, a macabre find marred the rural tranquillity. The cutters found themselves staring down at a body lying in a peat cutting about three feet below the surface of the bog. They called the police. But Peter Glob also hastened to the scene.

This time there was little doubt of the bog man's antiquity. For one thing he wore an ancient type of leather cap made of eight pieces of skin sewn together and held on with a hide chin-strap. Also he lay just above a layer of "dog's flesh," as Danes call a reddish peat layer formed by a particular kind of moss early on in the Iron Age. Like the Grauballe man, the Tollund man had been placed in an old peat working. But he had died much earlier: about 2000 years ago.

This makes the preservation of his head truly astonishing. No other head 2000 years old has remained so well preserved. The left side of the face was somewhat creased, but the right side—the side that had been lying downward—could have belonged to a living, breathing individual. Its serene, intelligent expression suggested a gentle, thoughtful, even noble personality. Each pore, each furrow, each wrinkle of experience around the eyes reinforced the illusion that Tollund man was still alive. So, too, did the day's growth of bristle visible on chin and upper lip. The calmly closed eyes and the tranquil expression on the mouth suggested that the corpse was merely asleep. The body's peaceful, curled-up attitude conveyed the same impression.

At first glance you would think that death had occurred naturally, and unsuspected. But a plaited leather noose around the neck told a different story. Later, pathologists' reports suggested that death had come by hanging and not by simple strangulation.

A further life was doomed when people took away the body to be studied. To do this, the Danes built a massive crate around the slab of peat enshrining the Tollund man. Then helpers man-handled the load, weighing nearly a ton, onto a horse-drawn cart. The work overstrained one individual's heart and he collapsed and died. The bog had yielded an old corpse but claimed a new life in return.

Like the Grauballe man, the Tollund man himself proved to contain few clues to suggest how and why he had been killed. Apart from his cap he wore no more than a leather belt. His gut revealed nothing but the relics of a last meal, again of seeds eaten in winter. Here, then, lay another Iron Age man who had met a

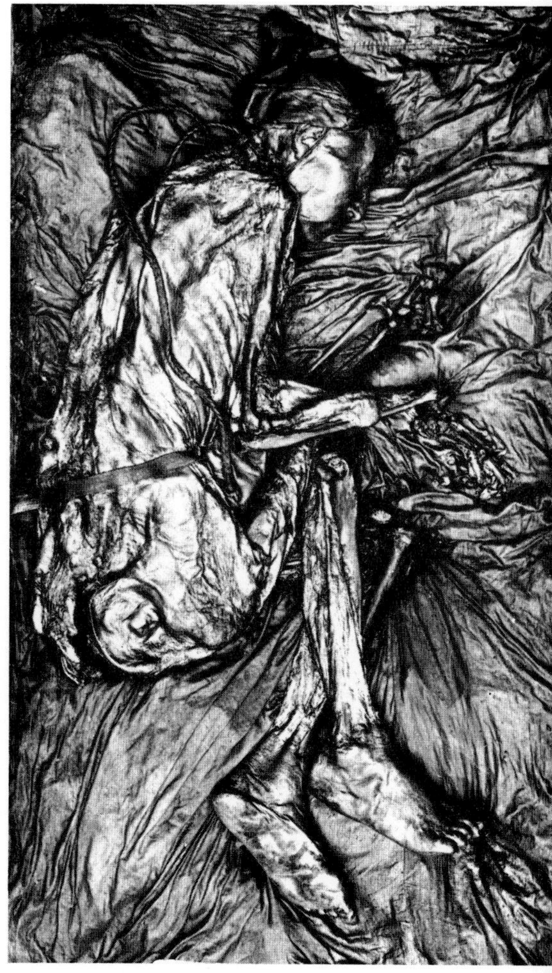

Above: Tollund man as he lay when first completely uncovered. He was so well preserved that the police were called to investigate, as if he were the recent victim of a modern murder. The noose found around his neck was the cause of death, by hanging. The body lay 50 yards out from firm ground not far above the clean sand floor of the bog. (Silkeborg Museum/Photo Lars Bay)

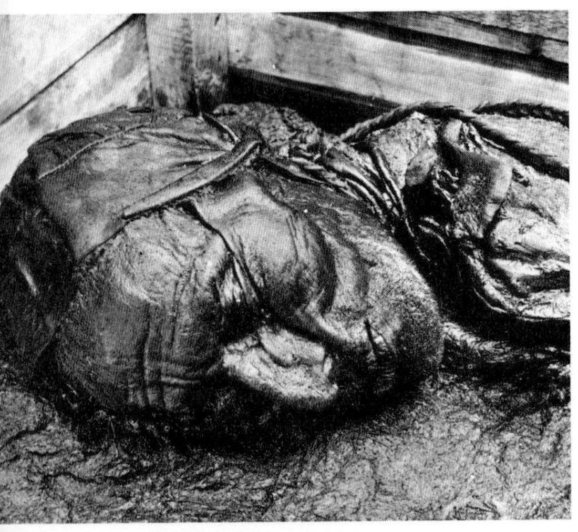

Above: the head of Tollund man, the only part of his body that has been preserved. In the process the proportions of the head and facial features were completely retained, but the head as a whole shrank by about 12 percent.

violent end. Was he murder victim, human sacrifice, or executed criminal?

Both these famous finds have been at least in part preserved. Scientists soaked Tollund man's head for six months in water containing acetic acid and formalin. During the next six months they switched to alcohol and toluol; then to toluol and paraffin; finally to toluol and heated wax. A year after the preservation processes began the head had shrunk a little but kept its shape superbly. Today visitors can meet this Iron Age man face to face in Silkeborg Museum about six miles from Tollund Fen.

The Grauballe man fared even better: scientists decided to save his entire body by completing the natural process of preservation already far advanced by 1600 years of bog submersion. Nineteen months' soaking in an oak bath containing tannic acid came first, then a month in distilled water containing Turkish red oil. Next came impregnation with lanolin and other substances. Lastly parts of the body received injections of collodion. The Grauballe man was now ready to go on public show in his own special room in the Museum of Prehistory at Aarhus.

These bog men found in the early 1950s were the first to be salvaged with such care, but not the first to be found. From time immemorial, tanned, well-preserved corpses had, as it were, popped up from Danish bogs to startle peat diggers. More than 150 such bodies are known to have sprung from the fens in the last two centuries alone.

But before archaeology found its feet, people had no idea how old many of these were. They simply shunned the corpses as devils, or gave them Christian reburial. Serious study of these bog corpses is rather a novel development. This means that we have lost a great deal of evidence. Nonetheless enough survives to enlarge the picture provided by the Tollund and Grauballe men and to provide more clues to their deaths and disposal.

The decade before their discovery yielded three finds in one Danish bog alone. This is less surprising when we remember that the Danes stepped up peat cutting for fuel in and just after World War II. This time the location was Borremose (Borre Fen), a great flat expanse of low land in north-central Denmark. In 1946

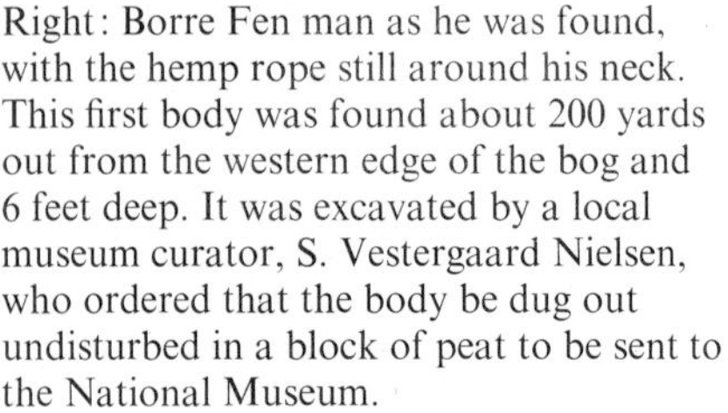

Right: Borre Fen man as he was found, with the hemp rope still around his neck. This first body was found about 200 yards out from the western edge of the bog and 6 feet deep. It was excavated by a local museum curator, S. Vestergaard Nielsen, who ordered that the body be dug out undisturbed in a block of peat to be sent to the National Museum.

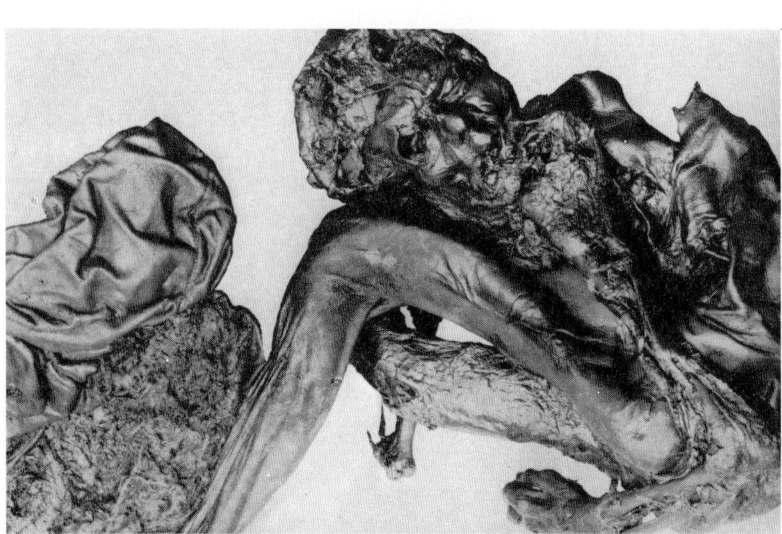

Battering at Borre Fen

peat cutters came on a small well-preserved man about six feet deep in soft peat. Research showed that some 2000 years ago someone had thrown his corpse into an already ancient and birch-overgrown peat working. Tanning had turned his skin to black leather, but one eyeball was still yellowish white. Several details will be already familiar from what you read earlier. For instance, a day's stubble covered the lower part of his face. His hands showed no trace of hard manual work. His intestines contained a vegetarian meal consisting of weed and other seeds that would have been eaten in winter. He had died from hanging or strangling. The death weapon in this case was a hemp rope with a slip knot. There was also bone damage, and the man had been naked.

But in some ways this find differed from those of the Tollund and Grauballe men. Two sheepskin capes, one with a collar, lay rolled by the Borre Fen man's feet, and beneath his head lay a fragment of cloth. Then, too, a birch branch about three feet long had been placed on his body.

Left: the Iron Age woman excavated from Borre Fen in 1947. Buried about 6.5 feet below the surface of the bog, she lay face down with her head to the north and feet to the south. The skull was crushed into pieces and the brain matter visible.

Below: the 1948 find of a plump woman's body in Borre Fen. She is shown face up after excavation. The head lay to the east with the right arm bent up against the face.

A year later the second Borre Fen body emerged, less than a mile northeast of the first. It lay face down in yet another old peat working. But this time the corpse was that of a woman, with long hair dyed red-brown by the bog water. A shawl, blanket, and bits of cloth covered the lower part of her naked body, which rested on a birch-bark sheet. Bronze and amber ornaments fixed to a leather strap had hung from her neck. The skull had been pulverized and the right leg broken. Nearby lay the tiny bones of an infant, also a clay pot that helped archaeologists determine that both had died about the same time as the Borre Fen man. Short sticks had been placed over the woman.

The third Borre Fen body turned up in 1948, less than a mile south of the first. This, too, bore the same approximate date as the others. Like the second find, the corpse was female. Her plump body lay face down, under a belted blanket used as a skirt. Someone had smashed her face and partly scalped her.

Women as well as men, then, had ended up in bogs in Iron Age Denmark. Brutal battering seems to have killed the two Borre Fen women, while strangling or throat-cutting had done away with all three men so far described. Was this chance, or part of a pattern? If part of a pattern, what was its meaning? And why had someone placed sticks near two of the corpses?

Legend of Queen Gunhild

The answers to some of these questions begin to emerge as we probe back through time. In 1942 a young woman curled up "like a question mark" was extracted from a "dog's flesh" peat layer in Bred Fen, east of Borre Fen. Her hair was plaited and coiled high on her head beneath a little woollen bonnet. Other relics led her discoverers to think that someone had dumped her into the bog naked and trussed but uninjured, maybe to drown.

The same year yielded an early middle-aged man, from Søgard Fen in central Denmark. He lay on a bed of downy bog-cotton flowers, with sandals and a cap, and wrapped—not dressed—in three leather capes, one fewer than those found with a bog body at Karlbyneder in eastern Denmark, in the early 1900s.

Right: the coiled hair and woollen bonnet of a young woman found at Bred Fen in 1942. The body was wrapped in cloth so that only the head showed. She appeared to have been 20 to 25 years old and about 5.5 feet tall.

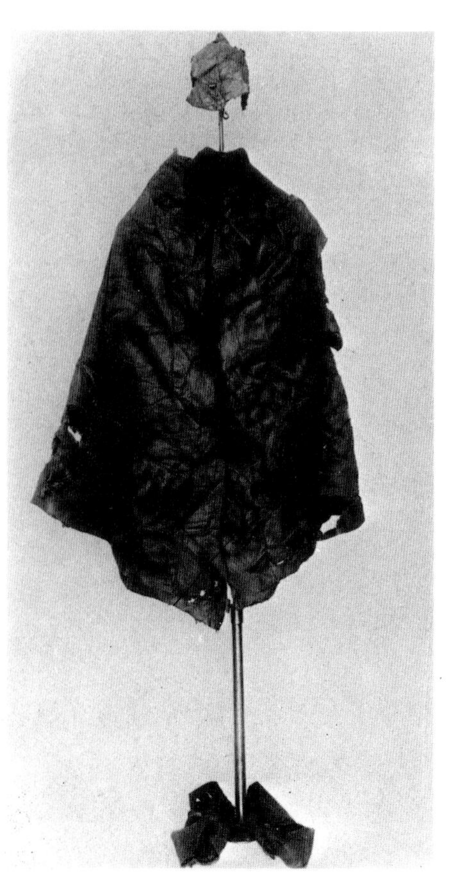

Below: the cape and boots of the man aged 30 to 35 years, found in Søgard Fen in Central Jutland in 1942. He lay face down on an inch-thick layer of bog cotton, the flower which in a fairy tale was used to clothe the princes who had been turned into wild swans.

Four years previously a bog man with a curious hair style had appeared, a mere stone's throw from where Tollund man's body was later recovered. He wore his hair pulled into a knot at the left side of the back of the head. Someone had strangled or hanged him with a leather strap and wrapped him in skins before dropping him into the bog.

The grisly trail of bog body finds leads us back through the 19th century. It grows fainter the farther we leave behind mass literacy, telephones, cars, and cameras, which between them ensure that scientists learn of, reach, and visually record the latest bog body before it rots or someone reburies it as just another unknown corpse.

This last is what happened to a supposed murder victim discovered in 1893 at Rørbaek in northern Denmark. The bog man was reinterred, but rediscovered by chance when a plow struck the coffin 70 years later. By then, though, only bones and hair remained of what, a lifetime earlier, had been a well-preserved body. Better luck had come in 1892 when a bog man with hair, shoes, and some clothing was photographed where he lay, in a bog just north of Tollund Fen. The photograph—the first of any Danish bog man—still survives.

Although most bodies were lost to posterity, people sometimes preserved durable objects discovered with the corpses. Glass beads and a bronze pin forming part of a neck decoration 1700 years old survive from a woman's body found in 1843 on the Danish island of Falster.

Above: the first photograph of a Danish bog man taken in May, 1892 at Nederfrederiksmose. Bodies have been found at some 35 sites in Denmark alone. Before this time if bodies were found in the peat they were briefly the marvel of the local people and were then carted off to the nearest churchyard and buried there.

Denmark's National Museum also has a check skirt, horn comb, and other articles discovered in 1879 with an early Iron Age woman. She lay in Huldre Bog in East Jutland, with a willow stake on her breast. Branches and stakes survive too from the 19th-century find of "Queen Gunhild"—whose supposed corpse was discovered in central Denmark. Old tales told how her political enemies had had the 10th-century Norse queen savaged and drowned in a bog. Scientists soon demolished the "Queen Gunhild" attribution. But, significantly, we know from ancient tradition that people pinned down dead witches with stakes to stop their ghosts walking. This could help to explain the finds of sticks near this corpse and those of some other Iron Age bodies.

Sticks, clothes, and personal ornaments make up almost all of the few surviving relics of 19th-century bog body finds. But we also have valuable written accounts going back to the late 18th century. Thus we know that in 1797 southwest Denmark produced a short, stocky corpse with curly red hair. Two leather capes rested on top of him and three hazel sticks lay beside his body. We have a much more detailed account of a bog man found in 1773. He lay naked with hands placed as though tied behind him. His throat had been cut to the bone, and the killers had laid twigs or sticks on his carcass.

The researcher who counted 150 bodies known from Danish bogs also studied the same phenomenon in other countries. He credited what are now East and West Germany with a still larger number and listed over 70 from the British Isles, 50 from the

Above: horn comb discovered in 1879 with a woman's body in Huldre Bog, part of the most complete Iron Age woman's costume found in Denmark. The bog itself lies between hills crowned by ancient burial mounds. It retains a certain air of mystery even now—its name comes from the word *huldre*, a kind of fairy that is outwardly beautiful but able to bewitch with illusions of happiness.

Netherlands, and 20 from Norway and Sweden. Europe's grand known total he put at 700—more than three-quarters of them from northwestern Europe. Some represent victims of recent accidents or murders, and soldiers and airmen killed in the world wars. A very few go back 5000 years or more to the Stone Age. But most were Iron Age men and women, largely from the millenium beginning about 500 B.C.

County Down, Ireland, produced the first detailed account of a find outside Denmark. In 1780 a peat cutter found a small female skeleton at the base of a small mountain bog. Hair, clothing, and ornaments suggested a woman of rank, perhaps a Danish noblewoman from the time of the Viking invasions. This century Galway yielded a fine 400-year-old corpse with clothing and stomach contents intact. But such finds generally lack the hallmarks of the brutal murders described for Iron Age Denmark. It is as we move east from Ireland across northwestern Europe that signs of this practice increase.

Several bog bodies have cropped up west of the River Ems. They include the double discovery in 1904 of a naked man and woman at Werdingerveen in the Dutch province of Drenthe. Of the man, only the skin (with signs of a wound near the heart) had survived. The woman's skin and hair were a gleaming brown. Assen Museum preserves the remains of this find.

Perhaps the richest non-Danish source of Iron Age bog people is the Schleswig-Holstein region just south of Denmark's present boundary with West Germany. From here, in 1640, came the first bog body to be recorded. In 1790 peat cutters at Bunsok came on a corpse caged by poles and sticks. More than 80 years later, a near-naked man with a skull fracture emerged from Rendswühren Fen near Kiel. He became the subject for the

Right: the bog man found in 1871 at Rendswühren Fen near Kiel in Germany. On his left leg lay a piece of leather with the pelt facing inward, bound with leather thongs. He was covered with a large rectangular woollen cloth and a cape made from skins covered his head, which had a triangular hole in the forehead.

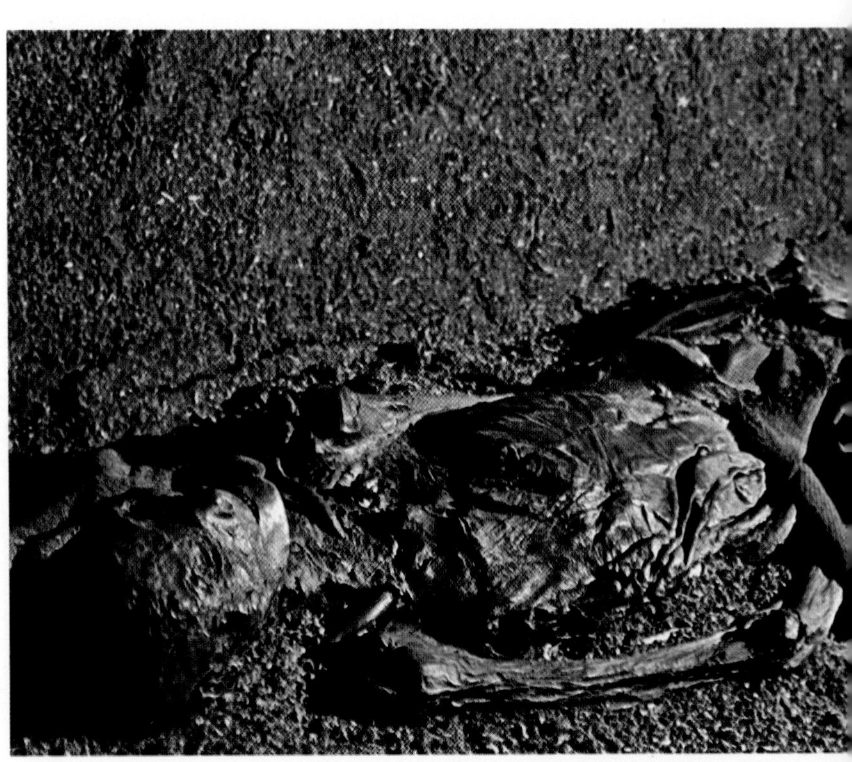

Body Preserved by Smoking

world's first bog-body photograph, and people preserved him—in a fashion—by smoking. His skeleton, with its taut shroud of shriveled skin, survives in a Schleswig museum. Here, too, lies the tanned skin of the Damendorf man—minus the skeleton, which had entirely dissolved.

The Eckernförde region that produced him has been the source of many other discoveries. Among the most striking of these was a naked, 14-year-old girl with bandaged eyes, who had seemingly been drowned in a shallow peat pit. A heavy stone weighed down her body. Bone studies showed she had suffered from malnutrition in the cold, damp winters of nearly 1900 years ago. Less than a month after peat workers discovered her corpse in May 1952, the same Windeby bog revealed a man's body hardly any distance away. He had been pinned down with forked branches and hazel wand had been used to choke him to death.

As a last Schleswig-Holstein example we may mention an even more gruesome object from near Osterby. This was the severed

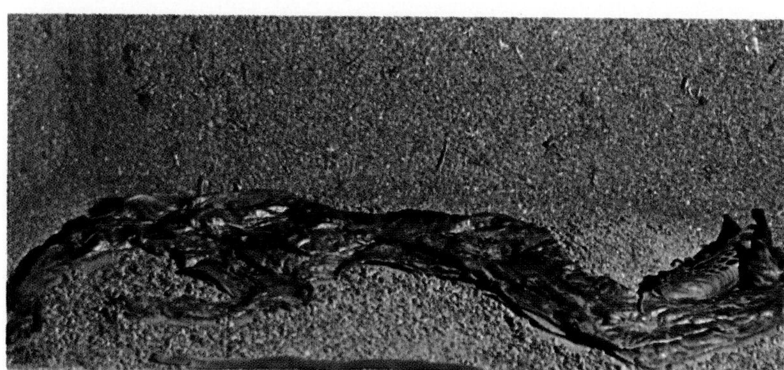

Left: the skin of Damendorf man, whose skeleton had completely dissolved. Only his skin, leather belt, and shoes survived. A split nearly an inch long in the region of the heart may be related to the cause of his death. Below: body of the young girl found at Windeby bog in 1952. The body was excavated in a single huge block of peat and transferred to the Schleswig-Holstein Museum in a hearse. Curious bystanders lined the road, giving the effect of mourners paying their last respects. The left side of her scalp had been shaved.

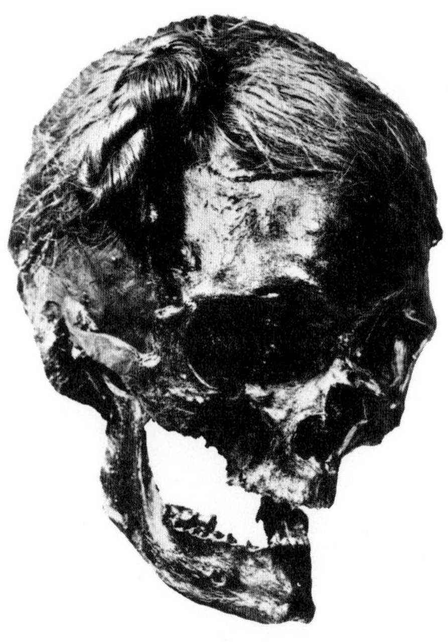

Above: the man's head from Osterby, with its 11-inch-long hair tied in a "Swabian knot." Discovered in 1948, the head was wrapped in a sewn deerskin cape and had been cut off with a sharp implement or weapon—the marks were still visible on the bone.

Below: sarcophagus carving of around the 2nd century, showing a battle between the Romans and Germans. The details of dress are borne out by the bog finds. The Germanic warriors wear capes, shirt and trousers, or sleeveless tunics.

head of a man with long, graying hair, drawn together on the right-hand side and ingeniously tied in an elaborate knot. This reminds us of the 1938 Tollund Fen find.

The bog bodies themselves, then, reveal certain patterns, but not what these signify. To grasp who these Iron Age people were and how they had lived and died we must enlist the aid of other sources of information. One is the collection of archaeological finds of clothes, tools, and buildings made and used near the bogs while these were reaping their macabre harvest. Our other aid consists of contemporary Latin writings, especially by the Roman historian Cornelius Tacitus. Archaeology has proved Tacitus to be a cautious and broadly reliable writer. Tacitus in his work *Germania* briefly describes the Germanic tribes that held northern Europe in his day. It therefore embraces the very people, places, and time that concern us.

Prehistorians now believe that the Iron Age Germanic peoples derived largely from the Battle Axe people—speakers of Indo-European tongues who migrated from southern Russia more than 4000 years ago, penetrating into east, central, and parts of northern Europe. Intermarriage between the newcomers and established Europeans produced the Germanic tribes. Those of the southern Baltic area built a rich Bronze Age culture largely based on trade in Baltic amber with the wealthy Mediterranean civilizations. Some families seemingly grew rich and powerful from a monopoly of bronze.

About 500 B.C. all this was changing. Celts drove a wedge between the northerners and their southern markets. From Celts, though, the Germanic peoples learned to make cheap, serviceable tools from abundant iron. With trade hamstrung and bronze devalued, the ruling class in and near Denmark lost wealth. Meanwhile the northern climate worsened. Cold, wet weather ushered in the Iron Age. Winning a living from the land became difficult. For these reasons the old class structure probably broke

down and a poor, more egalitarian society of hardy, sturdy fisherfolk and farmers was left to grapple for its living with a hostile land and sea.

What did these people look like? Tacitus tells us that the Germanic peoples were tall and strongly built, with fierce blue eyes and reddish hair. But bog body finds reveal that this picture is oversimple. Some adults were short by modern standards. A poor winter diet left traces of malnutrition. Also, teeth suffered harsh wear from grit in flour produced by grinding grain with stone implements.

Most men went clean-shaven. Women often had bobbed hair. Bog body finds of both sexes normally reveal reddish, peat-stained hair. But the severed graying head from Osterby had had blond hair. Peter Glob describes "Queen Gunhild's" hair as dark brown, and the Grauballe man had probably been dark-haired as well.

The two finds of heads with curiously knotted hair tally with description by Tacitus of the Swabian knot known also from ancient sculptures. Invented by the Swabian tribe and copied by their Germanic brothers, this hair style lent extra height to its wearers and thus made them appear more frightening in battle.

Germanic men dressed simply. Men found in the bogs were usually naked, covered only with one or more short skin shoulder capes. Julius Caesar encountered Germanic warriors inadequately clad like this, and Tacitus wrote that most German men wore just a cloak or cape pinned by a brooch or thorn. They spent days by their fires in nothing else—no mean survival feat if performed in the cold, wet winters of the early Iron Age. Only the rich, said Tacitus, wore underclothes. These were long and skintight. But bog finds show that at least some early Iron Age men had coats, leggings, shoes, and caps. Tunics and trousers seemingly came later. But the naked, belted corpse of Tollund man may well have worn a linen suit of flax or nettle fibre, long since dissolved by soil-acids.

We know much more about what the women wore. Tacitus describes low-cut, sleeveless, linen outer garments with a purple pattern. Roman sculptures show similar clothing. Best of all, two fine sets of Early Iron Age clothing survive from eastern Denmark. One was a long, woven, sleeveless gown gathered at the shoulders by brooches, and with a fold to serve as a hood—a style brought in from Greece where women were using similar dresses when the wearer of this one was dropped in a Danish bog 2400 years ago. The other costume comprised a plaid skirt woven from wools of contrasting browns, a shawl with a bird's bone pin, and two furry skin capes. Some women also wore caps. But bog bodies generally lacked ornaments.

From the Roman historian Tacitus we learn that Germanic tribes lived in farming villages of houses detached, not abutting according to the Roman practice. He noted: "Every man leaves an open space around his house, perhaps as a precaution against the risk of fire."

The remains of just such an Iron Age village have come to light at Borre Fen in northern Denmark. This small, moated settlement of 20 turf-walled houses, maybe roofed with thatch, stood on an island in the marsh, guarded by an earth wall and a wooden

Clothing of the Germanic Tribes

Above: the women's clothing found at Huldre Bog. The sleeveless garment would be folded outward over the shoulders for use as a hood. One lambskin cape was worn next to the skin and another as an outer garment. A check skirt was fastened to the body with a leather strap.

Indo-European Fertility Rites

Right: a reconstructed prehistoric village at Lejre about 20 miles west of Copenhagen, Denmark. A workshop for houses characteristic of the Iron Age, the site includes about a dozen houses rebuilt from remains found in different parts of Denmark. The village is encircled by a common fence, and each farm also has its own fence. A central village green and smaller houses for storage have been added.

Above: Lejre researchers dressed in woollens and swathed in animal hides eat beside an open hearth fire. The grist stones, storage jar, clay andiron (foreground), and meat smoking over the fire—all these would be familiar to Northmen of the Iron Age. The fire would have been the center of activity throughout the winter. Skins of oxen and horses suspended over the fire helped keep flying sparks from reaching the dry roof thatch.

fence. Each morning, the men probably crossed the marsh by causeway to the fields and pastures where they tended cattle and toiled to grow grain on family plots. Meanwhile, back at home, the women threshed and ground grain; baked bread; made cheese and beer; molded and baked clay pots; and wove cloth on simple looms. At night, men literally drove cattle and other livestock indoors, where the creatures' body heat combined with peat fires to ward off the damp, penetrating cold. Then the peasants supped off porridge, cheese, possibly some meat, washed down by an alcoholic liquor made from grain.

We can well imagine that at times like this men drank heavily and gambled to forget their day's drudgery. "Drinking bouts lasting all day and night are not considered in any way disgraceful" wrote Tacitus.

When crops failed and starvation loomed, whole bands of Northmen roamed far afield, seeking plunder where they could. Indeed in 113 B.C. the Cimbri and Teutonic tribes from all over northern Denmark rampaged south deep into Europe, invading France and Spain. Their troops repeatedly crushed Roman armies until they were annihilated in northern Italy. Such exploits led Tacitus to see warfare as the favorite mode of life among these hardy, brave barbarians.

In reality, most Northmen were usually peasants, working desperately hard to win enough food from the land to tide them through the winter. Small wonder that the tribes inhabiting Denmark and the northern part of Germany did their utmost to appease their chief deity—Nerthus, an earth mother goddess who made crops grow and animals bear young in spring.

Probably the Iron Age Danes inherited their cult from Middle Eastern people who revered the same deity under such names as Ishtar and Astarte. In each case, the goddess supposedly assured summer plenty, but only if you offered her some sacrifice. And it had to be the right sacrifice, made in the right place, at the right time of year, in the right way, by the right person.

Tacitus again holds clues to what went on. Of Nerthus' worshipers he wrote: "They believe that she takes part in human affairs, riding in a chariot among her people. On an island of the sea stands an inviolate grove, in which, veiled with a cloth, is a chariot that none but the priest may touch. The priest can feel the presence of the goddess in this holy of holies, and attends her with deepest reverence as her chariot is drawn along by cows. Then follow days of rejoicing and merrymaking in every place that she condescends to visit and sojourn in. No one goes to war, no one takes up arms; every iron object is locked away. Then, and then only, are peace and quiet known and welcomed, until the goddess, when she has had enough of the society of men, is restored to her sacred precinct by the priest. After that the chariot, the vestments, and (believe it if you will) the goddess herself are cleansed in a secluded lake. The service is performed by slaves who are immediately afterwards drowned in the lake. Thus mystery begets terror and a pious reluctance to ask what that sight can be which is seen only by men doomed to die."

In slightly garbled form, Tacitus thus describes a typical ancient Indo-European fertility rite symbolizing the holy spring marriage of sky and earth from which would flow a fruitful summer. First, the god and goddess journeyed by wagon in procession around the countryside. The goddess was possibly abstract or an image hidden in the cart. The god, her husband, would have been a priest or some other specially selected man. Wherever they passed, people acclaimed their holy union. But its consummation came with a ceremonial climax—a man's life offered to the goddess. Who but her husband would have been most fitting for this sacrifice?

Many finds help us to piece together such a picture. Danish bogs have yielded numerous Iron Age carts, tossed in, piecemeal, as sacrifices, notably in northern Zealand, the large island east of mainland Denmark. From here came two superbly ornamented wagons each with a single seat of honor, arguably for the goddess or her image.

Above: invasion of Italy by the Cimbri, who attacked central and western Europe in the years 115–101 B.C. They won several victories over the Romans before they were beaten by the Roman general Marius at Vercelli. The Cimbrian warriors were said to be tall with blue eyes and fair hair, frank and credulous in character, but ferocious and fearless in battle.

Left: the Dejbjerg wagon, discovered in the 1880s, perhaps used to transport the goddess in a fertility rite. The fine craftsmanship and opulent decoration show that this was not used for ordinary work, and may have been built purposely for sacrifice in the bog.

Below: contemporary representation of the sacred ritual marriage which is the solemn climax of the goddess' spring journey. Cut upon a flat stone some 2500 years ago, a man and woman are shown stretching out their arms to each other. Behind the woman is a tree or ear of corn, and the whole scene is surrounded by the sacred sign of the goddess, the twisted neck ring.

Proof that many bodies belonged to sacrificial victims include the nooses around the necks of the Tollund man and other bog men. Several such ropes remind us strongly of the bronze torques separately tossed in bogs as sacrificial offerings. Moreover torques feature as necklets on a Bronze Age image of the naked goddess, and on goddess heads depicted on the Gundestrup cauldron. This famous Celtic work of art was offered up to Nerthus in a Danish bog close to the Iron Age village of Borre Fen from where three of the bog bodies mentioned earlier derived. Then, too, there is an early Iron Age illustration of the twisted neck ring scratched upon a disk-shaped stone around the embracing figures of a man and woman. A giant ear of corn behind the woman identifies her with a force that makes plants grow. The twisted neck ring, then, was the hallmark of the goddess of fertility. Strangling someone with a twisted rope meant consecrating him or her to Nerthus.

The curiously varied seed meals eaten by the Tollund and Grauballe men may have represented special sacrificial meals, not just a lack of protein at the end of winter. The timing of their deaths is right for spring sacrifices. Then, too, the delicate, unworn hands of several victims suggests that these were priests or at least no ordinary peasants.

That theirs were no simple burials we know, too, from the fact that early Iron Age Danes normally cremated bodies, while later Iron Age peoples buried dead, but furnished them with tools and ornaments. Most bog burials lacked either.

Lastly, people chose bogs for sacrifices because these wooded hollows were landmarks in a tree-denuded landscape. "Their holy places are woods and groves," says Tacitus.

Sometimes, apparently, the victim was not preordained but picked by chance. Tacitus describes how the Germanics cast lots with chips of wood—a forceful reminder of the debarked slips of wood beneath one Borre Fen woman's body.

But were all the Iron Age bog bodies simply offered up as sacrifices, or did some die for other reasons? Slit throats, drown-

Right: the silver Gundestrup cauldron, showing gods and goddesses, cult processions, sacrificial scenes, and animal combats—a complete picture of the Celtic world of deities and the rituals associated with their worship. The cauldron was found in pieces in the small bog of Raeve north of Borre Fen.

Sacrificial Bridegrooms?

Left: detail from the bronze Rynkeby cauldron found in 1845. The woman, probably the fertility goddess, wears the torque or neck rink which is her symbol.

ing, and decapitation perhaps suggests no more than local differences in the killing methods used. But Tacitus explained some such deaths otherwise. Describing Germanic capital punishments he wrote: "Traitors and deserters are hanged on trees; cowards, shirkers, and sodomites are pressed down under a wicker hurdle into the slimy mud of a bog." The idea was for state offenders to suffer public punishments, while "deeds of shame" were buried out of sight. Elsewhere Tacitus describes how husbands punished unfaithful wives by shaving off their hair and driving them naked through the street. The bog bodies—unclad, some shorn, some pinned down by branches—indeed awaken echoes of these practices.

Nonetheless, the circumstantial evidence is strong that Tollund man and many more bog people had died as sacrificial bridegrooms of the goddess Nerthus to ensure that crops would grow and men would thrive through the year ahead.

Folk memories of these barbaric rites had faded by the early 1900s. But people in one Danish parish recalled a curious spring custom. Sir James Frazer describes it in *The Golden Bough*. A little girl was crowned with flowers and dressed as a bride, with a little boy as her groom. With "outriders" on hobbyhorses, they journeyed in procession from one farmhouse to another. At each farmhouse people gave the couple gifts of food. Farmers' wives arranged a wedding feast and we read that "the children danced merrily in clogs on the stamped clay floor till the sun rose and the birds began to sing."

Iron Age ceremonies linked with ritual murder persisted, then, even into our own Industrial Age. Christian children performed them in innocence, for the bogs had long ceased to claim bodies.

Chapter 11
The Mysterious Mountain

When 19th-century Europeans first saw the strange mound that loomed over the surrounding Javanese landscape, they found it hard to believe that it was more than a mere hilltop. Excavation and restoration, mainly by Dutch archaeologists, soon showed it was much more than that. Today Borobudur is one of the wonders of the Orient, a symbol in stone of the cosmic system of Mahayana Buddhism, a huge edifice built over 1000 years ago, and richly covered in carvings which, says one Indian historian, would stretch for three miles. How these reliefs have been deciphered and the true significance of Borobudur revealed are the subject of this chapter.

For centuries the strange stone mound had loomed above the plain. Earthquakes and tropical downpours had loosened its rocks, and from the cracks between them sprouted a lush growth of bushes and trees. A traveler crossing the rice fields and palm groves below might have been struck by the wooded hill's curious symmetry, but his gaze would more likely fall beyond, on the weirdly shaped ring of dark mountains almost surrounding the fresh green Kedu Plain of south-central Java, one of the large islands that today make up Indonesia. From one peak a smoke plume by day and a red glow at night betray the mountains' volcanic origin.

To the local villagers, though, the nearby wooded hill held a special significance. They knew that its stones bore ancient carvings of human figures, for they could see pinnacles and statues peeping from the trees. Moreover they believed that visiting the place brought bad luck. Javanese history describes how in 1709 the king of Mataram besieged, defeated, and killed a rebellious subject and his followers who had made a stand on the hill. In 1757 the crown prince of Jogjakarta is said to have visited the hill where he took pity upon a "knight" imprisoned there in a "cage"—actually a statue in a latticed stone "bell." Soon afterward the prince fell sick and died. Superstition of this kind helped to cloak the place in mystery.

Local legend proved no deterrent to the curiosity of Java's colonizing Europeans. By the mid-18th century the Dutch effec-

Opposite: a Buddha at Borobudur. In the Buddha's left hand is a red flower placed there by a pilgrim. Modern visitors follow the same sequence as did their ancient ancestors, and to facilitate its appreciation the magnificent monument is being restored by the government of Indonesia with the help of Unesco.

Above: Sir Thomas Stamford Raffles (1781-1826), founder of Singapore and lieutenant governor of Java from 1811 until 1816. He described the Javanese as "a highly polished people, considerably advanced in science, highly inquisitive, and full of penetration." Raffles set in motion the recovery of Borobudur from obscurity and decay.

tively ruled Java, but the British East India Company took over temporarily for what proved the closing stages of the Napoleonic Wars. It was a British Lieutenant Governor, Sir Thomas Stamford Raffles, the man who later founded and administered Singapore, who first probed the true nature of the stony hill. Raffles was making a tour of inspection in central Java in 1814 when he heard about Borobudur—the local name for the tree-clad monument. Raffles knew that parts of Java teemed with ancient shrines and temples, but this one sounded intriguingly larger than anything he had encountered. Unable to visit Borobudur himself, he left its exploration to a capable Dutch engineer officer called Cornelius who was experienced in Javanese antiquities. Cornelius hired 200 reluctant villagers and set to work to clear away the vegetation covering the hill. Threat of subsidence prevented his removing all obstructions, but in two months Borobudur had largely emerged from 1000 years of oblivion. Weathering and subsidence had had a shattering effect. Floors sagged, walls leaned crazily, and structures lay in tumbled mounds like houses hit by a bomb blast.

More work was needed to make plain every detail of this strangely sprawling edifice. By 1835 the local Dutch administrator had completed Cornelius' clearing operation. Neglect followed. But between 1907 and 1911 the Dutch government paid for a heroic reconstruction job by Thomas Van Erp, a Dutch army engineer. The building revealed by all these efforts was a Buddhist monument larger and more splendid than any other in the world, and unusual enough to pose tantalizing questions about its purpose.

Borobudur consists of a shallow, stepped pyramid surmounted by a big bell-like Buddhist structure called a *stupa*, and embellished with statues and reliefs on an amazing scale. Borobudur occupies a total of 10 levels. The bottom six are square terraces, each recessed toward the ends. The next three terraces form concentric circles. The 10th and topmost level comprises the central stupa, while the lowest terrace is simply a broad platform path. Terraces two to five form galleries with stone Buddhas facing outward from niches in the upper level of their balustrades, with scenes done in stone relief on each inner wall and the inner surface of each balustrade. Stone stairways—one located in the center of each side of the monuments—lead up through these galleries to reach the 6th square terrace. From there you climb up to the three tiered circular terraces adorned only by Buddha statues half hidden in perforated bell-like structures called

Uncovering Borobudur

Above: the central stupa at the time of the Van Erp restoration project. His was mainly a holding operation—better drainage of rainwater, urgent repairs, and partial restoration—but his results revealed much of the monument's potential.

Left: view of Borobudur from the avenue, photographed at the beginning of the century. This was before Van Erp's major reconstruction effort which began in 1907.

dagobas. The crowning stupa is plain with solid walls.

Borobudur's Buddhist builders had clearly worked before the 15th century, for by that time Islam had ousted Buddhism and Hinduism, until then the chief religions of the Javanese. But who were these builders? When, how, and why had they actually raised this splendid monument? Archaeologists have found no clear-cut contemporary account of its construction. But they have discovered indirect evidence of the buildings' date in the inscriptions accompanying some of its reliefs. Distinctive features of the script matched those already known from royal charters issued in Java about the year A.D. 800. Old Javanese inscriptions suggested to the French scholar J. G. de Casparis that men had founded Borobudur in A.D. 824 in the reign of Samaratunga. Samaratunga's powerful Sailendra Dynasty of central Java was at its height at that time. Sailendra rulers had clearly approved the building of the monument, even if they had not constructed it themselves.

No one knows for certain just who the Sailendras were. Some historians think they could have been a native Javan dynasty, but most believe that they were immigrants, perhaps from southern India or from Indochina. Their name favors the second possibility, because "Sailendra" is Sanskrit for "King of the Mountain." This was the old imperial title held by rulers of the Indianized Indochinese kingdom of Funan which fell early in the 7th century. Some historians suggest that the collapse of this mainland power inspired the ambitious young island dynasty to seize Funan's former title for itself. Others claim that the Sailendras were a Javanese continuation of the Funan dynasty.

But whatever their origins, there was no doubting the Sailendras' ambition. Based in central Java, from the mid-8th

Above: a stairway providing access to the upper part of the monument, photographed before restoration at the beginning of the century. Stairways are built into the middle of each side of the pyramid.

Right: restored stupas of Borobudur. The Buddhist stupa is heavily laden with religious symbolism—it encloses the body and represents the Buddha in the state of nirvana. The ground plan of a stupa often resembles the mandala, a metaphysical diagram of the world. The small stupas of Borobudur contain seated statues of the Buddha, all in the identical pose of teaching.

Kings of the Mountain

Left: detail of a relief from Borobudur of a Sailendra sailing vessel. The tripod mast and heavy outrigger are characteristic of Javanese ships of about 800 A.D. When there was no wind rowers used poles which were passed through holes in the bridge. The ships were often as long as 65 feet.

century they made their power felt far beyond. The Sailendras came to dominate the ports of northeast Java, from where their sailing vessels ranged overseas to raid or threaten Cambodia and the Malay peninsula before A.D. 800. By 850—probably because of a dynastic marriage—Sailendras gained control of the powerful Sumatran-based empire of Sri Vijaya, and transferred their government to the Sumatran center, Palembang.

Meanwhile, as followers of Mahayana Buddhism, an Indian creed that had won a foothold on Java by the middle 700s, some of the Sailendras fostered a rich flowering of Buddhist art and architecture in the form of monuments and temples.

From evidence on other sites it seems that, though Sailendras were probably the patrons of Borobudur, Buddhist priests from India—or somewhere well versed in Indian techniques of art and architecture—designed and supervised the making of the building. There is evidence that some priests specialized as architects and others as sculptors. These experts would have had copies of Indian treatises on art and architecture to work from, and probably trained Javanese builders and wood carvers in the skills so strikingly apparent in the building and decoration of Borobudur.

Borobudur's size, shape, and content give us a fair idea of the task that faced the architects and workmen, and how they went about it. Their object was to cap a hill in terraced stone. They built their terraces from a leveled base that flanked the summit of the hill, and used rubble to bulk out the hilltop core. Instead of quarrying, they hauled the more than 2,000,000 dark lava boulders from the beds of nearby rivers, first trimming them to size and shape. Instead of using mortar to join these stones together, they snugly fitted them in place by carving holes and corresponding knobs to join one stone to another. These joints proved strong enough to hold most stones together, even during earth tremors of the type all too familiar in Java. The builders

Above: Prambanan Temple in Java, a Buddhist temple similar to Borobudur in style and built not long after. Built for the first Mataram dynasty early in the 10th century, it is a symmetrical structure surrounded by additional small temples. The influence of Indian styles is strong in both architecture and sculpture. Greatly ruined now, this sumptuous temple is dedicated to the god Tara.

Right: *makara* or gargoyle used as a water spout for drainage at Borobudur. The makaras represented sea monsters. Above this one is a Buddha statue placed in a niche, of which the first balustrades have 104, the second 104, the third 88, the fourth 72, and the fifth 64. Originally there were 432 statues.

showed considerable foresight in the way they drained the monument. To carry off the heavy tropical rainfall from the different stages they built 100 stone spouts intricately carved as gargoyles.

Once all the stones were in position, sculptors began chipping out the reliefs, usually starting at the top and working down. From the serene Buddha figures to lively scenes of everyday life, their images are mostly Indian in style. Art historians have traced this sculpture's origins back to the so-called Gandhara style that bloomed in northern India in the early centuries after Christ. But Gandhara sculpture, in its turn, was deeply influenced by the naturalistic statues of the Roman Empire. From Rome's eastern outpost, Syria, the Roman style of representing human figures found its way east deep into Asia. Roman art in turn owed debts to the styles of ancient Greece. Because Greek and Roman sculpture also influence the Church sculptures in medieval Europe, we can trace a link between the effigies in Christian cathedrals and Borobudur's Buddhist carvings.

At the same time, traditional Javanese culture left its imprint on the monument. Borobudur's sculptors interpreted divine figures in a softer, more realistic way than their Buddhist counterparts in India. More obviously Javanese are Borobudur's stepped, or corbeled, arches that frame different levels of the stairways. Surmounting and symbolically guarding each arch is

Javanese and Indian Styles

Left: a hunting scene from a relief at Chandi Mendut, a temple not far from Borobudur. It is the enlargement of a more ancient brick temple whose walls were enveloped by the stones of the present edifice. The theme of this relief, carved on the entrance ramp, is very old. Hunters in a field of grazing buffalo shoot with bows and arrows at a duck, which holds a turtle aloft.

a monstrous head, a symbol of the upper world, with bared fangs and bulging eyes. Descending from its body are two elephantine-headed, serpentine sea beasts that symbolize the underworld Such arches are common on early Javanese religious buildings

Van Erp reckoned that, all told, nearly 14,000 cubic feet of stone had gone into the building. Between its base more than 350 feet across, and the summit 100 feet above ground, sculptors eventually covered over a mile of stone with high relief, set up more than 500 statues, and made guardian lions, niches, pilasters, spouts, and many other features. Then workmen plastered the whole fantastic fabric with hard stucco to preserve it from the damaging effects of weather.

All this they did with muscle power applied to ropes, logs, levers, and such craftsmen's tools as mallets and chisels. One scholar has worked out that as many as 1500 sculptors, 4000 builders, 15,000 stone carriers, and 30,000 stone cutters must have worked for 21 years to raise a lesser structure on the Asian mainland. Who knows how many labored to build Borobudur, or how long it took them? De Casparis' researches into contemporary inscriptions seemed to give a building time of only 18 years between the supposed founding date of 824 and a Sailendra queen's provision of rice fields to support the structure's upkeep in 842. Such speed for so great an undertaking would have been almost miraculous.

To Western visitors, brought up against a Christian background, the result of all these labors seems alien yet oddly familiar. Borobudur's sculptured scenes and serene Buddha images appear curiously reminiscent of the Bible stories and saintly figures frozen in stone by the sculptors who enriched Europe's medieval churches and cathedrals. But mounting pinnacled Borobudur is more like climbing a church roof than walking through a nave. Apart from its central stupa, this stepped Buddhist monument lacks enclosed space. Moreover its square base bears no relation to a cruciform church. Nevertheless, scholars have shown that Borobudur indeed parallels the imagery and symbolism of a Christian place of worship.

Above: east flight of steps at Borobudur. At the beginning of each flight of steps a decorated corbeled arch forms an entrance porch. The arch of the third gallery (at the top of the photograph) is the only one intact. The guardian monster at the top "devours" the pilgrim as he ascends, symbolizing death and resurrection.

Right: the marriage of Siddhartha Gautama, before he became the Buddha or "enlightened one."

Below: Mahayana Buddhists worshiping in Sri Lanka. This sect developed the non-theistic philosophy of original Buddhism into a theist religion. It recognized many Buddhas as governing the world in stages, each living in a different paradise. Mahayanaism also venerates human Buddhas, including Gautama, who have come to teach men truth, and a large number of bodhisattvas, demigods of kindness who help men along the right path.

To understand how people used Borobudur it is first important to grasp some of the principles of Buddhist teaching. Its founder, in the 6th century B.C., was a North Indian prince, Siddhartha Gautama, who became the *Buddha*, or "enlightened one." The Buddha taught that human unhappiness sprang from selfish desire for illusory goals ranging from wealth to everlasting life. He preached moral, selfless moderation as a path toward escape from the otherwise unending cycle of birth and rebirth that binds us to this world of suffering and illusion. The Buddha's goal was *nirvana* or non-existence, a state in which the self is merged into the "Great Self" of the Universe.

Eventually Buddhism, like Christianity, split into different sects. The *Mahayana* (Great Vehicle) Buddhist sect which influenced the building of Borobudur stressed seeking the salvation of others as the Buddhist's true objective. As their example, Mahayana Buddhists cite the Buddha's own supposed successive saintly incarnations as a *Bodhisattva,* one with the enlightened nature. They aim to become Bodhisattvas, on the path to Buddhahood. This road, they think, will take them through the three spheres (*dhatu*) of the Universe. From lowest to highest these are *kamadhatu*, the "Sphere of the Desires;" *rupadhatu* or "Sphere of Forms;" and *arupadhatu* or "Sphere of Formlessness."

In 1929 the German scholar W. F. Stutterheim published his remarkable discovery that Borobudur symbolically represents all three of these cosmic spheres. He declared that the base represented *kamadhatu* ; terraces two to five pictured *rupadhatu* ; and levels six to ten symbolized *arupadhatu*.

Before 1885 no such knowledge had been possible. But in that year a Dutch archaeologist learned that the broad lowest terrace had been built out from the monument's true foot, concealing it from view. People were astonished to discover no less than 160 reliefs carved on the hidden base. Experts photographed these images in 1890. Workers then replaced the pavement. For scholars, the photographs provided enduring aids to studying the monument's significance. Plainly revealed upon the hidden base were scenes of people's good and evil deeds. Here, deeds of charity and holy pilgrimage, gossiping and murder reaped their just rewards and penalties, illustrated by events in heaven and in hell. Many panels also bore inscriptions telling sculptors how to illustrate the scenes. Scholars recognized these guides as quotations from a holy Buddhist text concerning *karma*—that is, the law of cause and effect by which people living in the earthly grip of desire earn rewards or punishments according to their deeds. Borobudur's lowest level thus symbolized *kamadhatu*—the sphere of desires, the lowest level in the Buddhist Universe.

Why the builders of the monuments had covered up the *karma* images remained a puzzle. Modern scholars have suggested several explanations. One suggests that priests wished to hide unelevating scenes from Buddhist monks or from a local Buddhist king, because they were either undesirable or unnecessary reminders of the baser side of human nature. Other scholars object that in this case it was scarcely necessary to mask the base in 90 million square feet of stone forming a platform over 20 feet wide. The massive nature of this afterthought surely implies some stronger need than simply tactful concealment. The likeliest explanation is that builders added the bottom terrace chiefly as a retaining wall to reinforce the pyramid and to halt its tendency to creep down the hillside and disintegrate.

Men may have built the terrace as a reinforcement, but its design undoubtedly enriched the structure. This broad platform leads the eye inevitably toward the steeply rising terraces above. Moreover it provided devotees with a broad path on which to walk around the monument before ascending through its rela-

The Path to Buddhahood

Below: 1835 drawing of Borobudur. Hartmann, a Dutch administrator of the Kedu region, arranged for the cleaning of the galleries and removal of much of the debris which covered the monument so that, by the time this drawing was done, the entire temple was free of its disfiguring covering.

Above: a scene from the life of Buddha, a relief from Borobudur. They are of two types—narrative and decorative. The 1460 narrative panels are arranged in 11 rows that go all around the monument for a total length of about 3000 yards.

tively narrow passageways. Thus, as one writer on Borobudur suggests, the platform symbolized the easy, open, but unworthy earthly life of *kamadhatu*, in contrast to the narrower and more demanding path of Buddhism represented by the upper levels of the monument.

The second to fifth terraces represent *rupadhatu*, the sphere of forms. Here, visitors find corridors riotously flanked with images —1300 separate panels of narrative reliefs and more than 1200 of decorative reliefs, with more than 4500 feet of continuous frieze at a higher level. Above that, more than 1400 ornamental tiles adorn the cornices. The balustrades' outer facades feature 432 seated Buddha statues in niches surmounted by small stupas that help to give the monument its many-spired effect.

To the uninitiated the result is beautiful but bewildering. However, Dutch scholars of Buddhist theology have shown that the square terraces were not pointlessly ornate; they hold a vital message for Buddhist pilgrims well versed in ancient Sanskrit texts. At each level the carvings help that message to unfold. In every gallery the main or inner wall narrative reliefs read from right to left; the outer wall or balustrade reliefs, from left to right. Put simply, the burden of their message is the Buddha's progress toward the Buddhahood. To find out where this theme starts, you enter the first gallery from the eastern stairway, turn left and follow the main wall. This bears 120 "strip cartoons in stone" illustrating the Buddha's life. These carvings include the birth of Prince Siddhartha and the Bodhisattva's final incarnation and trace his progress to the condition of enlightenment in which he finally became the Buddha. Below this story, carved high up on the first gallery's 10-foot-high inner wall, we find another 120 panels—this time drawn from two groups of tales collectively called *jatakas* and *avadanas*. The *jatakas* tell how the Buddha was born and reborn in previous incarnations, sometimes as man, sometimes as animal. In each life, he was a Bodhisattva who gained increasing merit by his virtuous deeds. *Avadanas* differ from jatakas in that their chief protagonist is not the Bodhisattva but some other saintly figure. Most of the panels on the first gallery's lower wall come from the avadanas.

The first gallery's outer wall—the balustrade—is wholly taken up by 500 panels depicting jataka and avadana scenes from the Buddha's former lives. A typical example of such stories is the Bodhisattva's incarnation as a hare who sacrificed himself by leaping into a fire to provide food for a starving priest.

More jatakas and avadanas illustrate the second gallery's outer wall, but a new theme features on its almost 10-foot-high inner wall. Drawn from *Gandavyuha*, a holy Mahayana Buddhist text, these 128 large reliefs trace the patient quest for Ultimate Truth pursued by Sudhaṇa, a wealthy merchant's youthful son. Sudhana wanders from teacher to teacher. Each instructs him and answers his questions in new ways. But he remains unsatisfied. At last he meets the Bodhisattva Maitreya, the future Buddha, and Sudhana ends his wanderings though not his story.

Both walls of the third and fourth galleries follow with Sudhana's increasingly sublime experiences. The third gallery shows him in Maitreya's splendid palace, a celestial realm where miracles occur. The fourth gallery shows Sudhana under his final

Cartoon Strips in Stone

Left: Prince Sudhana with his attendants in a hunting party, from a relief at Borobudur. The first 20 panels in the lower series on the wall of the first gallery depict "The Saintly Deeds of Prince Sudhana" of North Panchala, and this scene relates to the prince's rescue of a beautiful princess whom he later married.

teacher, the Bodhisattva Samantabhadra, and at last attaining the Ultimate Truth—the object of his long search.

Thus as the devout walked around and up the monument they reached increasingly exalted themes. Finally they stepped up to the sixth and highest of the square terraces and left behind the images on the walls of the terraces below—the sphere of forms.

In contrast to the closed, square, ornately decorated galleries below, the pilgrims now saw ahead the open, round, unornamented surfaces of the top three levels and their crowning stupa—shapes that symbolize *arupadhatu*, the sphere of formlessness. As one writer put it, on these upper levels form "is absent or surpassed"—a notion strengthened by the symbolism of the circular bases that the stupas rest upon. Borobudur's Buddhist builders probably saw a square as occupying fixed limits and symbolizing the world of tangible phenomena. To them a circle, on the other hand, seemed boundless, and symbolic of the infinite. Here, Buddha images are no longer fully visible, as in the niches lower down. You have to peep through diamond-shaped slits to glimpse the 72 Buddhas seated in the stone dagobas concentrically placed on the three round platforms (32, 24, and 16 dagobas in ascending order). Each gap in a dagoba discloses only part of the Buddha it encloses, a reminder that the seeker after truth finds only parts of the elusive whole. The Buddha (if there were one) in the big, central stupa would be totally invisible behind the stupa's solid, doorless walls.

If the different meanings of its different levels reveal Borobudur as a richly complex monument, at least the Buddha statues might seem straightforward. At first glance all appear identical. All are serenely seated in a cross-legged pose. But close examination reveals subtle differences in the positions of their hands. Between them, the more than 500 statues depict five *mudras* or distinctive gestures, each with a special name and meaning connected with one of five so-called Dhyani, or transcendental Buddhas. For besides revering human Buddhas such as Gautama, Mahayana Buddhists believe in a whole pantheon of past, present, and future transcended Buddhas or "enlightened

Below: broken statue of the Buddha in the *Abhaya mudra* position, symbolizing the reassurance to refrain from fear. The open left hand is placed on the lap and the right hand is lifted up above the right thigh with the palm forward (here the right arm has been broken off). This is the pose of the Dhyani Buddha who is Lord of the North.

Above: a Dhyani Buddha among the stupas at Borobudur. This is an example of the Buddhas of the fifth balustrade, *Dharmachakra mudra*, symbolizing the turning of the Wheel of the Law. Both hands are held in front of the breast, the left hand below the right. The left hand is turned upward with the ring finger touching the thumb, while the ring finger of the right hand touches the little finger of the left. The position resembles the turning of a wheel, and is attributed to Vairocana, the Dhyani Buddha of the Zenith.

ones." Each Dhyani Buddha has its own place in the universe. Thus all 92 Buddha statues in the eastward-facing niches of the lower four balustrades have the left hand open on the lap and the right hand on the right knee, with fingers pointed downward—the so-called "earth-touching" or *Bhumisparsa mudra* related to an incident in Buddhist lore. This mudra identifies these images as Aksobyha, the Dhyani Buddha who dominates the East.

Similarly, the 92 northward-facing statues display the "fearless" mudra of Amoghasiddhi, Lord of the North, the 92 westward-facing Buddhas are in the meditative pose of Amitabha, the west's Dhyani Buddha. A similar number of "wish granting" Ratnasambhava Dhyani Buddhas face south.

Higher up, the Buddha pattern changes again significantly. From all sides of the fifth balustrade, Vairocana, the Dhyani Buddha of the Zenith, makes a teaching gesture. Facing out in all directions, these 64 Vairocana statues signify a power bounded by no spatial limits. This major Buddha of the monument reappears above in the 72 dagobas of the circular terraces, but with a different teaching gesture.

This brings us to the fascinating problem of the Buddha in the central stupa. Because the five Dhyani Buddhas are emanations of the *Adi* (Absolute or Supreme) Buddha, you might suppose his statue would be hidden here upon the summit. When Cornelius cleared Borobudur in 1814 he found a large hole in the stupa's wall. He went inside but left no record of having found a statue. By the 1850s, though, there were reports of one, and early in the 1900s Van Erp indeed removed a statue from the stupa. (It now stands beneath some trees outside the monument itself.) But here was no superbly carved evocation of the supreme

Buddha. Instead, the statue apparently displayed the earth-touching mudra of an Aksobhya. In fact just what is represented was unclear because the sculpture had been left unfinished. Its dress was crudely carved, its fingers incompletely formed, one arm was longer than the other, and the face was ugly.

Disconcerted by its imperfections, archaeologists decided that this Buddha was a reject statue that had been found and placed inside the stupa long after its construction, perhaps by someone ignorant of Buddhist symbolism. Quite possibly Borobudur's builders had left the central stupa empty to symbolize the Supreme Buddha, who is rarely shown in realistic form. But some writers believe the statue to be genuine, its very incompleteness illustrating man's inability to reach Eternal Truth.

Taken as a whole, then, Borobudur was a magic mountain to be climbed by Buddhist pilgrims. The different "cosmic" levels helped them to recreate their past lives and provided goals for future lives, climaxed by the Heavens of the summit.

But ground plan as well as different levels held symbolic meaning for the Mahayana Buddhist. One ingenious theorist has had the notion that Borobudur represented the Buddha's mythical birthplace—a lotus flower floating on a lake. This theorist believed that Borobudur's ground plan incorporated a lotus rosette and petals. Moreover, he held that Borobudur's hill had been an island in a lake that sprawled where Kedu Plain now stands. As supposed proof of this he remarked that several local villages and monuments stood just above the 700-foot contour line and some of the village names incorporated the word *tanjung* meaning "cape." Most scholars would dispute this theory.

Microcosm of the Universe

Less controversial is the notion that Borobudur's layout is that of a *mandala*. This Sanskrit word originally described a magic circle in which people invoked gods. To Mahayana Buddhists of the Vajrayana school a mandala came to mean a tablet containing circles and rectangles as a diagrammatic representation of the world's metaphysical form in a centralized structure that had developed outward from the middle. In such mandalas, the incorporated realistic Buddha images were in a way subsidiary to the overall abstract design, because pure form supposedly represented a higher level of reality than the illusory world of objects apprehended by our senses. Mahayana Buddhists would contemplate a mandala as an aid to meditation that would bring them closer to the essence of reality and to the original unity at the center of the cosmos. Could it be that the ground plan of Borobudur made it just such a microcosm of the universe, but a uniquely huge one carved out of stone?

For more than a century archaeologists sought to identify this bafflingly unusual structure with some well established type of building. Considered simply as a Buddhist monument, Borobudur seemed basically a stupa, a type of shrine reputedly originating in the Buddha's instructions for the disposal of his body after death. The Buddha told his followers to place his ashes in a stupa, depicting this by placing his inverted begging bowl upon the ground and standing his staff upon the bowl. From this guide, Buddhists hold, they learnt to build shrines as domes surmounted by a pinnacle. In time these stupas became more ornate. Some assumed a bell-like shape. A base was added, sometimes several

Below: ground plan of Borobudur, showing its resemblance to a mandala. A mandala is defined as a schematized representation of the cosmos, chiefly characterized by a concentric organization of geometric shapes, each of which contains an image of a deity.

Above: the central stupa at Borobudur.

Below: a worker chiseling around the supporting blocks at the foot of Borobudur as part of the 1971 Unesco restoration project. Archaeologists, stone disease specialists, geologists, biologists, and expert stonemasons from Europe and Asia were brought together to rebuild and restore the monument. An estimated cost of $5.5 million was shared between Japan, Indonesia, and various European countries.

one above another, to produce a low, stepped pyramid. A flight of steps up each side led to a path around which devotees walked below the central stupa. Between A.D. 150 and 400 such stepped structures were built at Gandhara in northwest India and in central Asia. Their influence spread eastward, and undoubtedly affected the builders of Borobudur. This supports the theory that Borobudur was simply a stupa with a base big and ornate enough to dwarf the bell-like central shrine. Paul Mus, a French scholar writing in the 1930s, saw its shape as a hemisphere—and thus by implication as a stupa—with a smaller stupa as its crown.

But Borobudur's elaborately stepped lower levels clearly called for a different explanation. The French architectural historian Henri Parmentier suggested in the 1930s the architects had meant to crown the terraces with an immense dome, but that the subsidence of lower walls forced them instead to cap the monument with a smaller shrine surrounded by still smaller satellites.

Other scholars saw Borobudur primarily as a royal tomb or temple. Some emphasized its full name *Chandi* Borobudur, stressing the local tendency to equate chandis with royal tombs containing the ashes of dead Javanese kings. However, recent study suggests that a chandi was originally a Javanese temple, often dedicated to a king worshiped as a god. In line with such traditions, one German architect supposed that Chandi Borobudur was basically a stepped pyramid surmounted by a temple. Its three successive levels (the Buddhist spheres of desires, forms, and formlessness) could thus also represent earth, atmosphere, and heaven, as symbolized by the different levels of a chandi.

Thus two seemingly conflicting theories arose: one that the structure was a chandi, the other that it was essentially a stupa.

New light on the problem emerged through a careful study of the meaning of the building's name. Some scholars sought to reconstruct its name from Boro (a local village) and Budur—a Buddhist sanctuary mentioned in a medieval Javanese manuscript. But both combined in Javanese would have produced the place name Budur Boro. Sir Thomas Stamford Raffles, who rediscovered Borobudur, tried equating Budur with the modern *buda* meaning "ancient," to produce "Ancient Boro." Alternatively, he thought that *boro* could mean "Great" and *budur*, "Buddha"—hence "Great Buddha." Suggested former spellings of *boro* inspired some writers to come up with other possibilities, including "The Honorable Buddha," "The Many Buddhas," "The Monastery of Budur." (Ruins of a monastery have been found nearby, but the monument itself was plainly not one.)

In 1950 De Casparis announced a new solution to the problem. Studying earlier origins of the words "boro" and "budur" he traced them back to two stone inscriptions on the great stone complex dated about A.D. 842. Both bore the jaw-breaking word *Bhumisambharabhudhara*. Embedded in it, De Casparis recognized the name we know in the shortened form of Borobudur. Intriguingly, the monument's long original name meant "The Mountain of the Accumulation of Virtue in the Ten Stages of the Bodhisattva." Taking the crowning stupa as one stage, Borobudur *does* have 10 stages, each to the Mahayana Buddhist corresponding to one of the 10 stages through which the Bodhisattva passes on the road to Buddhahood.

Virtue in Ten Stages

But two other meanings can be read into the old inscription. First, it could imply a terraced mountain. Secondly, it could mean "kings of the mountain"—the Sailendras in whose kingdom it was built. Prehistoric Indonesians saw stepped pyramids as symbols of the mountain homes of dead ancestors. To De Casparis, Borobudur represented a marriage between old Javanese beliefs and the new faith of the Buddhist missionaries.

Significantly, the Sailendra king who reigned in 842 was the tenth king of his dynasty. He might have built his 10-stage monument to glorify his ancestors and his own divine Bodhisattva.

Borobudur's royal builder could thereby have hoped to gain merit and to advance along the path to Buddhahood. In the hands of Buddhist priest-architects and sculptors, the result was part chandi, part stupa: a unique microcosm of the universe where Buddhist pilgrims who walked around each successive terrace retraced the Buddha's path toward enlightenment.

Astonishingly, Borobudur may have dropped into neglect 1000 years ago, soon after the Sailendras moved their capital to Sumatra. Only the patient detective work of modern archaeologists and other scholars has rediscovered and restored the building. In addition, their labors have explained the mysterious meaning of what its Indonesian biographer Dr. Soekmono has aptly called "a monument for all mankind."

Left: aerial view photographed in 1924 of Borobudur after it was restored by the Dutch under Van Erp. An account of his reconstruction efforts states, "Buddhism and monumental religious sculpture have disappeared from Java, and to counterfeit the decoration would have been to falsify a historical document."

Chapter 12
King Arthur: Man or Myth?

The story of King Arthur and the Knights of the Round Table is Great Britain's most famous myth. Even today, the name of "Camelot," Arthur's palace, has a magical, evocative ring. But how far, factually, is the legend true? Was there even such a king? And where exactly was the evocatively named Camelot? Only recently have historians and archaeologists begun to look seriously for answers to these and other questions. This chapter looks at the evidence: the early written version of the myth; the digs at the reputed sites of Camelot; the verdict of historians. The result is a tantalizing piece of historical detective work.

"He drew his sword Caliburn, called upon the name of the Blessed Virgin, and rushed forward at full speed into the thickest ranks of the enemy. Every man whom he struck, calling upon God as he did so, he killed at a single blow. He did not slacken his onslaught until he had dispatched four hundred and seventy men with his sword Caliburn. When the Britons saw this, they poured after him in close formation dealing death on every side. . . ."

King Arthur's defeat of Saxon invaders in southwest England is full of a superhuman heroism typical of the book it comes from: Geoffrey of Monmouth's *History of the Kings of Britain*. It was this 12th-century mixture of fantasy and fact that gave us the Arthurian legend as we know it today.

Behind the legend stands the dim figure of a 5th-century British warrior who may have led Romanized, Christian, Celtic peoples in a last great stand against barbarian Anglo-Saxon invaders. From Denmark and Germany wave upon wave of these militant migrants had invaded England after Roman rule collapsed there in about A.D. 400. In the hands of historians, poets, and romancers, Arthur grew from a little-known war leader to a great national hero whose exploits shone forth from an otherwise obscure, gloomy corner of British history. Arthur's deeds inspired pride in their nation's remote but glorious past among future generations of British readers—including the English, against whose Anglo-Saxon ancestors Arthur had traditionally

Opposite: *The Battle Between King Arthur and Sir Modred* by W. Hatherell. Both Arthur and Modred are said to have died as a consequence of this fight, which took place during the Battle of Camlann, thought to be in Cornwall in southwestern England.

Right: *The Quest for the Holy Grail* by the 19th-century British Pre-Raphaelite painter Sir Edward Burne-Jones. The quest occupied the time and energy of many knights of Arthur's kingdom, but in the end it was found by the pure Sir Galahad and by Sir Parsifal.

Below: romanticized view of King Arthur hunting with his knights. His legendary exploits formed the basis for richly woven stories by poets such as Malory and the Romantic Alfred Lord Tennyson. Here Arthur is presented as a civilized, generous, beloved king of a court made up of chivalrous and honorable knights.

fought. The man and his legend still hold a strange fascination.

But did he ever live? Do the tales woven around him enshrine a man or a myth? Recent studies of old texts and sites linked with the Arthurian legend lead some scholars to answer "yes" to both questions; others remain skeptical. To explore the question of Arthur's identity, let us first see something of how the tales told about him took shape.

The oldest-known written evidence of Arthur consists of scanty references in early medieval copies by monks of much older manuscripts, most of them handed down by word of mouth. Three manuscripts are especially important. The first is a copy of a mid-6th-century Latin work by a monk named Gildas—a tedious and largely inaccurate writer who mentions a British defeat of the Saxons at the siege of Mount Badon. Gildas credits no individual leader with this victory, which apparently halted for a while the Saxon advance across England. The second source, the 10th-century *Welsh Annals*, firmly links Arthur's name with the Battle of Badon. They refer, too, to "the strife of Camlann in which Arthur and Medraut (Modred) perished." Such annals were based on yearly entries kept by monks in the Dark Ages to help them reckon the dates of Church feast days. They are often reliable guides to actual people and events. But because their starting points were often arbitrary, putting accurate dates to the events they describe is sometimes difficult.

The third early source is a *History of the Britons* compiled in the early 800s in North Wales by Nennius, a cleric translating already ancient Welsh tales into Latin. Nennius calls Arthur the Britons' *dux bellorum* (commander-in-chief), not king, at Mount Badon. Nennius goes on to list 11 more battles in which Arthur fought, based it seems on an old Welsh poem. Much of his account appears authentic, but Nennius also describes "mar-

The Original Arthurian Tales

vels," including Arthur's son's grave which apparently altered in length each time Nennius measured it. Already, it seems, we are crossing the border from fact to fantasy.

By the time Nennius wrote his *History*, Welsh legends had firmly enshrined Arthur as a Celtic hero overcoming giants, witches, and monsters. Written in the 10th century, the poem *The Spoils of Annwn* features Arthur's overseas quest to the land of the dead for a magic cauldron—the prototype, perhaps, for the Holy Grail, a vessel that figures in later Arthurian legend. Celtic tales, too, told of heroes like Gwalchmai and Llenlleawc, patterns for the Arthurian knights Gawain and Lancelot. Arthur's wife Guinevere first appeared in Celtic form, as Gwenhwyfar. But what is lacking is any real proof that such characters did indeed exist.

By 1100 Arthurian tales told in Wales had also reached France and beyond. In Italy, a doorway at Modena Cathedral actually featured a sculpture showing Guinevere rescued by Arthur, Gawain, and Kay.

It was in the 12th century that Arthur's adventures began to assume their familiar literary shape. In 1125 an English chronicler named William of Malmesbury called for an authentic account of the man then hailed as Britain's national hero. He hoped that an authenticated biography and the discovery of Arthur's unknown burial place would discredit such fantasies as the legend that Arthur would one day return. Written about 1135, Geoffrey of Monmouth's lively *History of the Kings of Britain* claimed to be just such a factual account. However, the book was a stew concocted from old Celtic legends and histories and spiced by the writer's own vivid imagination.

Geoffrey tells how Merlin the magician helped the British king Uther Pendragon seduce Igerna, the wife of the Duke of Cornwall. From this union Arthur was born at Tintagel Castle.

Above: Merlin by the late-19th-century British artist Aubrey Beardsley. This ornamental illustration is one of a series done for an edition of *Morte d'Arthur*.

Romantic Tales of Chivalry

Right: the birth of King Arthur, from an oak carving in the King's Robing Room in the British Parliament's House of Lords, by H. Armstead. According to a Cornish legend, Arthur was born at Tintagel, the son of Uther Pendragon and Igerna, wife of the Duke of Cornwall. According to this story, Merlin helped the seduction by making him look like Igerna's husband, and Uther later married Igerna after his men had killed the Duke in battle.

Above: the coronation of King Arthur, from an illuminated medieval French manuscript. Whether crowned because he pulled a magic sword from a stone or because he was the king's son, the romance of Arthur's reign has been embellished by centuries of chroniclers.

Crowned king at the age of 15, Arthur subdued much of Europe with his knights and his sword Caliburn (also called Excalibur). He set up court at Caerleon in Wales. At Camblam Arthur killed his rebellious son Modred, the fruit of an incestuous liaison, but was himself mortally wounded and taken to the Isle of Avalon to be tended. Brave, generous, and chivalrous, and with a mysterious beginning and ending, Geoffrey's Arthur emerged as a world figure, appealing hugely to the medieval love of chivalry, adventure, and mystery.

Subsequent writers embellished the story. In 1155 Robert Wace's French translation of Geoffrey's history anticipates the wounded Arthur's return from Avalon, and mentions for the first time the now famous Round Table. Less than half a century later Layamon's English version of Wace explained the table as a device to stop precedence quarrels among Arthur's knights. It also had Arthur shipped to Avalon by Morgan, a fairy queen. The tale that the boy Arthur won Britain's crown by drawing a sword from a stone emerged in the early 1200s, in Robert de Borron's *Merlin.*

Meanwhile other legends inspired the late 12th-century French romancer Chrétien de Troyes to write long poems about the amours and wondrous adventures—including the quest for the Holy Grail—of the chivalrous knights of Arthur's court at Camelot. Chrétien demoted Arthur himself to an impotent figurehead, whose wife was seduced by Lancelot.

Arthurian stories snowballed during the Middle Ages. They found their richest expression in Sir Thomas Malory's 15th-century English *Morte d'Arthur* (Death of Arthur). This work sets its last poignant scene in Glastonbury, Somerset, renowned as the Arthurian Avalon long before Malory wrote.

Plainly, much of the matter in most of these Arthurian stories is fiction—so much in fact that some people believe that historians simply invented Arthur to plug a gap in Britain's national history. But at least Arthurian legend was based on old Celtic tales of remembered events: some lost, others garbled during the centuries of retelling before men wrote them down.

Some scholars seeking to sift fact from folklore believe old documents do prove that Arthur lived. But skeptics find many of their arguments tortuous and unconvincing. For instance, whole theories have been underpinned by a medieval scribe's supposed misspelling of a single word.

At least, the Arthurians maintain, we have the names of actual places linked with Arthur's name. Several stand out: Tintagel, where he was apparently born; Camelot and Caerleon, where he held court; Glastonbury, where he died. Then there are the 13 battle sites listed in Nennius and the Welsh annals.

These sites, Arthurian scholars supposed, might hold archaeological clues helping to prove that the hero had once truly lived, reigned, and fought.

In some cases the first difficulty was finding a site to fit its place name. Tintagel at least posed no such problem. Geoffrey of Monmouth, who first linked Tintagel with Arthur, described a castle standing high on a coast and surrounded by sea except for a

Below: the first kiss of Lancelot and Guinevere, from a late-14th-century French manuscript. Arthur himself merely provided the framework in medieval stories of courtly love between one of his knights and the queen or for tales of the chivalrous exploits of his band of knights of the Round Table.

Above: Roman latrines and barracks at Caerleon, Wales. Geoffrey of Monmouth chose to site Arthur's court in Caerleon, within 20 miles of his own birthplace. Below: the remains of the inner ward of Tintagel Castle, supposedly the birthplace of King Arthur. The mainland is in the background and the archway at left. The right-angled foundations at the far right are those of the walls of the Great Hall, a 12th-century building which stood within the inner ward. The southern end has fallen over the cliff.

rocky isthmus joining its rock to the mainland. This description exactly fits a particular headland in North Cornwall. The headland formed part of the manor of Bossinney, listed in 1086 in *Domesday Book*. *Domesday Book* mentioned no headland castle, but archaeological studies begun in the 1800s revealed traces of ancient fortification, as well as later works. You can still see the huge bank that once commanded the landward approaches to the headland. A deep ditch fronts the bank and a palisade once crowned it. To reach the headland, people had to thread their way along a narrow passage between the ditch end and a steep-sided rock. On the peninsula itself there are traces of a great stone hall and a small chapel comprising simply nave and chancel. There were also no doubt smaller, wooden buildings which have long since disappeared. Disappointingly, however, it turned out that this stronghold was built at least 600 years later than Arthurian times. Carved stonework discovered there in the 1800s suggests a date of about 1150 for the complex. That makes it the undoubted remains of a castle built by Henry I's illegitimate son Reginald soon after 1141 when Henry created him Earl of Cornwall. Significantly, Earl Reginald's half-brother Earl Robert of Gloucester was Geoffrey of Monmouth's patron. Almost certainly, then, Geoffrey located Arthur's birth at Tintagel to flatter the royal family whose patronage he valued. It is true Geoffrey first wrote his account of Arthur before the medieval castle had been built, but that version of his history has disappeared. Geoffrey probably produced the surviving version in about 1145, adding Tintagel as a topical—and tactful—afterthought.

If Tintagel was indeed first fortified as late as the 1140s, then it hardly seems likely that Arthur could have been born there. But evidence that there were stone buildings on the site as early as the 400s supports the claims of the Arthurians. Excavations in the

Arthur Born at Tintagel?

early 1930s unearthed not only medieval ruins, but traces of no less than eight earlier monastic structures, all protected by the same bank and ditch that the medieval builders later reinforced. Among the ruins, the archaeologists found what they believed were the remains of monks' cells, a sacristy, a guest house, a library, and a dining hall. Proof of the monastery's date—and of its affluence—lies in numerous fragments of imported pottery found on the site. These include Samian ware of Roman times, some with crosses stamped inside the base indicating a Christian use; big Mediterranean-type jars for holding wine and olive oil; and mortars used for mashing food, probably French in origin.

The presence of such imported pottery strongly suggests that the monastery at Tintagel flourished in the late 400s and early 500s. A Celtic settlement therefore stood upon Tintagel at about the year of Arthur's reputed birth. Moreover, this was no ordinary settlement, but probably the largest complex of its kind anywhere in Celtic Britain. Even the skeptics must find these facts remarkable. In spite of the lack of trustworthy written proof, many people may still feel that Arthur and Tintagel must have been connected, though scarcely in the way that Geoffrey described: few mothers give birth in a monastery.

Locating the place where Arthur is reputed to have been born proved a good deal easier than the next task—that is, establishing just where the shadowy monarch held court. Where was that world-famous Camelot? Caerleon, Winchester, and London have all been named by medieval writers. Caerleon does indeed contain impressive ruins, but they were Roman, and the so-called "Round Table" there is in fact what remains of a Roman amphitheater. Winchester Castle contains a massive circular table of ancient oak. Could this be the vital clue? Unfortunately, radiocarbon dating carried out in the 1970s demonstrated that the

Above: the Round Table of Winchester Castle. Around the Tudor rose in the center (added at a later date) is the legend "Thys is the rownde table of Kyng Arthur with XXIV of hys namyde knygttes." Arthur himself is seated above.

Left: Arthur and his knights at the Round Table, from a 13th-century manuscript. In the center is the Holy Grail. The table may have been round in order to prevent fights over precedence among the king's followers.

Excavation at Cadbury Hill

timber was after all of medieval date. The explanation is that from the 13th century growing interest in Arthuriana resulted in numerous courtly entertainments called Round Tables, where men and women imitated the feasts, dances, and jousting that they imagined had enlivened Arthur's court. In 1348, for example, England's Edward III instigated the Order of the Garter partly to revive the traditions of Arthurian knighthood. Later still, England's Tudor kings claimed Arthur as an ancestor (they were after all partly Welsh, which was something) and indeed a painted Tudor rose appears in the center of Winchester's Round Table.

Camelot's claim to be the seat of Arthur's rule is not made easier by the fact that there is no town or city in England or Wales of that name. Chrétien de Troyes was vague about its setting. Malory—evidently influenced by the Table there—equated Camelot with Winchester. Other writers claimed that Camelot could still be seen in Wales—a reference, some think, to Caerleon's (or maybe Caerwent's) ancient Roman walls.

In 1542 an antiquarian named John Leland suggested another possibility. He wrote: "At South Cadbury stands Camallate, sometime a famous town or castle. The people can tell nothing there but that they have heard say that Arthur much resorted to Camallate." No one can be certain why Leland placed Camelot at South Cadbury in Somerset, in southwest England. It may have been, as he wrote, that the local people simply believed that it had been there. Perhaps a combination of local place-names and geographical features influenced him. He certainly corrupted the "Camel" of two local villages called Queen Camel and West Camel into "Camallate." He may well have been impressed with nearby Cadbury Hill, a steep-sided limestone peak some 500 feet high which dominates the surrounding countryside. Crowning the hill is South Cadbury Castle. No castle stood here in Leland's time, for the banks and ditches, now largely wooded, that ring the hill are the remains of an Iron Age fort built on the summit before the Romans came to Britain in 55 B.C.

In Leland's time, it seems, a good deal of largely unrecorded legend was gathering about the hill. Later written tradition locates Arthur's palace on the level summit; forges a subterranean link between two hillside wells; and holds that the hill is hollow and that Arthur and his knights lay asleep inside, to emerge in time of national need.

Whatever Cadbury Hill's Arthurian connections might have been, its Iron Age fort alone suggested this to be a site worth investigation. Accordingly, for one reason or another, archaeologists have been burrowing in the hill on and off since the late 19th century.

In 1890, South Cadbury's rector reported opening a hut-dwelling on the summit and discovering a flagstone that—contrary to workers' expectations—did not lead to King Arthur's cave. Twenty-three years later a somewhat sketchy but better documented dig revealed pottery attributed to late Celtic times. But justification for large-scale excavation emerged only in the 1950s when plowing turned up surface finds including scraps of Tintagel-type pottery and a piece of glass from Dark Age France. It was not much. But it was enough to convince Ralegh Radford,

Below: Arthur and his knights returning to Camelot, from a 16th-century Flemish manuscript. The site of Camelot is widely believed to be at South Cadbury, Somerset, first suggested by the antiquarian John Leland in 1542.

Left: archaeological excavations at South Cadbury Castle. At left is Ralegh Radford and in the center is Leslie Alcock, professor of archaeology at the University College, Cardiff, in South Wales. The castle crowns an isolated hill about 500 feet high near the border between the counties of Somerset and Dorset.

a leading British archaeologist, that South Cadbury Castle had indeed been Camelot. Moreover in 1955 an aerial photographic survey revealed dark patches on the pale, cultivated summit—crop-marks betraying extensive areas of ancient soil disturbance. Interest in a major excavation now gained momentum.

In 1965 leading archaeologists and Arthurian scholars formed the Camelot Research Committee which found enough money to finance a trial dig in 1966, under Leslie Alcock, an authority on the archaeology of Dark Age Britain. What followed proved so fruitful that the project ran on to 1970.

The first problem was deciding where to work. The 18-acre summit was too big to excavate entirely. The team thus set out to find those areas most likely to reward investigation. Surveyors drew up a contour plan, and the archaeologists used a banjo-shaped metal detector to criss-cross the hilltop in a search for buried metal objects. At the same time, local variations in the soil's electrical conductivity showed up the sites of old, filled-in post-holes where upright building supports had once stood.

The first season's digging hinted at a long but remote history of habitation. Neolithic, Bronze Age, and Iron Age peoples had all left their mark upon the hill. More importantly for the Camelot Research Committee, so had Celtic peoples of Arthurian times. The personal possessions found seemed unexciting: a small misshapen iron knife and fragments of Tintagel-type pottery. Significantly, though, these fragments came from each of the three trial sites. This suggested extensive Dark Age occupation by a relatively wealthy group. But what most excited some archaeologists were the remains of a Dark Age defensive wall and other structures uncovered during the five seasons' work.

Trenches cut across the inner defensive rampart revealed seven phases of building and rebuilding between pre-Roman and medieval times. One rampart in particular produced the kind of evidence that enabled scholars to say with certainty that it had been a barrier erected in Arthurian times by Celts, presumably against the Saxons. It survived as a rather low narrow mound of rubble, but in places it was plain that the outer surface had been

Below: volunteers uncovering bones at the Cadbury Castle dig in one of the smaller trenches on the east side of the hill fort.

Right: Leslie Alcock, director of the dig, and a model of the South Cadbury site. He is pointing to an illustration of the type of house believed to have been built at the time.

Below: a bronze pin with double-spiral head and a gilt bronze letter "A" found at Cadbury. The brooch is believed to date from the 9th or 8th century B.C., but the "A" is Roman, possibly from the 3rd or 4th century A.D.

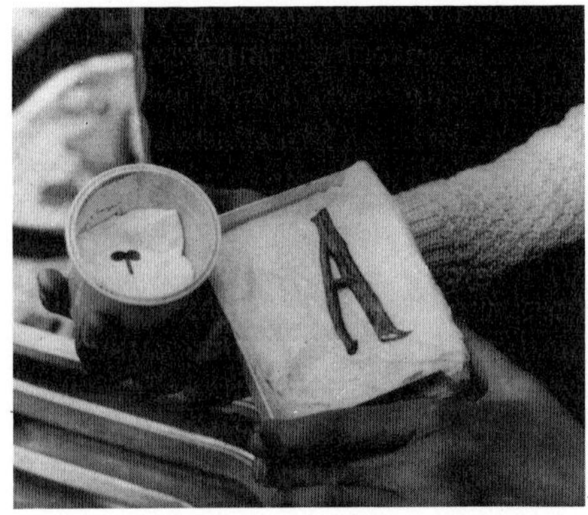

faced by stones, with gaps once filled by posts—supports for a timber breastwork built above the rubble mound. Moreover alignments of the stones inside the core revealed that the walls had consisted of a timber framework held in place by rubble heaped up on the beams. Presumably defenders would have stood, protected by the breastwork, on a wooden platform placed above the stonework. The fort's Celtic builders had evidently lacked the Romans' skill in dressing stones and bonding them with mortar. Instead, they plundered dressed stones from nearby Roman ruins, and in particular a temple standing on a hill. They then built their drystone wall somewhat in the fashion of the pre-Roman Britons. Unsophisticated, maybe, but impressive nonetheless, for their defense extended some 1200 yards, surrounding the entire surface of the hilltop. Leslie Alcock felt that the sheer size of the area enclosed implied that South Cadbury had acted as a base for an army large by late Celtic British standards—possibly created from the independent Celtic kingdoms' small fighting forces, gathered at this strategically important site to halt the Saxons' attacks on southwestern Britain.

Tell-tale soil stains derived from rotted timbers reinforce this picture of military strength by helping archaeologists to visualize the impressive gate tower that commanded the southwest entrance to the fort. We must imagine here a narrow wooden passage led into the wall, closed by two pairs of doors and capped by a protected lookout platform raised above the general level of the rampart.

Late on in the excavations another exciting find appeared. Pits and post-holes confusingly covered the summit center—burrowings spread out over several centuries. From this confusion close study extracted a pattern made up of rows of post-holes. In Arthurian times these holes had evidently held posts supporting a timber hall over 60 feet long and half as wide, with a screen near one end separating one-third from the rest. Wooden posts had apparently helped to support a thatched roof laid on a wooden framework. In this primitive hall the camp's commander-in-chief had almost certainly held counsel and issued commands. Arthur himself, perhaps?

This barnlike building is a far cry from the splendid palaces in

Isle of Avalon?

which writers describe Arthur holding court. But the real Camelot—if it ever existed—may well have been more like a "Wild West" frontier fort than a sophisticated city.

Twelve miles northwest from Cadbury Hill the steep-sided mass of Glastonbury Tor rises above the fields of the north Somerset plain. In Arthurian times the hill was a peninsula flanked by shallow sea and marsh. Antique lettering on some modern maps identifies Glastonbury Tor as the Isle of Avalon, where the mortally wounded Arthur was traditionally carried. Here, too, the legend states that he died and his body was buried low down on the hill's western flank. Reports of Arthur's links with Glastonbury date from about 1150, when Caradoc of Llancarfan wrote a *Life of St. Gildas*. Caradoc describes how the Abbot of Glastonbury helped Arthur rescue Guinevere from King Melwas, her abductor. But people seem to have connected Glastonbury with Avalon in the 1190s. By then, the monks of Glastonbury Abbey claimed to have found the bones of Arthur and Guinevere buried near the abbey church's Lady Chapel. Gerald of Wales, who visited the abbey soon afterward, claimed that he saw the bones. He also mentioned a golden lock of hair that turned to powder when seized from the grave.

Thirty years later, Ralph of Coggeshall described the exhumation. But the least fanciful account—based largely on oral tradition—appeared a century later. This was by Adam of Domerham, a Glastonbury monk. On two important points accounts agreed: a lead cross had marked the grave, and the grave had been sited between two ancient pyramids. Otherwise the versions differed tantalizingly. A "hollowed oak" had held the bodies, claimed Gerald; Ralph referred to a sarcophagus. Ralph wrote

Left: *The Death of Arthur* by the 19th-century Scottish painter James Archer. Here Arthur is prepared for his journey to the Isle of Avalon by three queens as his boat approaches. According to Malory the king tells his last faithful supporter, "I will into the vale of Avilion, to heal me of my grievous wound; and if thou never hear more of me, pray for my soul." The three queens are Arthur's sister Morgan le Fay, the Queen of Northgalis, and the Queen of the Wastelands.

Searching for Arthur's Grave

Right: Glastonbury Abbey, site of the Lady Chapel and Arthur's grave. Arthur's connection with Glastonbury was first recorded in the *Life of St. Gildas* about 1150.

Above: 17th-century engraving of a cross, since lost, from Camden's *Britannia*, said to have been found in Arthur's grave at Glastonbury.

that the Latin text upon the cross had read: "Here lies the famous King Arthur, in the Isle of Avalon buried." Gerald phrased the inscription differently and included a mention of Guinevere.

To honor their famous find the monks installed them in a superbly carved double tomb within the abbey church. Adam of Domerham's account tells what happened next. At Easter 1278, King Edward I watched while the tomb was opened and the bones removed. Arthur's were "of great size" and Guinevere's "of marvellous beauty." Edward ceremonially laid the bones in caskets, minus the skulls which were removed for public veneration. The tomb containing the caskets was then resited before the high altar.

During the Reformation, religious zealots smashed the tomb, and no one knows what happened to the bones. Researchers came across the tomb's foundations in 1931 in the ruined abbey. Traces of the original burial persisted, too. John Leland saw what was claimed to be the cross after 1540. An engraving of it features in William Camden's *Britannia* early in the 1600s. The cross apparently survived at Wells until the 18th century and then simply vanished.

However, in 1962 archaeologists discovered what could have been the very grave from which the medieval monks had lifted Arthur's bones. Digging into the old cemetery south of the site of Glastonbury's Lady Chapel they found traces of a broad pit that may have held the base of a massive cross. Some three yards south of this lay fragments of an ancient mausoleum. Cross and mausoleum were probably the "pyramids" already mentioned. Writing early in the 12th century, William of Malmesbury had implied that both were really crosses, built up in several stages.

Between the two, archaeologists found a large hole had been dug and filled in about 1190. Proof of that date were distinctive stone chips lying in the hole—waste struck from masonry by the chisels of masons constructing the nearby Lady Chapel in the 1180s.

Here, then was Arthur's grave. Or was it? Skeptics claim that the 12th-century monks had forged both grave and antique lettering upon the cross. They had the motive: they badly needed cash to make good fire damage done in 1184. By claiming to hold Arthur's bones they would attract pilgrims—and donations—to Glastonbury.

However, supporters of the monks' account claim that the cross, although post-Arthurian, really did predate the medieval exhumation. They argue that St. Dunstan, then Abbot of Glastonbury, could have had it made about 945 when he removed old grave markers in the course of building up the level of the cemetery. From Arthur's burial, so this theory goes, St. Dunstan took away a stone slab bearing a simple 6th-century inscription and replaced it with the cross—a more elaborate memorial in keeping with Arthur's growing reputation. Disappointingly, no Arthurian period pottery turned up at Glastonbury Abbey. But a dig on the top of nearby Glastonbury Tor bared scraps of amphoras, old hearths, and other proofs of Dark Age settlement. Who the settlers were, however, remains a mystery.

So far we have looked at the evidence for Arthur's supposed birthplace, his capital, and the place where he was buried. The other sites associated with his name are chiefly battlefields. Dark Age battles were generally fought at strategically important river crossings. Those linked with Arthur's name suggest he campaigned all over Britain. Of the 13 battles named in early works, 12 are victories from the old Welsh list reported in Nennius' *History of the Britons*; the 13th and last is the final "Camlann" cited in the *Welsh Annals*. Unfortunately Nennius does not say who Arthur conquered and it is hard to find the sites described. His first battle took place at the mouth of the River Glein. There were two English rivers called Glen but there were doubtless more before the Anglo-Saxons changed their names. So we have no idea where Arthur fought his first battle.

Nennius sites the next four battles on the River Dubglas in a

Below left: the excavation of Glastonbury Tor as photographed by the archaeologist Philip Rahtz. This site is beneath the church on the summit of the hill. The team found imported Mediterranean pottery, iron and bone objects, a bronze head, fragments of a crucible, and Roman tile fragments, all dating from the Dark Ages—the Arthurian period.

Below: stone head dating from the Dark Ages, one of the artifacts found at Glastonbury Tor. Such proofs of settlement during Arthur's time were not found on the site of Glastonbury Abbey itself.

Above: Arthur's Seat, a hill rising near Holyrood Palace at Edinburgh, Scotland. It is in the shape of a recumbent lion. The hill is one of the many sites in Scotland associated with Arthur, although historical connections are extremely doubtful.

district named as Linnuis. Some scholars suggest that Linnuis was one of two Roman sites called Lindum. The more likely of the two would place the battle in a Scottish valley called Glen Douglas near Loch Lomond. There, Arthur could have fought against the Scottish kingdom of Dalriada though four times seems improbable. Another explanation is that Linnuis is a scribe's misspelling of *lininuis*, a word supposedly derived from *Lindinienses*, the name of a tribal group living near two "Dubglas" rivers that cross the north Dorset Downs of southern England. Leslie Alcock argues that this would be a likely area for Arthur to engage Saxons advancing from the east.

The 6th, 8th, and 10th battles named by Nennius fit no known place names. But the 7th was "the battle of the Caledonian Forest" (the "wood of Celidon"). This must mean a battle fought in Scotland, which the Romans called "Caledonia." Just where it happened and who Arthur fought there we cannot say.

The 9th battle occurred in the "city of the legion" which scholars identify as either Chester or Caerleon. Arthur reputedly

Right: Arthur as a historical character holding back the Saxon invasion at Bath. He wins the gratitude of the inhabitants who would have been raped or killed if he had not come to their aid. Bath is believed to be the site of the Battle of Badon.

Locating the Battlesites

won his 10th victory at Agned. Geoffrey of Monmouth equates Agned with Edinburgh. The hill there called Arthur's Seat does hold traces of a Dark Age fort. But some old manuscripts name the battle site as Breguoin or Breguein—names that set the scholars scurrying off to places in England.

The last two battles were the crucial ones for Arthur. Mount Badon seems to have represented Arthur's greatest triumph. Here, he felled 960 men, single-handed, in one day, Nennius declares, in true heroic mein. The *Welsh Annals* imply that the whole battle lasted three days and nights, during which Arthur "carried the cross of our Lord Jesus Christ on his shoulders." Gildas calls the struggle a siege. Moreover, he makes it plain that Badon was a British, Christian victory against the invading Saxon heathens. The date of Badon is debatable—A.D. 490 or 518 appear the likeliest contenders. The place is also uncertain. It could have been one of the five Badburys (named from an Old English word for Badda's fort—Badda being possibly some legendary Saxon hero). Bath in Avon (or rather, a nearby hill) is another possibility because "Badon" would have been pronounced "Bathon" in the old British tongue.

This brings us to the last struggle—the "Camlann" of the *Welsh Annals* and Geoffrey of Monmouth's "Camlam." It was this evidently civil strife (variously dated 510 and 539) in which Arthur was killed and which apparently left the British kingdoms divided against their common Anglo-Saxon foes. The names of the Cornish River Camel and Somerset Cam have helped to make each popular as the likely battle site. Slaughterbridge near Camelford in Cornwall does have an old memorial stone called "Arthur's tomb." But place-name experts identify Camlann with Camboglanna, a Roman fort in northwest England and a likely site for civil war between two British armies.

The uncertainty surrounding Arthur's battle sites has led some scholars to dismiss the whole list as legendary. Others think that Arthur's name became attached to battles fought by several warriors. Others declare that he was a purely northern figure, and that all southern so-called Arthurian sites are spurious. Evidence for this theory comes largely from a sentence in Aneurin's 6th-century *Y Gododdin*. Describing the mighty warrior Gwawrddur, Aneurin wrote: "He glutted black ravens on the wall of the fort, though he was not Arthur." In other words, in battle Gwawrddur was as valiant as Arthur, slaughtering enough enemies to gorge the birds that feed on carrion. Traditionalists claim this shows that the Arthur of Tintagel and Camelot was already venerated as a national hero by the 9th century when *Y Gododdin* was probably first written down.

This chapter has merely nibbled at the mystery surrounding King Arthur. What underlying truths, if any, have we managed to expose? Certainly not the Arthur of medieval chivalry and splendor. Arthur was more probably commander-in-chief of a British force that briefly stemmed the westward-flowing Anglo-Saxon flood. He may possibly have been an obscure Scottish chieftain's son. One fact is certain: the only datable evidence for Arthur lies in archaeology and old manuscripts. The first provides no mention of his name. The second is scanty, ambiguous, and unreliable.

Below: "Arthur's Tomb" at Slaughterbridge, near Camelford, Cornwall. The river Camel is often claimed to be the site of the Battle of Camlann, from which the mortally wounded Arthur was borne away to be healed in Avalon. But uncertainty and lack of proof plague those who would like King Arthur to take his place as a genuine British hero.

SIRIA
Arabia petrea
Terreste mare
Arabia ferilis
Arabia felix
Mare Indicum
Barnacais. r.
Aethiopia subegitu.
Media thiopia
AFRICA
Quiloa
Bonaspes.
Mare bone spej.
EQVINO TIALIS
TROPICVS CAP RICORNI
MERI DI ES

Chapter 13
Who Was Prester John?

Few mysteries intrigued medieval Europeans more than the enigma of Prester John. Was there really a Christian king whose kingdom lay east of the Moslems who controlled the Holy Land? Could he really help them in their struggles against the infidel? When in about 1165 a letter appeared addressed to the Christian Emperor of Byzantium, the legend began to take firmer shape. And when the Pope replied 12 years later the Christian king in the east took on the trappings of reality. But was Prester John a genuine priest-king ruling a Christian empire in Asia, or even Africa? In this chapter the author sets out to answer the question: Who exactly was Prester John?

When Bishop Otto of Freising in Bavaria met Bishop Hugh of Jabala in Syria near Rome in the year 1145, the Syrian bishop had a most extraordinary tale to tell. A few years earlier, said Bishop Hugh, a Christian priest-king from somewhere east of Persia had won a series of shattering victories against the Samiardi, two brothers one of whom was king of the Medes, the other of the Persians. He had seized their capital of Egbattana, now the city of Hamadan in what is now Iran, and had then gone on to crush a combined army of Medes, Persians, and Assyrians in a three-day battle. The mysterious priest-king had then set out with his army to help the Church of Jerusalem, where at that time Crusading knights from Europe were isolated in a Moslem-dominated and hostile part of the Middle East. Finding his path barred by the River Tigris, the king had headed north, upstream. For years he waited for the river to freeze over so that he could march his army across. But the Tigris had not frozen over. At last, the disappointed priest-king gave up his plan to join forces with the Europeans, and returned home.

Bishop Otto learned that this monarch was known as "Presbyter Iohannes"—that is, Priest, or Prester, John. John was supposedly descended from the Magi of the New Testament and he ruled their subject peoples "in glory and prosperity."

For European Christians living at the time of the Crusades this story had a special significance. It suggested that beyond Europe's Moslem enemies lay a Christian kingdom—strong, militant, and

Opposite: 16th-century map of the east coast of Africa showing Prester John seated on his throne in the mountains north of the equator. Mapmakers used him along with mythical beasts and fabulous monsters to populate the distant and unexplored corners of the earth.

Right: a 15th-century rendition of the siege of Jerusalem in 1099 by the European troops of the First Crusade. Prester John was reputed to have tried to help the Christian Church in Jerusalem but had been prevented from doing so because his troops were unable to cross the Tigris river.

Below: Nestorian religious painting of a woman with typically Chinese features. The Nestorian form of Christianity spread through central Asia as far east as Mongolia and China centuries before the arrival of Catholic missionaries. After the Moslem invasion of Persia the Asian Christians were a force in the area until the 1300s.

sympathetic to the cause of the Crusades. Not surprisingly, the story fascinated its German hearer.

Bishop Otto had no cause to disbelieve the story. He knew that Moslem powers ruled most of southwest Asia. But he knew too that Christian communities had sprung up there before the Moslems came to power, and still flourished. Modern historians have shown that Christianity somehow crossed the mountains and deserts of central Asia, and had briefly thrived in China in the 8th century. But unlike the Roman Catholic and Greek Orthodox Christians of the West, these Asian Christians were Nestorians. Named after a doctrine supposedly put forward by Nestorius, a 5th-century Patriarch of Constantinople, Nestorians believed that Christ's divine and human natures were separate, not identical as Western churches hold. This heresy was one reason why Western Christians knew so little about what went on among the Christians of the East. There were other reasons. Lack of trade and Moslem hostility in Africa and Asia had left medieval Christian Europe largely unaware of other lands and peoples. The Crusades opened a small window on the Eastern world, but little more than rumors of what lay beyond the Holy Land traveled westward. These rumors dealt mostly with monsters, infidels, and wealth beyond belief.

Bishop Otto was better read, better traveled, and more skeptical than most of his contemporaries, but Bishop Hugh's extraordinary tale of Prester John impressed him so much that the Bavarian bishop incorporated it in a chronicle that he was then writing. That is where modern scholars found Bishop Hugh's account of an incident which some believe sparked off the quest that followed: a centuries-long search by Europeans for Prester John and his successors.

Historians have found that facts support Hugh's story, but that the real events and characters were not those Hugh described. His brothers "Samiardi" were actually one individual—the Seljuk Turkish Sultan Sanjar. The conqueror of Sanjar's Moslem army was not Prester John but a Mongol Khan named Ye-lu-ta-shih of the Kara Khitai tribe. The scholar Gustav Oppert has tried deriving the name Prester John from Ye-lu-ta-shih's title *Gur Khan* via a supposed Syriac mistranslation *Yuhanan*, the Syriac for "John." But there is no real evidence to support this bit of verbal juggling. Moreover, it seems unlikely that Ye-lu-ta-shih had been a Christian, let alone a priestly Christian king. In his book on Prester John, the American scholar Vsevolod Slessarev points out that this Mongol's contemporaries described him either as a believer in the Persian-based faith called Manichaeism or as a Buddhist. Slessarev suggests that Ye-lu-ta-shih was probably a Buddhist, because Buddhism would have influenced the Mongol's Chinese education. Finally, the battle of 1141 in which Ye-lu-ta-shih had crushed the greatest Moslem soldier of his day occurred nowhere near the city now called Hamadan, but east of Samarkand, in central Asia.

So far Prester John may seem vague and shadowy. But the 12th century also produced the priest-king in more definite form. This form is an extraordinary letter supposedly sent by Prester John to the Byzantine Emperor Manuel I. Some versions of the letter addressed it jointly to Manuel and his counterpart in Western Europe, the German Holy Roman Emperor Frederick Barbarossa. We don't know when the letter first appeared. The 13th-century French chronicler Albéric of Trois Fontaines put the date at about 1165, but Albéric's evidence is often unreliable. All we can say with certainty is that the original letter was addressed to Manuel, who reigned between 1143 and 1180.

Rumors of Nestorians

Below: a weird collection of fabulous beasts including the legendary unicorn, an illumination from *The Book of Marco Polo* as included in a French manuscript. Europeans imagined that the uncharted areas of the East were inhabited by all sorts of monsters.

Theſe Letters following were tranſlated into *Latine*, by *Pa. Iouius*, and reuiewed after alſo and publiſhed by *Damianus à Goes*, and in *Italian* by *Ramuſio*. That which is omitted, is the ſame with that in the former Letter.

* *Breu.*

* *Madagaſcar.*

The Letters of *Dauid*, the Mightie Emperour of *Æthiopia*, vnto *Emanuel* King, of *Portugall*, &c. Written in the yeere 1521. as alſo to King *Iohn* and Pope *Clement*.

IN the name of God the Father, who was from Euerlaſting, and hath no beginning, &c.

Theſe Letters are ſent from me Athani Tingil, *&c. Emperour of the great and high* Æthiopia, *and of mightie Kingdomes, Dominions, and Territories, King of* Xoa, *of* Caſſate, *of* Fatigar, *of* Angote, *of* * Baru, *of* Baaliganze, *of* Aden, *of* Vangue, *of* Goiame, *(where* Nilus *ſpringeth) of* Amara, *of* Baguemedri, *of* Ambeaa, *of* Vagne, *of* Tigremahon, *of* Sabaym, *from whence came the Queene of* Saba, *of* Bernagaes, *and Lord euen to the Countrey of* Nubia, *bordering vpon* Egypt. *Theſe Letters are directed vnto the moſt mightie, moſt excellent, and victorious King,* Don Emanuel, *who dwelleth in the loue of God, and remayneth ſtedfaſt in the Catholike Faith, the Sonne of the Apoſtles* Peter *and* Paul, *the King of* Portugall *and* Algarbi, *a louer of Chriſtians, an Enemie, Iudge, Emperour, and Vanquiſher of the* Moores *and* Gentiles *of* Africa *and* Guinea, *of the Cape of* Buona Speranza, *and of the Ile* * *of the Moone, alſo of the Red Sea of* Arabia, Perſia, *and* Ormuz, *of the greater* India, *and of all places, Ilands, and Countries adiacent, the deſtroyer of the* Moores, *and ſtout Pagans, the Lord of Fortreſſes, high Caſtles and Walls, the Inlarger of the Faith of Ieſus Chriſt. Peace be vnto thee, King* Emanuel, *who relying vpon the aſſiſtance of God, deſtroyeſt the* Moores; *and with thy ſhips, thy Souldiers and Captaines, expelleſt them in all places the faithleſſe Dogs. Peace be with the Queene thy Wife, beloued of Ieſu Chriſt, Seruant of the Virgine* Marie, *the Mother of the Sauiour of all people. Peace be to thy Sonnes, being now, as it were, in a freſh Garden, amidſt the flouriſhing Lillies, a Table furniſhed with all Dainties. Peace bee vnto your Daughters, which are adorned with Princely Robes, as Palaces are with Hangings of Tapiſtrie. Peace vnto your Kinſfolkes, the Off-ſpring of*

Right: the English text of a letter from the Emperor of Ethiopia to King João II of Portugal, written in 1521. At this time Ethiopia was thought to be the kingdom of Prester John.

Below: Frederick Barbarossa (1152–1190), one of the addressees of Prester John's celebrated letter to Christian monarchs of the West. One of the greatest of the Holy Roman emperors of the Middle Ages, Frederick was a crusader and opponent of the papacy. His power rested on his commanding personality and on the support he received from the German church and nobility.

This letter provided answers to many of the questions that must have puzzled Bishop Otto. From contemporary copies of it now in museums in London, Paris, and Vienna we learn something of Prester John himself. We learn too of the people and the lands he ruled, and of their natural and unnatural wonders.

The writer began by introducing himself as "John, Priest by the Almighty power of God and the Strength of Our Lord Jesus Christ, King of Kings and Lord of Lords." He greeted Manuel who he understood admired Prester John, and had wished to send John gifts. Prester John himself would now send gifts to Manuel. But he wanted to make sure that Manuel held the true faith. People regarded Manuel as a god, but Prester John knew that Manuel was mortal and subject to human infirmities. Manuel would be welcome to visit Prester John. John would place him in high office and load him with treasures should Manuel decide to return to Byzantium.

The writer then explained that Prester John surpassed everyone in virtue, wealth, and power. Much of the rest of the letter spells out the details of his splendor and humility. We learn for example that 70 kings acknowledged John as overlord. Seven kings, 62 dukes, and 265 counts and marquises served at John's dinner table every month in rotation. Twelve archbishops sat on his right at table and 20 bishops on his left. A patriarch acted as his house steward and his cup-bearer was an archbishop and king. Supreme ruler over all these dignitaries, John nonetheless humbly contented himself with the low ecclesiastical rank of priest and on his journeys he rode with a plain wooden cross carried before him.

His wealth lay in the abundant natural resources of his kingdom. Milk and honey flowed freely, and emeralds, sapphires, topazes, and many other precious stones abounded in the River Indus. "For gold, silver, precious stones, animals of every kind . . . we believe there is not our equal under heaven." John's palace demonstrated this wealth with its rare woods, fireproof ebony roof, sardonyx palace gates, crystal windows, and tables of gold for courtiers and of emeralds for the emperor himself.

But John's empire embraced wonders beyond mere wealth.

Letter from Prester John

Left: map from the Ebstorf monastery in Germany, thought to have been drawn around 1250. Its attempt to place on one chart all that was known or believed about the world, combined with the ignorance of Europeans about many parts of the globe, result in its representation of the Garden of Eden (top center) as equal in importance to Jerusalem, seen here as the center of the world.

Upon a plain stood a hollow stone containing water that cured any Christian bathing in it, whatever his disease. There were other marvels, too, which multiplied with the many versions of the letter that appeared and circulated in the Middle Ages. We read of hares as big as sheep; birds that carried whole oxen to their nests to feed their young; horned, four-eyed men; dog-headed men; Amazons; pygmies; centaurs; unicorns; the Phoenix; gold-digging ants; and salamanders that entered fire and spun threads from which fine silks were woven.

The letter gives us some idea of where these miracles abounded. From his capital at Susa in Persia John ruled "the three Indias." This vague realm was often subdivided into Nearer, Middle, and Farther India. These places apparently correspond with what we now call northern India, Ethiopia, and southern India, for medieval Europeans considered that all Africa east of the Nile formed part of Asia, and that no sea separated Ethiopia from India.

In this rich empire, poverty, envy, avarice, theft, and lying were unknown, and peace and justice flourished. Prester John was warlike in the service of the Cross. He could muster 140,000 mounted troops and 1,400,000 infantry. With this army he planned to march to Jerusalem and punish the Christians' Moslem enemies.

No one now believes the letter to be genuine. Scholarly detective work revealed that its author had lifted much of his material

Envoy from Pope Alexander

from existing medieval sources—among them tales of Alexander the Great, a Latin work on gems, and contemporary accounts of the wonders of the East. Moreover, at the time the letter was written, there was no splendid, thriving capital at Susa. This old Persian city lay half in ruins.

The letter's borrowings, errors, and use of language suggest to most historians that the writer was probably a West European acquainted with the Near East and hostile to the Greeks of the Byzantine Empire. What exactly made him write a hoax letter? Some scholars have suggested that the author had a moral aim: to stress the virtues of Prester John's imaginary Christian kingdom as an object lesson to the West, where Holy Roman Church and Holy Roman Empire were in a state of conflict. The writer may also have hoped to raise the flagging spirits of the Christian crusaders by hinting at a powerful ally to the east. But many think his letter just an exercise in literary composition. Whoever he was and whatever his motive, this hoaxer had an immense influence upon the history of Africa and Asia. For the great age of European exploration and empire-building largely began with the hunt for the fabled Land of Prester John described in the letter.

However, the first, abortive mission may have had another origin. In September 1177 Pope Alexander III wrote a letter to "John, illustrious and magnificent King of the Indians." From a surviving copy of the text, we learn that the Pope had heard of John's Christian faith and eagerness to conform to Roman Catholic orthodoxy. The Pope stressed as a major source of his information not the extraordinary letter but his own physician Philip, a traveled man who had visited John's kingdom or somewhere near it. Happy to help John, Alexander now sent him Philip as a messenger. He asked John to respond by sending envoys. We do not know what happened to Philip or even where he went. We can however guess at his destination. Professor Charles Beckingham, a British authority on African and Asian history, has shown that Pope Alexander's reference to Indians

Right: the ruins of the Persian city of Susa, once the capital of the Achaemenid Empire and chief residence of Darius I and his successors. The city was once the flourishing center of a district famous for silk, sugar cane, and oranges. At the time of Prester John's letter the city was in a state of decline.

might have meant Georgians, Nubians, or Ethiopians but certainly not inhabitants of the Indian subcontinent. Closer study convinced Beckingham that Philip's likeliest goal had been Ethiopia.

In 1221, though, came news of an event that once more focused Europe's eyes on Asia as the home of Prester John. From Bishop Jacques de Vitry and Cardinal Pelagius—both with a crusading army in Egypt—came letters describing a recent defeat of Moslem forces by "King David." Spice and gem importers trading with the Holy Land from farther east had spread the tale. They reported that Samarkand and other eastern Moslem cities had

Below: Pope Alexander III and Frederick I Barbarossa, two of Prester John's correspondents. This scene shows Frederick acknowledging Alexander as the true pope after his decisive defeat at Legnano in 1176, which paved the way for the Peace of Venice in the following year.

Tales of Ung Khan

Right: illustration from a book describing journeys to the Orient dating from the 17th century. This shows the tent of the khan at his camp in Mongolia, surrounded by a wooden stockade.

Below: Kublai Khan handing a golden seal, a 15-inch gold strip inscribed to the glory of the khan of khans, to the Polo brothers (Marco's father and uncle) at his capital of Cambaluc on their first trip to the East. It was like a passport, entitling them to food, lodging, fresh horses, and an escort anywhere within the Mongol empire.

already fallen to this king, whose troops now marched upon Baghdad. Many people speculated that David must be Prester John's son or maybe grandson. De Vitry even thought that David was Prester John himself.

For De Vitry's crusading force, embroiled in what proved a disastrous campaign, the rumor of a Christian victory may well have been the result of wishful thinking. We now know that the warrior king whose Asian campaign inspired the rumor was a ruthless and most un-Christian Mongol empire-builder named Genghis Khan. But Mongol victories did more than help spread rumors of the legendary Prester John. They made it possible for Christian travelers to go in search of him. This was because under Mongol rule, one power for the first time unified all central Asia and even welcomed Christian travelers. Most came as missionaries or traders, but the land of Prester John was clearly one of their objectives.

In 1245 a Franciscan friar named John de Carpini rode 3000 miles in less than four months to reach the Mongol Khan's camp deep in what is now Mongolia. In 1253, William of Rubruck, another Franciscan, followed in Carpini's footsteps. Then in about 1270 the famous Venetian traveler Marco Polo passed through central Asia on his way to China. Rubruck and Polo both heard tales that put Prester John in a new light. They learned of a battle in which Genghis Khan had killed his Mongol Christian overlord Ung, or Ung Khan. It seems quite likely that there had been such a Christian Mongol ruler. A 13th-century Syrian chronicler called Gregory Abulfaraj recorded a letter of A.D. 1009 describing the conversion to Nestorian Christianity of a king of the Mongol Kerait tribe. Abulfaraj claimed that the Kerait ruler of around A.D. 1200 held the title *Ung Khan* which Abulfaraj interpreted to mean "King John." Some modern scholars have identified Ung Khan with "Prester John." But Ung Khan—or more accurately Wang Khan—was a Chinese title not conferred upon the Kerait king until 1190 at the earliest, long after references to Prester John appeared in Western Europe.

However there was more than one candidate for the title Prester John. For instance, Rubruck favored a former Mongol

king whose Chinese name Ta-Yang-Khan means "Great King John." Marco Polo reported that Prester John still reigned in the country of the Keraits, but as a vassal of the Great Khan. Other travelers came up with other candidates. About 1326 Friar Odoric of Pordenone made a great trek across Asia in which he claimed to have visited a land still ruled by Prester John, but Odoric declared that "not one-hundredth part is true that is told of him."

Some travelers went farther. Finding no Christian king or wealthy kingdom in the heart of Asia, they began to wonder whether Prester John reigned there at all. One such skeptic was Jordanus de Sévérac. This Dominican friar visited India about the time that Odoric was crossing central Asia. De Sévérac found no trace of Prester John in India, but heard that a Christian monarch, presumably a descendant with the title "Prester John," lived in Ethiopia—in other words in what remained of John's old empire of the three Indias recorded in the letter sent by Prester John to the Byzantine emperor. To Christians now catching up on world affairs, it seemed likely that Mongol conquests

Above: imaginary portrayal of the battle between Ung Khan and Genghis Khan. Marco Polo and William of Rubruck both reported that a Christian Ung or Wang Khan had once been an overlord of the great conqueror but had been defeated and killed by him. Ung Khan was often identified with the mysterious Prester John.

Prince Henry the Navigator

Above: Prince Henry the Navigator, third son of King João I of Portugal, who was born in 1394. He was a patron and organizing force behind various explorers, and he established a school of navigation and mapmaking using his position and personal wealth. Prince Henry was eager to find a sea route around the continent of Africa to reach the East, and he was very interested in the reports of Prester John's kingdom in Africa.

had driven John into this obscure "middle" region of his empire. De Sévérac fleshed out the new hypothesis with a fanciful account of vassal kings and wild beasts. Once more European estimates of Prester John rode high. Anything seemed possible in Ethiopia, a land as little known to Europeans of the 14th century as Mongolia had been a century or so before. From Ethiopian pilgrims to Jerusalem, West Europeans at least knew that Ethiopia had a Christian king. They knew he sometimes fought the Moslem powers that blocked European travel to his country. In addition rumors suggested that the Nile rose in Ethiopia, and that Prester John could, if he wished, divert this river, so reducing Moslem Egypt to a desert.

Understandably, European Christians felt such a monarch well worth cultivating as a possible ally. But first they had to find his kingdom. Curiously enough the nation that sought him most persistently was Portugal, the kingdom at the westernmost end of Europe and farthest from Ethiopia. The Portuguese leader who launched this search was Prince Henry the Navigator—a scholar with a burning spirit of adventure. Henry's conquest of the rich Moorish port of Ceuta in North Africa in 1415 fully opened the young prince's eyes to the wealth shipped westward from India by Moslem Arab merchants. What Henry found in Ceuta helped fire the prince with ambition. He would bypass the Arab-speaking middlemen and their hostile Moslem lands, and reach the riches of the East directly. At the same time he would find and make an alliance with Prester John, whose kingdom lay somewhere on the way to India, where the spices came from. Together they would crush their Moslem enemies.

Hostile Moslems barred overland routes between Europe and India, and Italians monopolized east Mediterranean trade. Henry had to find another route, so he gathered around him scholars, travelers, and even Moslem prisoners. From them he acquired much-needed information. Then he sent sailors south down the coast of West Africa to find a sea route to the East.

Henry's ambitions probably gained fresh impetus in 1452 when an ambassador from Prester John supposedly arrived in Portugal. This report seems unsubstantiated, though other records tell of Ethiopian ambassadors to Spain and Italy about this time. In 1455 a Genoese in Portugal wrote a letter claiming that Prester John lived six days' travel inland from the coast of Gambia. This was the first text to attempt to localize the Ethiopian monarch. Five years later Henry died, his aims unrealized. However, his ships had probed far south, and after Henry's death King João II kept up the search for India and Prester John.

The breakthrough came in 1488 when storms hurled Bartolomeu Dias' frail caravels around the southern tip of Africa. But this was only part of a two-pronged Portuguese expedition. King João was already looking for another route to Prester John. Travelers had told him that 750 miles west of the African kingdom of Benin in what is now Guinea lived the immensely powerful King Ogané. We now know that Ogané was probably the king of Ife, another West African state, but João believed the man was Prester John. Maps suggested that his kingdom must lie south of Egypt. Accordingly, João sent two monks to reach John overland via Jerusalem which then lay in Moslem hands.

Unable to speak Arabic, the monks got no farther.

Stubbornly, João tried again, this time sending two lay adventurers who spoke fluent Arabic. Pero da Covilham, previously a diplomat and spy, and his companion Afonso de Paiva left Portugal and headed east early in May 1487, just three months before Bartolomeu Dias headed south on his historic voyage. The emissaries carried with them a letter to Prester John, a map on which to mark his kingdom when they found it, and 400 *cruzados* in cash and letter of credit. Disguised as dealers in honey, the couple daringly cut adrift from Christendom and mingled with its Moslem enemies. They arrived in Cairo, then, wearing Moslem dress, pressed on to Aden. There they parted. Afonso de Paiva was to go direct to Ethiopia and Prester John, Pero da Covilham to sail by Arab dhow to India to trace the rich export trade in spices to its source. Both planned to meet in Cairo and return home.

The scheme misfired. Pero da Covilham succeeded in the first part of his mission. He reached Cannanore, where ginger came from, and Calicut—a port where half-naked men rode elephants, built thatched huts, and shipped pepper from the palm-fringed shore. After visiting East Africa, Da Covilham returned to Cairo only to find that Afonso de Paiva had died there. We shall never know whether or not Afonso's mission to Ethiopia had succeeded.

Pero da Covilham prepared to take ship home to Portugal and his long-neglected wife. He never arrived. Two Jews brought a secret message from King João insisting that he should return only after making every effort possible to track down Prester John. Obediently the weary traveler retraced his Red Sea journey. Da Covilham landed at Zeila in what is now northwest Somalia and in 1494 reached the court of Prester John, or rather, of the Ethiopian emperor, Alexander. But Alexander soon died, and his successor refused Da Covilham permission to leave the country. There he spent his last years, made comfortable by a black wife and lands provided by his captors.

Portugal was not to be in ignorance of "Prester John" for much

Above: Bartolomeu Dias on his historic voyage around the southern tip of Africa. He managed to sail from Lisbon in Portugal down the west coast of Africa, stopping at the mouth of the Congo river, and around the Cape of Good Hope to anchor in Mossel Bay east of the continent.

Below: the port of Calicut in the late 1400s, then the most important port on the Malabar coast. There were no docks, so the Portuguese ships of Pero da Covilham had to anchor offshore.

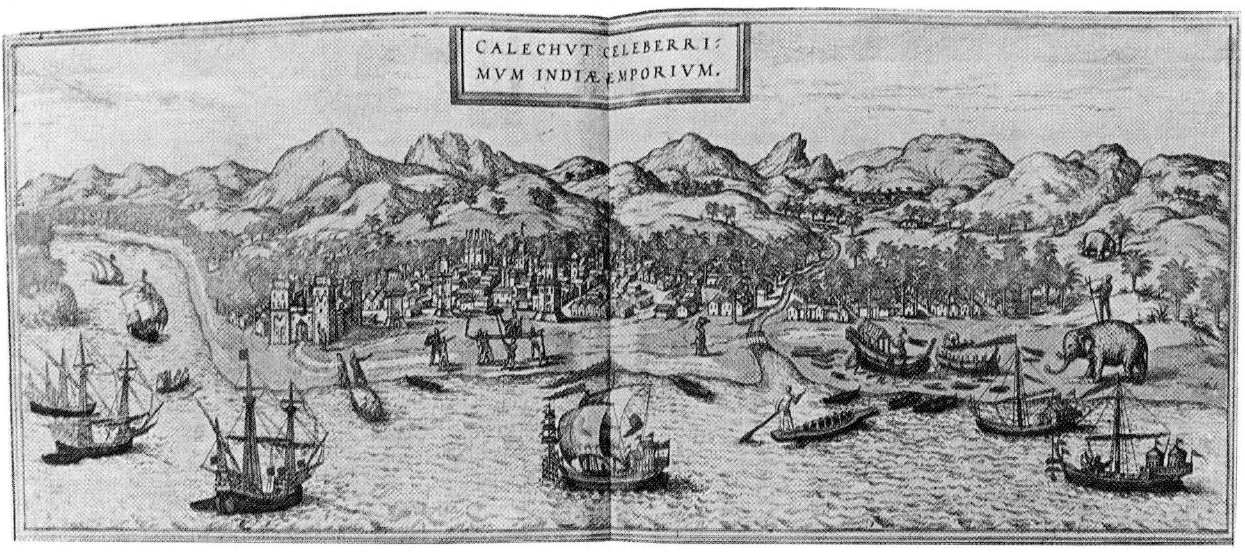

Above: Alfonso de Albuquerque, the second Portuguese viceroy of India, who governed for six years. He firmly established the Portuguese in the subcontinent and did much to gain control of the valuable spice trade. Albuquerque forwarded a letter from the Ethiopian regent to King Manuel of Portugal.

longer, once Dias and Vasco da Gama between them had opened up the sea route to East Africa. In 1506 two Portuguese with a Tunisian Moor as guide sailed around Africa, landed at Guardafui on the very tip of the Horn of Africa, and set off inland to Ethiopia. None ever reappeared in Portugal, but two of them at least reached Ethiopia. We know this from a letter written to the king of Portugal by the Ethiopian regent, Helena. Carried by messenger, this letter reached Afonso de Albuquerque, by then Portugal's forceful governor in India in 1512. Albuquerque forwarded the letter and its messenger to Portugal. When they arrived in 1514 King Manuel gave both a rapturous reception, and planned a formal embassy to Ethiopia. Unbelievably, six years passed through naval bungling before the embassy arrived at the Red Sea port of Massawa—then just a mosque and a few stone buildings. A small, mixed group of ambassadors set off into the interior. They included a doctor, painter, organist, fencer, several craftsmen, and a chaplain—Padre Francisco Alvares. Alvares' account of what followed finally revealed the kingdom of Prester John to Portugal. It proved a nation very different from the empire of medieval legend.

From Massawa the party headed inland to the provincial capital of Debaroa, a route that took them up steep mountain paths and out onto a high plateau with fertile fields. Traveling by mule and camel, the ambassadors pressed on through Tigre Province. Here they marveled at tiny chapels carved into the sides of almost sheer-sided peaks and at local dark-skinned women wearing little more than beads.

For five months, the party traveled through a mountain kingdom of humble villages and wealthy churches, but no towns. At last they met the object of their quest: Lebna Dengel Dawit, whose name they simplified to "David." Disappointingly they

Right: some of the most spectacular sights of the Portuguese embassy's journey to the kingdom of Prester John were the hermits' cells and churches hewn from the rock. Here is a monolithic church at Lalibela, Ethiopia.

found that the Abyssinians entitled him not Prester John but simply "emperor." Disappointingly, too, his palace proved to be a tent, his capital a mere camp. For the emperor and his court were constantly on tour around the country as affairs of state or wars demanded. More disconcerting still, the man seemed greedy. Instead of showering his visitors with gifts in the spirit of the legendary Prester John, the Emperor of Ethiopia at first demanded gifts from them. He particularly wanted pepper, because spices served as money in this kingdom. But the emperor was certainly Christian, and, if not himself a priest, at least an influence on Church affairs. "David" maintained the custom of annual rebaptism by total immersion—a practice started by his grandfather against the wishes of the Patriarch of Abyssinia. The emperor dressed in an imperial style befitting Prester John, as the Portuguese discovered on the only time he deigned to show himself. They saw a young man colored like a russet apple, richly dressed, holding a silver cross, and with a gold and silver crown upon his head. Eventually, too, he showed something of the mythical Prester John's generosity, presenting gifts of gold and silver to the embassy when at last they departed after an enforced stay of several years. The Portuguese reached Lisbon in 1527, more than a century after Henry the Navigator had initiated the hunt for Prester John in Africa.

The ambassadors dispelled the myth that Ethiopia's emperor was rich and powerful. But had they really tracked down the original Prester John's descendant? Some writers have thought so, and that the "John" of Prester John came from the Ethiopian phrase *Zan hoy* ("My King"), misheard as *Gianni* by Italian merchants visiting Jerusalem or Alexandria, hence "Jean" in French and "John" in English. But there are strong doubts that Ethiopians addressed their emperor as *Zan hoy* before the 16th century.

In any case a closer look at early references to Prester John brings us once more back to Asia as the legend's likely starting point. Dr. Slessarev's study of Bishop Hugh's account—the oldest known reference to the priest-king John—suggested that a real-life Mongol general had somehow got mixed up with a legendary figure holding an emerald scepter and related to the Magi. These latter items hint at links with legends of St. Thomas, the Apostle, who is believed to have preached the Gospel in India in the 1st century A.D., and to have died a martyr there. One story of his martyrdom involves an Indian king's rich but pious son called Vizan (John). The story tells how Thomas converted Vizan and ordained him deacon. When Thomas died Vizan became one of Thomas' two spiritual successors and leaders of the Church in India. Could the legend of a priest-king Prester John have sprung from such a source? Slessarev believes that it could.

Other scholars have dug far deeper back in time to find the Prester's origins. A French historian, Professor Georges Florovsky, traced the name "Presbyter John" as far back as St. John's epistles. The name, Florovsky felt, became the basis of the myth. The legend of the all-powerful priest-king had simply taken shape and changed according to the spirit of the different ages that had passed it on.

Mission to Ethiopia

Below: detail of Prester John as an African king, from a map of the Mediterranean by Maggiolo in 1563. The map placed the fabled priest-king's kingdom in East Africa.

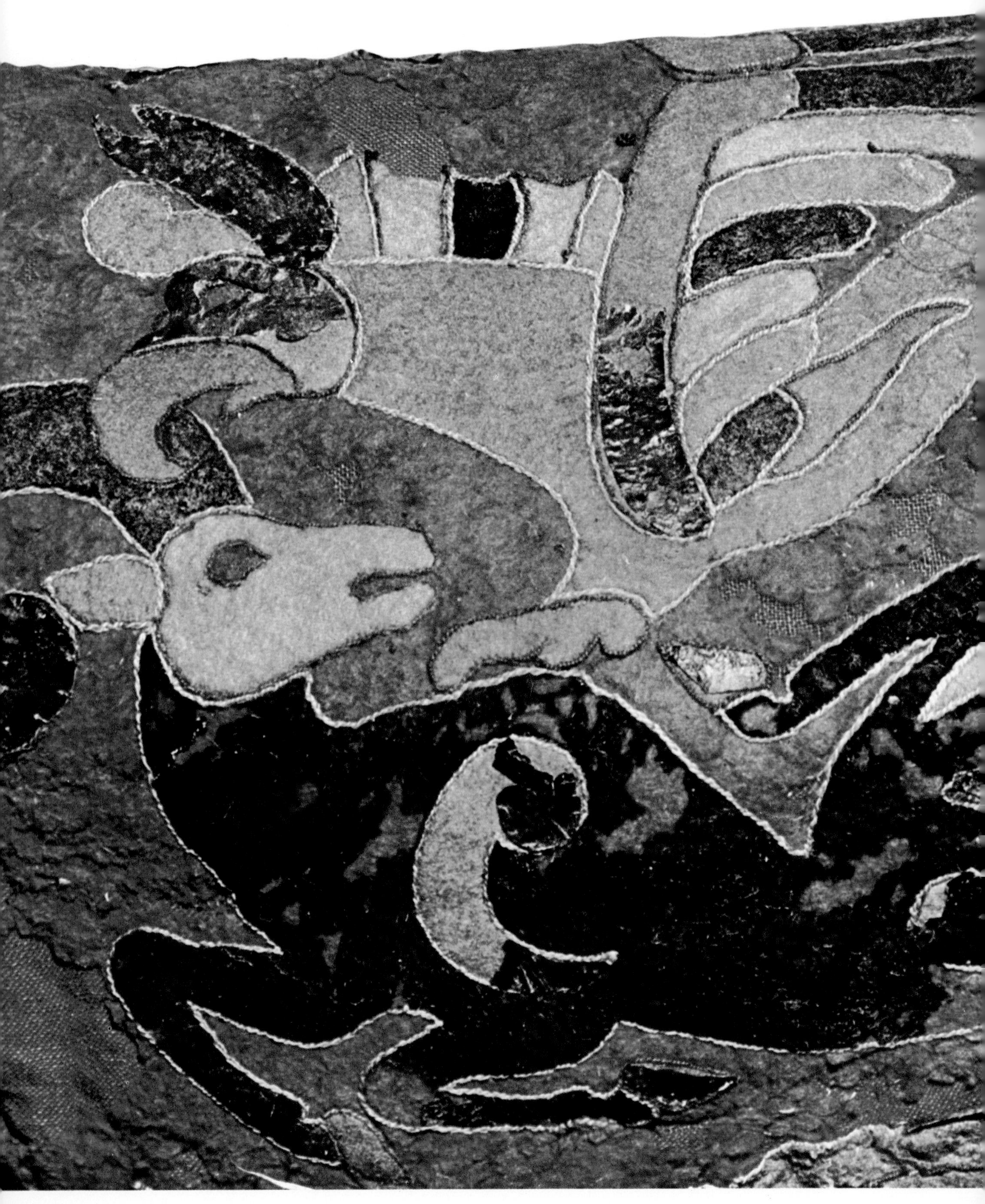

Chapter 14
A World of Mysteries

Archaeology today is a booming industry. The enormous public interest in such exhibitions as those of the tomb treasures of Tutankhamen or Bronze Age China, the Israelis' patriotic incentive to find out the truth about Masada, the international rescue fund organized to salvage the temples at Abu Simbel in Egypt—all this interest provides a boost to the solving of further mysteries. There is no shortage of such mysteries. This final chapter describes finds and investigations in three very different parts of the world—the grasslands of southern Siberia, the tropical forests of Mexico, and the dry waterless desert of central Australia.

In 1865 a Russian historian, Vasily Radlov, became curious about a number of man-made mounds he had found in the remote Altai Mountains of southern Siberia. They were almost certainly ancient burial mounds, but whose? The settled peoples of Europe had built similar mounds over the graves of their dead 2000 years or more previously. But at that time only mounted nomadic tribesmen ranged the pastures and great forests of central Asia, just north of what is today the Soviet Union's frontier with China. Who then had built these mysterious mounds in the Altai Mountains?

Because the nomads of central Asia had built no cities and used no form of writing they left few clues about how they lived. Most of what 19th-century scholars knew of these ancient horsemen came therefore from indirect sources. Chief among these sources was the Greek historian Herodotus, who had learned a good deal about eastern Europe's nomads, the Scythians, when he visited the coast of the Black Sea in about 450 B.C. Open grassland then stretched from eastern Europe right across central Asia, so it seemed likely that the Scythians' culture resembled that of other nomadic tribes farther east. The trouble was that many of Herodotus' stories seemed too strange to be taken seriously. One such story is his account of a Scythian chief's barbaric and elaborate burial. He describes in detail how the Scythians had embalmed the body, strangled some of the chief's household staff and horses, and buried them all, together with

Opposite: picture of an eagle-griffin seizing a mountain goat which adorned a saddle cover found in a Pazyryk barrow. The Soviet archaeologist Rudenko found this artifact, fantastically embellished with these imaginary animals in fine red felt, among other remains of the Altai horsemen of southern Russia.

Below: magnificent gold comb found in the Solokha burial mound in central Russia. The hair of the members of some tribes was combed rather than shaven, and some combs were highly decorated. Scythian warriors are here portrayed on the handle.

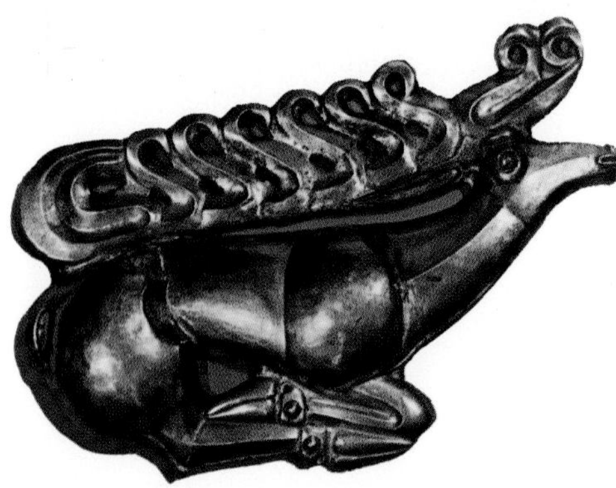

Above: a deer ornament from a bridle found in the barrow at Kostromskaya. The retracted legs, head thrust forward, and antlers crowned with tines to form a motif of their own are all characteristic of Scythian art.

gold and other treasures, in a mound of earth.

Why could archaeologists not verify this account simply by digging up a royal Scythian barrow? Southern Russia is full of Scythian burials, but the difficulty is that most were plundered long ago by robbers. However, in 1862 archaeologists working at Chertomiyk in southern Russia did find a splendid Scythian tomb almost intact, with dead horses and retainers just as Herodotus had described. But apart from a few gold ornaments dug up and sold by treasure-hunters, the Altai Mountains' tombs far to the east remained unknown to archaeologists. So when Radlov dug into a large mound at the remote Altai locality of Katanda he was digging where none but possibly thieves had gone before.

Radlov knew that boulders covering the mound or barrow distinguished it as a Scythian burial, but he was not prepared for what he found. Digging down into the mound he reached a thick lens of ice, in spite of the fact that winter had not even started. To melt the ice he poured hot water on it. Then, peering through the opaque window of melting ice, Radlov caught sight of dead bodies dressed in clothes and around them furniture and other objects. Unfortunately, decay set in soon after Radlov's hasty exposure of the tomb. Only his story and a few tattered fabrics remained as records of his astonishing discovery of an ancient burial preserved by ice.

For 60 years Radlov's reports gathered dust. His accounts eventually came to the attention of the Soviet archaeologist Sergei Ivanovich Rudenko. In 1924 Rudenko visited the Pazyryk Valley near Katanda. There he found no fewer than 40 mounds like those described by Radlov. Rudenko proceeded more cautiously than Radlov, delaying full-scale scientific excavation of his first Pazyryk mound until 1929. Later, in the years after World War II, he excavated four more barrows in this remote valley more than 5000 feet above sea level. All the tombs showed the same general pattern of construction. All consisted of a low-roofed subterranean "log cabin" paved with thick wooden blocks, and roofed by timbers covered with layers of birch bark and then branches or felt, surmounted by a low earth mound capped by boulders to produce a man-high cairn up to 150 feet across. Rudenko calculated that over 200 cubic yards of stone had gone into the building of the first and largest barrow that he excavated.

Digging down into the chambers, Rudenko and his team struck ice just as Radlov had done in the 1860s. But this time, instead of simply melting the ice, they patiently extracted it piece by piece. Their care was rewarded by the discovery of fragile objects of skin, leather, wood, and fabric that would have perished long ago had they been exposed to open air or to the damp atmosphere of an ordinary burial. These finds helped Rudenko build a picture of how a nomadic pastoral people had lived and dressed perhaps 2400 years ago.

Against the southern wall of each "log cabin" a human body lay with rug and felt blankets in a hollowed-out larch trunk coffin. The bodies had been embalmed just as Herodotus had described. The brains had been removed, together with other internal tissue, and the skin stuffed with grass, herbs, and moss. The nomads had then stitched up incisions in the skin by means of hair or tendon threads. Two of the mounds held two chieftains' bodies, tattooed with fantastic animal forms by means of soot rubbed into rows of holes pricked in the skin. In one mound there was a collapsed birchwood cart with spoked wheels. Herodotus described how a wagon was used to carry dead Scythian chiefs from tribe to tribe before burial.

Clothes found with the bodies were of fur, felt, leather, or plant fiber. Men's clothes included soft leather caftans, plant-fiber shirts, tunics, peaked caps, and thick felt stockings. Women were dressed in similar caftans and stockings and one had leopard-fur boots. Furnishings were easily portable, among them stools, collapsible tables, brightly-dyed felt wall hangings, mats, and rugs including the world's oldest known woollen pile carpets. One mound contained a square carpet of Persian design with velvety pile and a geometric pattern featuring rosettes, animals, and horsemen. Carpets, clothing, saddle covers, even coffins, had been fantastically embellished with forms of animals and imaginary monsters or geometric designs. These were carved in relief or done in colored leather or felt and then sewn onto the objects they adorned.

Burial cabins and their contents almost certainly represented the furnished homes actually occupied by the Altai horsemen for at least part of the year. But hints that they were also tent-dwelling nomadic herdsmen lay in their easily transportable possessions. Moreover, to secure good pasture all the year, the flocks and herds of the horsemen would have made long seasonal migrations. Maybe it was on such treks that the riders obtained the silk Chinese saddlecloths and woollen Persian rugs found in the burial mounds—goods manufactured as much as 2000 miles away. Had they bartered for such goods with horses? Close to

Tattoos Preserved

Below: a reconstruction of the tattoos on the bodies of Scythian chieftains. This man, most of whose skin was preserved in the freezing temperature of one of the Pazyryk mounds, had both arms and one leg decorated with designs in the "animal style" of the Scythians.

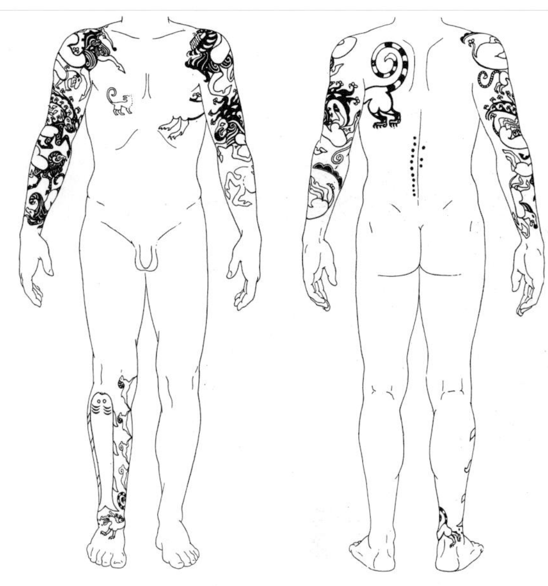

Left: tattoo of a fantastic monster, a deer with the beak of an eagle and the tail of a cat, on the right arm of a man in one of the Pazyryk barrows found in 1948. The deer's antlers and the tail terminate in birds' heads. The tattooing probably indicates noble birth or the attainment of manhood.

Below: a typical Scythian carriage drawn by oxen. The carriage found at Pazyryk is not built along traditional lines.

Tombs Like Refrigerators

Right: Persian pile carpet found at Pazyryk. Measuring 6 feet by 1.5 feet, the carpet has borders of fallow deer and griffins. The stars that fill the center field are repeated with the colors reversed to separate the grazing deer from the mounted horsemen. There are 215 knots per square inch and the rug probably took about 18 months to make.

Above: detail from a carved cedar-trunk coffin found in a barrow at Bash-Adar. The texture of the fur and the tiger's stripes are shown by incised zigzag lines, like tongues of flame.

Below: to produce narcotic fumes inside their tents Scythian mourners heated stones in a fire, placed them in vessels like this, and then scattered hemp seeds over the stones. Hemp smoking was evidently practiced not only for purification but in everyday life by both men and women.

the burial chambers lay the bodies of riding horses so well preserved that Rudenko recognized that they were all bay or chestnut geldings, many of them well bred, and well fed on grain in the early spring when pasture was poor. Judging by their hooves, they had even been stabled before being slaughtered.

But the strangest discovery of all comprised charred hemp seeds and stones in bronze pots, found with small felt-covered tents. Herodotus provides a clue to their use. He describes how Scythian mourners would go into a tent, throw hemp seed on hot stones, inhale the vapor, and howl in what was obviously a drug-induced ecstasy.

Unfortunately, Rudenko never found many of the treasures that had been buried with their owners. Long before he found the graves, robbers had tunneled down into the mounds. They had lopped off corpses' limbs and heads to seize necklaces and other body ornaments. Rudenko believed that the treasures that they left were only scraps compared with what they took away. But ironically, if it had not been for the break-in that occurred soon after burial, each tomb's perishable contents would not have been so well-preserved. Originally, each tomb was designed to serve as a kind of natural refrigerator. In winter, cold air sank between its crowning stones and froze the soil below—in summer, the sun's heat could not penetrate the stones to melt the soil. But when thieves dug a shaft down through the mound, the natural refrigerator became even more effective. Rainwater seeped in and froze inside the chamber, forming a lens of ice and so walling off the contents from outside agents of decay. Thanks to this accident of nature, archaeologists found a factual basis to support some of Herodotus' strange stories. At the same time these archaeologists have restored a lost chapter to the mysterious history of central Asia.

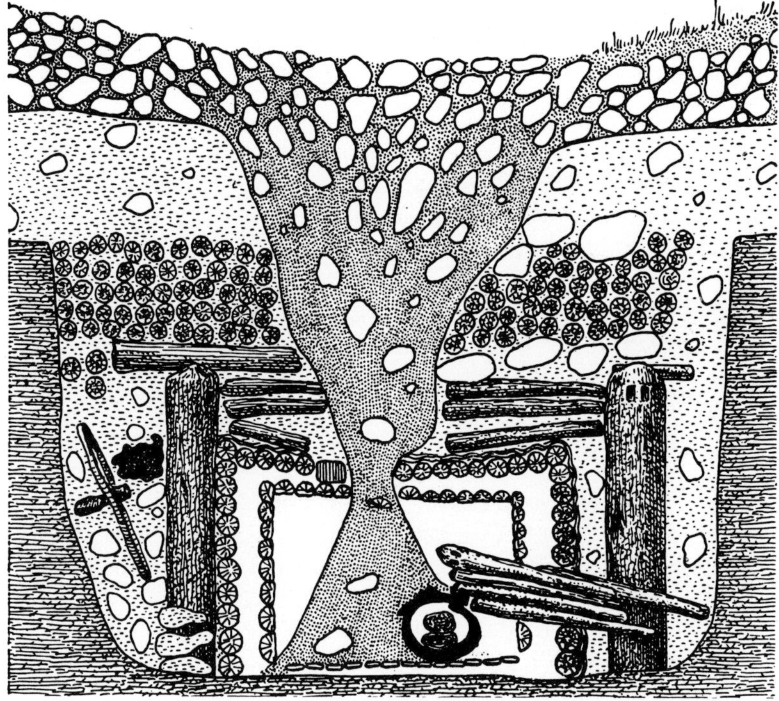

Left: a cross-section of the underground structure of a Pazyryk tomb. It consists of a heavy wood frame within which a double-walled burial chamber was built to house the coffin and household goods. Horses were sacrificed and piled along the north side of the pit. Every burial chamber at Pazyryk had been looted by robbers, who dug down to the layer of logs and then chopped their way inside.

Below: part of a Mayan manuscript calendar.

It was a very different kind of burial that added to our knowledge of a vanished culture halfway around the world from Pazyryk. Monumental buildings, carved hieroglyphs, and wall paintings survive to tell us of the Maya civilization built up in Central America by a Pre-Columbian Stone Age people—a people who devised a calendar more accurate than ours.

By 1949 archaeologists had found many of the Mayas' long-deserted pyramids in scrub and forest. In ancient Egypt, pyramids had served as royal tombs. But Amerindian people had topped their pyramids with temples in which they practiced rituals including human sacrifice. No Maya pyramid had also served as royal tomb—or so archaeologists believed in 1949, before Alberto Ruz explored Palenque's Temple of Inscriptions. Like their other former centers, the Maya had abandoned Palenque to the jungle 1000 or more years ago, possibly because soil exhaustion cut local crop yields.

As an archaeologist working for the Mexican government, Ruz was supervising Palenque's restoration. He had to contend with decayed buildings, heavily invaded by the forests that grow fast in this warm, wet region on the frontier of Mexico and Guatemala. The task proved huge, for Palenque had been a big reli-

The Temple of Inscriptions

Right: terracing of the later pyramid over that of the earlier pyramid of the Temple of Inscriptions at Palenque. Two workmen are repairing the lower terraces after they had collapsed.

Above: the stairway Ruz found beneath the stone slab leading down into the pyramid of the Temple of Inscriptions.

gious center rich in strange stone temples, complete with a road, an aqueduct, and steam baths. Ruz found its Temple of Inscriptions especially intriguing. Like other Maya temples, this stone building was a steep-sided pyramid, with steps leading to a crowning temple. This was a small structure roofed by stones that overlapped to form a high but narrow arch, for the Maya never mastered the true arch, and thus could never build large vaults and domes. Stone panels bearing the longest known Maya inscription made the Temple of Inscriptions unique and inspired its present name. But something less obvious caught Ruz's eye.

Most Maya temple floors were faced with stucco. This one consisted of abutting flagstones. The center stone was huge and at each end of it someone had drilled three holes, then plugged them with stones. Could the holes have held ropes for lowering the slab into position? If so, something important might be hidden beneath. Ruz determined to find out.

Beneath the slab Ruz first found a stairway leading down into the pyramid, but the shaft was blocked with a great mass of rocks and earth. It took months of toil to shift this obstruction. At last Ruz cleared 45 steps that went down to a landing with a sharp bend. Then came 21 more steps. Ruz had now descended over 70 feet to the level of the base of the pyramid. Meanwhile he had been making some discoveries. At the top of the stairs people had left jade ear plugs and a reddened stone as an offering. At the foot of the stairs lay other offerings, a pearl, jade beads, pottery, and shells containing red paint. A stucco tube snaked mysteri-

Right: mural at Bonampak, Mexico showing a child having its head artificially deformed (in the arms of the woman on the platform at left). This was the fashion among the aristocracy and several such skulls were found in the Temple of Inscriptions.

ously down the stairs and continued beyond.

Then came fresh obstacles: first a wall had to be demolished, then a stone-and-lime-packed corridor laboriously cleared. In a stone chest at the far end lay the bones of five youths and a girl, their heads artificially deformed and the teeth gem-encrusted, in the manner of the Maya nobility. Beyond these evidently sacrificial victims loomed a blank wall, several feet thick, its only entrance sealed by a triangular stone slab seven feet high. Ruz's heart beat faster as he tried to guess what lay beyond.

At last, on June 15, 1952, men heaved the stone aside and Ruz stepped through into a wonderland. Torchlight revealed a roomy crypt 30 feet long, 12 feet wide, and over 20 feet high. To Ruz the man-made cave seemed carved from ice. Rainwater seeping through the limestone rocks over thousands of years had faced the crypt with a gleaming crust of calcium carbonate, while the floor and ceiling were festooned with stalactites and stalagmites. Study of the walls nonetheless revealed a procession of nine larger-than-life stucco reliefs, representing the Mayas' so-called lords of darkness.

Most of the crypt floor was taken up by what seemed to be a massive altar capped by a carved stone slab nearly 12 feet long, more than 6 feet across and weighing several tons. Reliefs carved

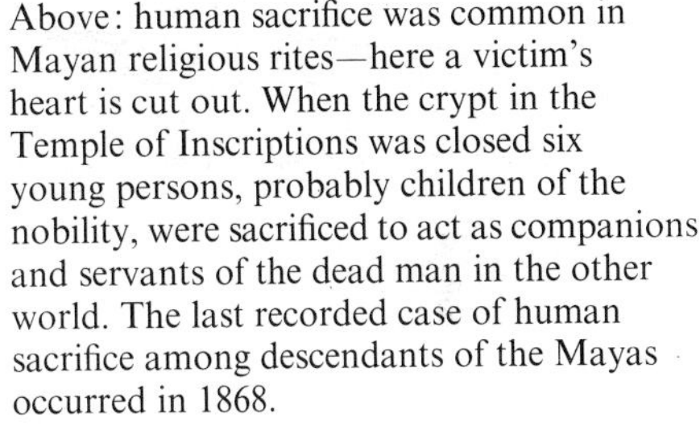

Above: human sacrifice was common in Mayan religious rites—here a victim's heart is cut out. When the crypt in the Temple of Inscriptions was closed six young persons, probably children of the nobility, were sacrificed to act as companions and servants of the dead man in the other world. The last recorded case of human sacrifice among descendants of the Mayas occurred in 1868.

Left: general view of the crypt showing the vaulting and the lid of the sarcophagus, which was covered with elaborate symbolic Mayan carving of the 7th century A.D.

Above: jade mosaic mask found in the crypt of the Temple of Inscriptions. The dead person was buried with this placed directly over his face. The eyes are of shell with each iris of obsidian. The main characteristics of the face are realistic and may have resembled the dead man.

on its surface revealed a young man lying on the head of a monster. Here, too, were symbols representing life and death, and hieroglyphs dating the work to about A.D. 700. Human heads masked in jade mosaic lay on the slab.

Below it was another monolith propped on six stone blocks. Ruz now began to wonder whether the upper slab could conceal a burial. Lifting the slab would be difficult and dangerous, so instead, he had a workman drill through the lower slab to see if it was hollow. A wire thrust in the hole emerged with flakes of red paint. For the Maya red had stood for the east, the rising sun —and immortality. Ruz now knew that his altar was in fact a tomb. To see what lay within he somehow *had* to raise its five-ton lid. Ruz spent a sleepless night watching the lifting process, slowly accomplished with infinite care and patience by means of four truck jacks and tree-trunk sections wedged beneath the corners of the slab. At last the lid stood high enough for Ruz to peer down. He saw a polished oblong slab with projecting "ears." Ruz raised this inner lid, and marveled at what proved to be the contents of a great stone coffin. Lying on its reddened floor was the bejeweled skeleton of a man aged over 40. A jade diadem had crowned his head. A realistic jade mosaic face mask with shells for lips covered his face. A collar of jade beads carved as fruits and flowers had hung about his neck. Jade bracelets, rings, and beads had adorned breast, wrists, and fingers. Even the hairs on his head had been combed out and threaded through jade tubes.

The burial was plainly that of someone important—so important that the pyramid and temple had been built above his tomb after his burial, because measurements showed that the coffin would have been too big for men to have carried it down the narrow stairway. Most experts think the man had been a priest-king ruler of Palenque. The sacrifice of the noble youths and maiden would support this theory. So would the stucco "snake" that crawled from his sarcophagus up through the pyramid—a "soul duct" to let his spirit travel in and out. But, surprisingly for

Below: the Temple of Inscriptions as it is now, after restoration.

Stone Faces in the Desert

someone so exalted, the skull was not deformed and the teeth had not been filed and filled with jade as was the Maya custom with nobles. The shape of the body leads some anthropologists to doubt that he had been a Maya Indian at all. Alberto Ruz had solved the mystery of what lay hidden in the pyramid, but the question of the corpse's exact identity remains to intrigue us.

The third of the mysteries in this final chapter is centered upon the most recently-explored of the world's great land masses. The story began in 1961 when veteran mineral prospector Michael Terry, an experienced traveler in the outback, woke up one morning after a night under the stars in the hot desert heartland of Australia. He filled a bowl with water from one of the rare waterholes of the region, placed the bowl on a rock, and began to wash himself. The waterhole, known as the Thomas Reservoir, is a million-gallon rock basin in the Cleland Hills at the western end of the bald, red ridges of the Macdonnell Ranges. Suddenly Terry's eye was caught by a totally unexpected sight—a series of complex figures chipped out high on the nearby rock face. Terry could hardly believe what he saw.

Much of the surrounding area is an Aboriginal reserve, but apart from the rare gold digger or survey team, few people pass where Michael Terry now stood. He himself had been here earlier on camel back in 1932, but then the rock engravings had escaped his eye. Now they appeared in startling clarity, because the low sun of early morning cast shadows in their chipped depressions, which showed as dark outlines against the paler sunlit surfaces of the surrounding cliffs and boulders. The first figure to catch his astonished gaze was a larger-than-life human form chipped out horizontally from a cliff face at rooftop height, or higher.

Intrigued by his discovery he reasoned that surrounding rocks might bear more traces of such strange "graffiti." Very soon he found some. First he noticed a squat figure, with short legs, a backward-curving horn on its nose, and an uptilted tail. The creature resembled a rhinoceros. Then Terry noticed human heads with horns, and on the very rock that served his washbowl as a pedestal, Terry recognized a "two-way" human head with what appeared to be a beard when he squinted at it from one end, but a crown when looked at from the other.

Terry guessed that he had stumbled on something extraordinary. But he was no anthropologist, and those who were took much persuading before they would begin their own investigations. At last the Australian Institute of Aboriginal Studies agreed to back an expedition to the site. In 1967—six years after Terry had first glimpsed the stone faces in the desert—he retraced his journey to guide a team of anthropologists under Robert Edwards, a curator of the South Australian Museum.

The scientists' long desert trek proved more than justified. Quartering the ground around the pool, they counted no less than 16 human faces and another 341 rock carvings within a radius of a mere 400 yards. Beside human forms and faces, someone had laboriously chipped out shapes resembling animal and human footprints, as well as purely abstract forms.

But it was the faces that most excited Edwards. They were far livelier than the masklike visages previously recognized as the rock art of Australia's Aborigines. Some heads had been shaped

Above: general view of the Thomas Reservoir in the Cleland Hills of central Australia. The reservoir is a huge, rarely visited natural rock hole.

Who Were the Artists?

like hearts, one like an upside-down pear. Each eye was represented by a dot surrounded by a circle and sometimes by several concentric circles. Many heads had the corners of the mouth uptilted in a clownlike smile. Several jovial heads sported a long nose and short horns that jutted from the forehead. One rock bore two disembodied smiling faces with an intervening abstract design. Another surface displayed two faces—one gay, one glum—reminiscent of the masks of comedy and tragedy worn by Greek and Roman actors. "Comedy's" grinning mouth, round chin, and tiny nose contrasted with "Tragedy's" unsmiling mouth, angular chin, and dominating nose.

One cliff displayed what appeared to be a young child's attempt to draw a man. Beneath bulging brows, the head tapered to a neck supported by a narrow torso shaped like an ill-formed bowling pin, and sitting loosely on the pelvis. From the lower corners of the pelvis grew two short, stubby legs, one seemingly raised as if in dance. From the upper corners of the pelvis two trunk-like arms curved up and outward. All limbs were unadorned by digits, but paired "buttons" had been chipped into the body's central column and single buttons in the pelvis area.

Below: engravings of animal tracks and a lizard.

Robert Edwards noted several significant facts about the carvings. First, they had all been chipped out by means of the same technique. This made it likely that one group of people had created them. Secondly, weathering had produced the same color in the surfaces of both the chipped and unchipped rock surfaces. Earlier studies of carvings in an Israeli desert had shown that only many centuries of weathering could tone down a raw rock surface to match surrounding stone. Edwards therefore had good reason to believe that the carvings were ancient.

He also had ideas about the identity of the people who had made what he believed to be the most striking ancient engravings in Australia—uniquely different from and better executed than any done by Aborigines. Arguments that an advanced Aborigine group could have carved the images left Edwards unconvinced. He believed that the mysterious rock carvers were immigrants bringing with them skills developed outside Australia itself.

Could these immigrants have reached Australia before, and

Right: a heart-shaped face with large eyes and a cheerful expression (left) with a complex abstract pattern beside it.

been displaced by, the ancestors of the modern Aborigines? This seemed unlikely, implying that the Thomas Reservoir faces were older than the oldest known rock art outside Australia.

There was another possibility. The rock engravers could have been later arrivals from one of the island neighbors of Australia collectively called Melanesia. Edwards indeed remarked that just such engravings—chipped, weathered images of heart-shaped faces—had been found in Papua New Guinea—an island separated from Australia by a short sea crossing. Perhaps ancient Papuans had produced the carvings that Michael Terry had later found. But, if so, we may never know when, how, or why New Guinea's island carvers reached, made their mark upon, and vanished from the dry heart of Australia.

Perhaps it is fitting that this final story should describe an unsolved mystery of the past. For in this book we have ranged through centuries and across seas and continents from North America to central Java, from Danish peat bogs to the desert sands of Egypt, following the historians and archaeologists in their patient detective work. But the evidence for the past lies all around us, and there are still numerous riddles to be solved, new solutions to be found.

Above: the faces of Comedy (top) and Tragedy carved on one isolated rock face.

Left: the carved human figure resembling a child's drawing, with an inverted pear-shaped head on a narrow torso.

Index

References to illustrations are shown in italics.

Picture Credits

Key to picture positions: (T) top (C) center (B) bottom; and in combinations, e.g. (TR) top right (BL) bottom left.

A.A.A. Photo 25, 73; Aerofilms 48(T); Aldus Archives 19(R), 24, 46(T), 48(L) (B), 49, 98, 102(BR), 103(T), 109, 209, 222(B), 226, 238(T), 243(BR), 244(B); © Aldus Books (Gordon Cramp) 28(BL), (Jeff Goodman) 222(T), 225, (Michael Holford) 99(B), (David Montgomery) 55(T), (Sidney W. Woods, after reconstruction by Felix Thomas) 82; B. Arthaud, Paris 110(T); Associated Press, London 51(TR), 134, 139(R), 180(T), 208(B), 219(B), 220(T); Australian Institute for Aboriginal Studies/Robert Edwards 249–251; Bavaria Verlag 37(L), 98(R), 113; Photos Bibliothèque Nationale, Paris 215, 229, 234(B); Bildarchiv Süddeutscher Verlag 15(TR), 122; Bodleian Library, Oxford (MS. Bodley 264, fol.231v.) 235, (MS. Tanner 17ff99) 167; Reproduced by permission of the Trustees of the British Museum 17(R), 18(B), 41, 77(R), 78(B), 80, 87(R), 89, 92(BR), 101(B), 103(B), 120(L), 129, 160(R), 163(R), 245(B); British Museum (Michael Holford Library photo) 105(T), (Photos © Aldus Books) 39, (R. B. Fleming) 231, (John Freeman) 230(T), 247(T), (Michael Holford) 237(B), (Michael Jaanus) 165(B), 234(T); Bulloz 10(T), 99(T), 152(T), 217(B); Camera Press (Werner Braun) 123, (*Observer*) 127, 131(T), 133; Photos J.-L. Charmet 60, 86(B), 228(T), 239; Musée du Louvre/Chuzeville 76; By courtesy of the City Art Gallery, Bristol 158; By courtesy of City of Birmingham Museums and Art Gallery 212–213(T); City of Manchester Art Galleries 221; Peter Clayton 13(R), 15(TL), 23, 28(BR), 30(L), 31(T), 32, 33(L), 102(BL); Bruce Coleman Ltd. (Charlie Ott) 51(B), (Leonard Lee Rue) 165(T); Colorific (Alan Clifton) 217(T), (Penny Tweedie) 128(B); Confederation Life Collection 154; Reprinted with permission from *The Courier-Journal and Louisville Times* 174(B), 175(T); Ektodike Athenon 174(T); Robert Estall 44(R), 45(TL), 47(B), 50(B), 52–53, 57(TL), 171(T), 172–173, 216(T), (Malcolm Aird) 42, (Charles Leigh-Bennet) 152(B); Mary Evans Picture Library 10(B), 11(R), 12(T), 14(B), 30(R), 45(B), 67, 70(L), 78(T), 79, 85, 86(T), 87(L), 105(B), 107, 111, 159(B), 161, 203, 213(B), 224(B); Explorer 62(BL); Werner Forman Archive 41(R), 114, 199, 204; Honor Frost 146–147, 149(T), 150, 151(T); Giraudon 90, (Musée du Louvre) 22(R); Photos Griffith Institute, Ashmolean Museum 33(R), 34, 35(T), 36, 37(R); Susan Griggs Agency (Nathan Benn) 169(TR), (Cotton Coulson) 169(B), (Ian Yeomans) 168, 169(TL); Photos Sonia Halliday 63(R), 69; 74, 106(T), 143, (Jane Taylor) 118, 124; Robert Harding Associates 16(B), 26, 63(L), 83(T), 96(T), 98(L), 192(B), (Robert Cundy) 246(CL), 247(B), (F. L. Kenett) 38(B), (John G. Ross) 31(B), (J. Rufus) 141; Hirmer Fotoarchiv 91(R); Historical Pictures Service 20–21(T), 91(L), 106(B), 191(T), 237(T); Historisk-Arkaeologisk Forsøgscenter, Lejre 190; Michael Holford Library photos 19(L), 21(B); I.B.A. 14(T), 83(B); *Illustrated London News* 62(BR); Dr. Helge Ingstad 164(B), 166; Iraq Museum 102(T); Irish Tourist Office, London 168(T); Professor Yigael Yadin/Israel Exploration Society 125(B), 126, 130, 131(B), 135(T); E. Emrys Jones 160(L); The John Judkyn Memorial, Freshford Manor, Bath/Photo Mike Busselle © Aldus Books 156(B); Photo Peter Keen 8; Landesmuseum für Vor-und Frühgeschichte 186(B), 187, 188(T); Lennart Larsen 182(T); Dr. Euan Mackie 57(B); The MacQuitty Collection 194, 200(R), 202, 208(T), 232; The Mansell Collection, London 16(T), 28(T), 62(T), 71, 81, 140(B), 144, 149(B), 159(T), 210, 230(B); Robert Marx 142, 153(T); The Metropolitan Museum of Art, New York/Photo Picturepoint, London © Aldus Books 156(T); Minnesota Historical Society 164(T); Nasjonalgalleriet, Oslo/Courtesy Guy Krohg 162; National Gallery, London 64, 70(R); National Museums, Athens (Dimitrios Harissiadis) 138(T), (Dimitrios Harissiadis © Aldus Books) 138(B), (Robert F. Marx) 139(L); National Physical Laboratory 51(TL); National Portrait Gallery, London 196; Nationalmuseet, Denmark 182(B), 183–185, 186(T), 189, 191(B), 192(T), (P. V. Glob) 178(T); Novosti Press Agency 242, 244(TR); PAF International/Grik Betting 190(B); David Paramor, Newmarket 15(BR); Peabody Museum, Harvard University 246, (Photo Hillel Burger) 246(T); Petrie Collection, University College, London/Sydney W. Woods © Aldus Books 29; Photoresources 128(T), 193, 240, 243(BL), 244(TL), (British Museum) 88, 92(BL), (C. M. Dixon) 59, (Alan Ede) 238(B); Picturepoint, London 35(B), 93, 112, 117, 214(B), 218, 224(T); Politikens Presse Foto 178(B), 179; Popperfoto 45(TR), 47(T), 116, 140(T), 153(B), 170–171(B), 175(B), 197–198, 205(B), 216(B); *Radio Times* Hulton Picture Library 13(L), 22(L), 68, 72, 77(L), 84, 99, 101(T), 120(R), 212(B), 214(T); Professor Philip Rahtz 223; Gunter R. Reitz, Hannover 66; Roger-Viollet 12(B), 20(B); The Royal Library, Copenhagen 163(L); Photo Marshall Cavendish, reproduced by permission of The Master and Fellows, St. John's College, Cambridge 151(B); Scala 38(T), 98(L), 100, 188(B), 233; M. I. Artamonov, *Frozen Tombs of the Scythians*, May, 1965. Scientific American Inc. All rights reserved. 243(T), 245(T); Photo John Webb © Aldus Books, courtesy Scott Polar Research Institute, Cambridge, England 157; Flip Schulke/Seaphot, 136, 145; Ronald Sheridan 41(L), 54, 135(B), (Richard Sterling) 58(L); Silkeborg Museum/Photo Lars Bay 176, 181; The Slide Centre 46(B); Snark International 207; By permission of the Society of Antiquaries, London/Photo Cookson © Aldus Books 17(T); Staatliche Museen, Berlin 110(B); Staatliche Museen, Berlin-Dahlem 228(B); The Tate Gallery, London/Photo John Webb © Aldus Books 65; Professor Alexander Thom 44(L), 57(TR); Michael Tollemache Ltd., London/Photo Eileen Tweedy © Aldus Books 108; UPI (Compix) 50(T), 125(T), 219(T), 220(B); Ullstein Bilderdienst 148; Universitätsbibliothek, Heidelberg 170(L); Andrew Vargo 248(B); Mireille Vautier 200(L), 201, 205(T), 206, 248(T); Venezia Biblioteca Marciana/Photo Mauro Pucciarelli 236; Vorder-Asiatisches Museum, Berlin 115; Zefa (Dr. K. Biedermann) 121, (Werner Braun) 132, (E. Deckart) 58(R), (T. Schneiders) 55(L), (A. Wetzel) 56.